Kitty's
Countryside
DREAM

KITTY'S
Countryside
DREAM

CHRISTIE BARLOW

Bookouture

Published by Bookouture

An imprint of StoryFire Ltd.
23 Sussex Road, Ickenham, UB10 8PN
United Kingdom

www.bookouture.com

ISBN: 978-1-910751-65-7
eBook ISBN: 978-1-910751-64-0

For Anita Redfern,

Friendship is a real gift,

It's given with no expectations and no gratitude is needed.

Thank you for being my true friend.

THE THANK YOUS

As always an enormous thank you to the people I love most in the world – my family: Christian, Emily, Jack, Ruby, Tilly (Mop), Mum, Dad, Graham, Penny and Georgie. This book would never have been written without any of you, it's as simple as that. Your patience has never gone unnoticed while I have been locked away in the cave, writing.

A ruffle of the hair for Woody, my mad cocker spaniel, who is by my side every day and is unquestionably the best company ever.

I couldn't do this job alone and I want to express huge love to Bookouture. I am beyond blessed to be working with such a fantastic team. Many thanks to Claire Bord and Olly Rhodes for turning my stories in to books. I still can't believe it! I thank you from the bottom of my heart. My sincere thanks to both my agent Madeleine Milburn and my editor Lydia Vassar-Smith for your energy, vision, patience, continuous support and faith in me. Last but by no means least, a huge gin and tonic for Kim Nash, who I know I have driven to drink on many occasions in 2015! I love you Nash!

High fives to my wonderful friends, Anita Redfern, Lucy Davey, Nicola Rickus, Catherine Snook, Louise Speight, Chantal Chatfield, Sarah Lees, Suzanne Toner, Bev Smith and Alison Smithies. Your enthusiasm for my books and constant sharing of posts have not gone unnoticed, you all rock!

A special mention to Mike Denman who I think is a frightfully brilliant actor. After watching him stalk across England in the award-winning musical *The Bodyguard* I have visions of him one day not only playing James Bond but also Tom Drew from Kitty's Countryside Dream!

Being a writer has brought many opportunities my way, opportunities that I may never have had the chance to do before and for that I am eternally grateful. Due to the success of my first two books and my constant tweeting I was approached by The Zuri Project Uganda to become one of their ambassadors. They are a UK registered charity that supports the design, delivery and evaluation of a variety of locally led development projects in rural communities in Uganda that work towards improving community well-being and alleviating poverty. It's times like this I know I have the best job in the world and I was delighted and honoured to become an ambassador. So a sincere thank you Team Zuri: Martin Hewell, Ross Young, Greig Young, Anne Whewell, Chris Hogan, Rebecca Kealey, Danielle Cawood, Jenna Draper, Bhasker Patel and Sam Aldridge who not only do phenomenal work for the charity but support my writing and mention my books at every opportunity.

Big love to some very special people, all the wonderful readers, book bloggers and followers. You all mean the world to me and it is a pleasure to know you all.

Finally, Kitty's Countryside Dream would never have been written if it wasn't for Neil Roobottom, a farmer who sold me my very first chicken over eight years ago. Since then Neil has taught me everything I need to know about rearing and breeding chickens. Chickens have become a way of life in our house and it was my feathered friends who provided that little spark of inspiration for this story

CHAPTER 1

When I received the telephone call on 1 November 1985 it was unpredicted; it came out of the blue, but maybe destiny was calling – a fresh start, and a time to make something out of myself. I'd never travelled further than the local town before, never mind outside the county, and yet here I was two months later standing on the stone steps that led up to my new ground-floor flat. I stopped and stared at my surroundings. This particular January day there was a cutting chill in the air; the sky was grey with a very high chance of snow falling, according to the man who had been in deep conversation with the woman sitting opposite me on the train. Travelling from Cheshire to my new destination had been a blur. I settled on the train with my small battered suitcase lodged between my feet and my book clasped in my hand. I read for over an hour until I heard the announcement of the station over the tannoy. I had arrived in Rosefield, a quaint village on the edge of North Staffordshire.

I paused on the pavement and looked up at my new home – it was plain and simple yet unexpectedly pretty; my guess was the terraced houses were built in the early 1900s and sometime later converted into flats. The brightly coloured front doors were all adjacent to each other and adorned with identical stone steps leading to them. The sash windows with the larger panes of glass gave my new home a welcoming feel. A couple walked hand in hand, laughing as they wandered past me in the street, but I quickly ducked my head as they passed, keen to avoid eye contact. Delving deep into the pocket of my parka I retrieved the bunch of keys that had been handed over to me by the solicitor. Quickly I checked the address – I wanted to make sure I was in the correct street and standing outside the correct house. Mine, according to the tatty label attached by the fraying string, was the sage-coloured front door – a fine-looking door. I couldn't believe I had been given my own property; it seemed unreal.

Two months ago, I'd been summoned to the solicitors' office; I was told to bring my identification. After they confirmed I was indeed Kitty Lewis they congratulated me – I was now the proud owner of Bluebell Lodge and a separate ground-floor flat inherited from a grandmother that I was led to believe had died before I was born. According to the solicitor, she had owned both properties. It had been a whirlwind of a week, a week that had unleashed a whole different life for me.

The property must have been vacant for a while; there were newspapers sticking out of the letter box and an empty milk bottle sitting on the doorstep. It was now or never, leaving my old life behind. I was intrigued to uncover what was on the other side of the sage door – what did my new home have to offer?

Placing the rusty key in the lock, I pushed the door open. I didn't have any expectations; I had grasped the adventure on a whim. I no longer had a purpose in life. I'd surrendered my university place several years ago, giving up on my high hopes of becoming a doctor one day in order to nurse and care for my terminally ill mother. My mother had sadly passed away five months earlier, just a few days after my birthday, leaving me on my own. My eyes welled up with instant tears, the memories still raw. I missed her so much.

I was an only child, born to Alice and Julian, and I was, it had seemed, their absolute pride and joy. They constantly told me I was special, a gift, the child they never thought they would have. They had tried for many years for another baby but it just wasn't meant to be – I was to be their only one. My mother had dedicated her life to me when my father was tragically killed on his way home from work one evening in May – 12 May to be precise, a date I struggled to cope with each year. He was struck by an oncoming lorry that had veered off the road, hitting him and killing him instantly. He didn't suffer, according to the paramedics, which was the only comfort my mother and I could take from the devastation it caused. I was just ten years old at the time.

Struggling to push the front door open fully, I discovered a backlog of piled-up newspapers and leaflets. Bending down, I scooped my arm around the door and threw the hazardous mountain of paper up the hallway. With one last mammoth push I was in. I was instantly hit by the damp chilliness of the air inside; wrapping my arms around my body, I snuggled deep inside my coat, peering out wide-eyed, anxious to discover what my new home had to offer. It seemed unlikely any heat had passed through the cream-painted radiators in a while.

Flicking the light switch, I was relieved to find there was electricity; the bulb lit up the small hallway, which was painted in soft truffle. Although I didn't have my bearings yet, a strange feeling surged through my body; I felt like I belonged – I felt like I was at home. Glancing along the hallway, I saw a row of coat pegs, all empty except for a clear plastic umbrella hanging from the end hook. A small round hall table draped with an off-white lace cloth and an avocado-green dial telephone sat directly under the pegs. Picking up the receiver and placing it to my ear, I heard a dial tone – the line was still connected.

Cautiously peering around the door to the left, into what must have been the sitting room, I was pleasantly surprised. I wasn't sure what I'd expected, maybe a mountain of clutter, but the room contained minimal furniture – a green velvet sofa with a multicoloured crocheted blanket thrown over it, an armchair positioned to the side of the pattern-tiled fireplace. Moving towards the curtains, I swiftly pulled them apart. The daylight burst its way into the tiny living room, giving it a new lease of life. I blinked while my eyes refocused, adjusting to the light.

I was just getting my bearings when suddenly I heard a loud thud. It appeared to come from the next room. Startled, I stood still, frozen to the spot, straining to hear something else, but there was nothing, just the sound of silence.

'Pull yourself together, Kitty,' I said. Talking to myself was something I did often these days.

Over the last few years, looking after Mum had taken up almost all of my time. I was her sole carer. It had become a lonely existence, with only my books for company. Most of my friends had vanished over time, disappearing off to universities all over the country to enjoy newfound friendships and freedom. Their invites had been plentiful to begin with, but the more times I turned them down, the less they remembered to invite me. I couldn't blame them – what did I have to offer in the grand scheme of things? I didn't have any clue about fashion or make-up or men; the last few years of my life had been spent washing and clothing Mum and cooking her meals whilst battling with the daily household chores. It hadn't always been like this – there had been a time when I was a social butterfly and in my college days I flitted from one party to another. I enjoyed spending time with my friends, but once my mum was diagnosed with her illness everything changed rapidly. Without my dad, she only had me to rely on, and I wasn't going to let her down. Even though some of my memories were raw, they were also heartening. I was apprehensive about my new adventure, yet there was a tinge of excitement inside me too.

I walked towards another door situated at the back of the living room and cautiously pushed it open. Startled, I gasped. There before me were two round, beady eyes staring straight back at me. Catching my breath, I was relieved to find it was only a cat; it must have sought warmth away from the bitter chill of the January air. He meowed and padded towards me. Then he arched his back, brushing his furry white body against my legs. The tinkle of his collar suggested he belonged to someone. Reaching for his tag, I saw his name was Alfie and he belonged … well, he belonged to me, according to the battered, engraved gold tag attached to his red tartan collar. His address was my new address. This was a comforting welcome; I wasn't on my own. Sweeping him up into my arms, I snuggled him into my neck, stroking his fur whilst he purred contentedly, probably thankful he was no longer alone. He was a little on the scrawny side and I had no idea who had been feeding him. No doubt he had fended for himself by hunting for his food, but I was here now – I would care for him. I placed him on the floor and opened the kitchen cupboards; they were bare except for a bag of pasta and a box of cat biscuits. I shook the box and immediately Alfie jumped up onto the table, scrutinising my every move. I poured the biscuits into a bowl. Within a matter of seconds the bowl was empty and he sat on the table licking his paws. He appeared happy and I stroked his head.

The kitchen was homely: there was a round pine table positioned in the middle of the room with four chairs tucked away underneath; a Belfast sink to one end of the kitchen and oak-coloured units that ran all along the far wall; a fridge, a cooker and a wall clock that was still ticking. Opening the fridge door, I glanced inside. I retrieved the carton of milk sitting in the doorway, which was no longer in date, and placed it on top of the kitchen unit. Towards the back of the kitchen I noticed a bike, an old-fashioned one with a wicker basket attached to the front of it, propped up against the wall. It had been years since I had ridden a bike; in fact the last time I could even remember was when I raced around the block against my father. I had squealed with delight whilst we both pedalled furiously to catch up with the ice-cream van. Blinking back tears, I picked up Alfie from the table and cuddled him; he was still purring. I was glad of my new friend, my only friend for now.

Placing Alfie onto the floor, I walked back out into the hallway, but he was hot on my heels. The door to the bedroom was slightly ajar, and, peeping around it, I was pleased to see it was a charming room, the rosebud-patterned curtains tied back to reveal a view of the street. It was deserted; there wasn't a single car or person in sight. The bedroom's décor was dated but the room was clean and tidy. There was a double bed, a bedside table with a lamp and a freestanding wardrobe. I was relieved to discover the bed because, up until now, I'd had no clue as to where I was going to sleep tonight. I opened the wardrobe door; it was empty except for a few wire coat hangers and a bundle of clean sheets folded up on the top shelf. There was a small bathroom just off the bedroom and in a nutshell that was about it.

Since I was a child I had always had the familiarity of my family home. After my dad died, my mum would never leave; she swore blind they would have to carry her out of that house in a box. Her cherished memories were made there with my dad and while she lived there she felt he was always close by. Since her death I had put the house up for sale; it was too much for me to take on by myself. It was an emotional, heart-wrenching decision, but I needed to move on.

I was going to use the money to buy myself a flat that I could afford and find myself a job. The call from the solicitors came at the right time – it was better than winning the lottery. My childhood home was sold fully furnished and the new family were extremely grateful for the helping hand, as was I.

This flat was everything I needed and somehow it was mine. I wasn't sure how or why it belonged to me but I was here and here I was going to stay.

My mind was whirling and today's journey was beginning to take its toll. Lying my exhausted body down on top of the bed, I stared at the ceiling. I needed answers and I had no idea who was going to provide them. Since I was a small child my parents had told me my grandparents were deceased, so why, if this hadn't been the case and my grandmother had been very much alive, had I never met them?

Alfie jumped up and curled alongside the arch of my body. He too seemed pleased with the sudden turn of events – he had a new friend. Tomorrow, the second part of my adventure would begin. I was anxious to discover what would be uncovered at the mysterious Bluebell Lodge. Feeling my eyelids droop, I closed them tightly, and fell into a deep sleep, the most restful sleep I'd had since my mother had died.

CHAPTER 2

I woke up startled, forgetting where I was for a brief moment. Blinking, I stretched my arms then glanced down at my watch. It was 10 a.m. already. My stomach was in knots and I realised I hadn't eaten since yesterday lunchtime. My first priority had to be to locate the nearest shop and stock up on essentials.

Alfie must have read my mind because he uncurled himself and started to butt his head against my hand; he too must be famished.

This was it: my new life in Rosefield started today, and it was time to explore. Feeling anxious, I wished Mum were here. She'd been my only friend for so many years and here I was, all alone now except for Alfie.

Still, I was looking forward to the day ahead. I stretched my arms, threw back the covers and walked over to the window; the street was already full of life. Looking up at the sky for comfort, I felt close to Mum today. Blinking the tears away, I smiled; I felt as if she would be watching over me.

I splashed tepid water on my face and brushed my teeth – that would have to do for now. My other personal belongings were making their way to my new home by removal van; hopefully they would arrive in the next day or two.

Heading into the kitchen, I decided to take the bike. I checked the tyres; they were inflated, which was a good start. I steered the bike towards the front door, being careful not to damage any wallpaper. Tossing my purse into the basket, I bounced the bike down the steps and turned to lock the door behind me. Alfie was sitting there with his eyes wide, probably praying that I wasn't leaving him.

'I'll be back as soon as I can, don't worry,' I said softly, stroking his head. I laughed; it made a change actually speaking to another living creature. Since Mum's death the person I had been talking to most had been myself.

Closing the front door, I locked it behind me. I mounted the saddle and pocketed the key, then pushed off, placing my feet on the pedals. Deciding to cycle left, I headed off down the street.

'Here we go.'

It was mid-morning and people were bustling up and down, going about their business. A couple of ladies stood on the edge of the pavement and gave me a cheery wave when I cycled past, followed by a 'good morning'. I felt myself smile. Lifting my hand, I waved back with enthusiasm. I surprised myself; it felt like I hadn't interacted with strangers for years, No one knew me here and I was going to grab this fresh start with both hands. I cycled past numerous terraced houses; each one of them pretty, with a different coloured door, and very well maintained. A little further on there was a small arcade of shops: a butcher's, a baker's and a newsagent. I noticed a pub on the corner but that was still plunged in darkness and had not yet opened its doors for the lunchtime trade.

I braked outside the baker's and slid from the saddle, leaning the bike against the window. I retrieved my purse from the basket and entered the quaint little shop. Its glass cabinets were bursting with mouth-watering cakes, pastries and home-made sandwiches. The smell of freshly baked bread wafted through the shop, which instantly triggered the ache of hunger in the pit of my stomach. I purchased numerous items and the assistant packed them into a carrier bag. She rang up the amount on the till and I handed over the loose change from my purse. I exchanged smiles with her; she seemed pleasant enough. 'Enjoy your food,' she said, handing my receipt over the counter. I looked at the name on her badge: Lucinda. She looked around my age; maybe she'd be someone I could eventually ask about my new home and surroundings.

I'd purchased enough food for the next few days, but now for Alfie; I mustn't forget Alfie, the poor mite. The newsagent was next to the baker's. It wasn't the usual place to find cat food, but I decided to try there first. As I pushed the door open the bell tinkled above my head, alerting the assistant to my presence. This shop was like Aladdin's cave; it sold everything from hardware to milk and, yes, thankfully, cat food. I grabbed a packet from the bottom shelf and placed it on the counter, and then decided to add a bottle of wine and a couple of ready meals for myself. The assistant smiled at me. I promptly paid and thanked her. Throwing my bags into the basket, I mounted the saddle and pedalled back down the street exactly the same way I had come. Everyone seemed friendly, the high street was picturesque and I already felt at ease. Braking in front of my house, I hopped off the saddle and bounced the bike back up the steps towards the front door. Alfie was waiting patiently on the other side, purring, meowing, and most probably relieved I had returned, eagerly waiting to be fed.

I'd barely torn open the packet of food before Alfie began nudging my hand, trying to eat the contents. Once he had finished, his wide eyes were willing me to give him more. I too demolished my lunch quickly; the ache in my stomach began to diminish. Hugging a mug of tea, I relocated to the sofa and pondered my next move. The directions to Bluebell Lodge lay mapped out on the piece of paper in front of me. That was it – just directions, nothing more. I had already been informed that Bluebell Lodge was a farmhouse, the family home of the Porters and since Agnes Porter, my grandmother, had passed away, the estate was being managed by Tom Drew. The route didn't look difficult and judging by the map it was less than five minutes from the house, which was ideal because I had never owned a car. I had no idea what I was going to find, but I was intrigued to find out.

CHAPTER 3

Grasping the directions that the solicitor had provided in my hand, I set off on my bicycle for the second journey of the day. The map indicated I should bear right and carry on up the street. It was only a short journey and I suppose I could have walked but I felt nervous and wanted to discover what was waiting for me as quickly as possible. Looping to the right at the top of the high street, I followed the directions to a white house that was situated on the corner of a bridle path. I continued down a narrow dirt track, which was just about wide enough to drive a car down. Given my atrocious map-reading skills, I questioned the path. Hanging on to the handlebars, I wobbled the bike along the thin gravel trail. Only a stone's throw away from the village centre, the scenery all around me was breathtaking. There was nothing for miles except fields that stretched further than the eye could see and ponies that grazed on the round bales of hay dotted over the bare field.

I guessed that I must be near now, and as I swung around the bend, there, in front of me, was a wooden farm gate. I braked in front of the gate and glanced down at the map. Yes, this looked like the place. The gate was unlocked; a combination padlock was tossed to the side, lying on the ground. Stuffing the map into my pocket, I felt apprehensive. Looking beyond the gate, I could see a tarmacked driveway; it was much smoother than the path I'd just travelled along. There was a row of bare trees adorning the driveway; I imagined they would look extremely picturesque in the spring when they enjoyed their full bloom once more. Leaning the bike against my body, I kicked open the gate, my heart pounding and my hands sweating; I felt like I was trespassing. Pushing the bike beyond the gate, I walked slowly along the tarmac, taking in my surroundings.

Reaching the end of the road, I turned the corner and the pedal somehow managed to hit the back of my leg, throwing me off balance. I stumbled then heard a loud squawk and a mass of white feathers flew up in the air. I squealed, realising I had run over something. I was still off balance and fell to the ground with a bump. I let go of the handlebars and the bike toppled on top of me.

'Oh my gosh, are you OK? '

I was yanked to my feet by two strapping arms. Startled, I looked up. The arms belonged to the man standing before me. He was staring at me, waiting for a response.

Clearing his throat, he thrust his hand forward. 'Pleased to meet you, I'm Tom. Tom Drew.' Hearing the name, I knew this was the man managing the farm according to the notes from the solicitor.

Bewildered and feeling like a fool, I swallowed, hoping some words would escape my mouth. I grasped his hand and shook it shakily. 'Kitty' was the only word I could muster up.

I had no idea where he had sprung from. He was wearing a lumberjack shirt, the sleeves rolled up over his forearms. At a guess he was a little older than me, but not by much, maybe early thirties. He raked his hand through his floppy brown fringe and pushed it to one side, revealing the blue eyes that were looking down at me.

'Don't worry about Dotty. She's always had a mind of her own that one; you didn't hurt her.'

'Oh my, I am so sorry. I wasn't looking where I was going.' There was a bulk of feathers floating around, as well as a ball of fluff pecking at the grass to the side of the driveway. I thought it was a chicken, but the strange fur-like feathering gave it an unusual and somewhat comical appearance. The creature had feathered legs and, just for good measure, a powder-puff-like crest resembling a pompom on top of its head. I'd never seen a chicken close up before, except a roasted one on my dinner plate, usually covered in gravy.

Tom smiled and acknowledged my hesitation. He swept Dotty off the ground into his arms.

'Meet Dotty, age four. She's a silkie.'

'A silky what?'

He grinned at me.

'A silkie chicken.'

He had completely lost me now; I had no idea what he was referring to.

'It doesn't look that silky to me; in fact it looks covered in mud and very bedraggled, but I'm glad I didn't hurt her.'

The chicken began pecking at his shirt buttons. The beak looked lethal to me and very sharp; he was braver than me.

He raised his eyebrows then grinned. 'It's a breed of chicken, just like a spaniel is a breed of dog.'

'I knew that,' I mused. 'A bit like a packet of crisps? They have different flavours, ready salted ...'

I had no idea chickens came in different flavours, so to speak. A chicken was a chicken and they laid eggs. However, I nodded, trying to give the impression I was knowledgeable on such matters. Somehow I don't think Tom was fooled.

'Look, she's harmless enough; she has an extremely friendly nature. Have a hold.' Without warning, he thrust the chicken at me.

Hastily taking a step back, I lost my balance again and tripped over my bike for the second time today; before I knew it I was back on the ground with a hefty bump. This wasn't going well. I instantly wished I hadn't brought the bike.

By this point, Dotty had flown out of Tom's arms with a great deal of commotion and was safely minding her own business doing what chickens do best, scratching amongst the soil in the flower bed at the side of the pathway. She seemed happy enough.

'This is beginning to become a bit of a habit,' Tom said, laughing, and helped me to my feet again. 'I've never had a woman fall at my feet twice in less than five minutes.'

I smiled and brushed myself down, yet I was conscious my face was burning a deep red colour.

'How can I help you?' Tom enquired.

'I'm looking for a place called Bluebell Lodge, have you any idea where I might find it?'

'Look no further – this is Bluebell Lodge,' he replied, making a sweeping gesture with his hands. He eyed me up cautiously whilst wiping his brow.

'I'm the manager of the Lodge,' Tom proudly announced. 'The old bird left us recently – Mother Goose we called her – and she ran a tight ship for many years, highly respected in this area.'

'Mother Goose?'

'Agnes Porter. This place was her life; she ran it like clockwork for more years than anyone can remember.'

'Did she have any family?' I wasn't sure why that question suddenly slipped out of my mouth, as I knew what the answer was, but I wanted to work out what Tom knew.

'She was married to a man called Arthur. They owned the farm together, but he died of lung cancer many years ago. He smoked like a chimney, or so she told me. She was a kind lady, owned a little flat on the high street, but she biked here every day, come rain, shine or snow.

'I began working here after Arthur died. Agnes threw herself into this farm after he passed away. She was a private woman, didn't like to socialise, and a hard worker. This farm was her life.'

He paused for breath and, remembering my manners, I thrust out my hand again. 'Let me introduce myself properly: I'm Kitty Lewis, and you might be surprised to hear that Agnes Porter was my grandmother.'

Tom's eyes widened and his eyebrows waggled. I could see he was trying to process the information I had just shared. 'Wow, that was not what I was expecting.'

'To be honest it was a bit of a shock for me too. My parents never spoke of any living relatives. I was under the impression my grandmother had died before I was born – well that's what my parents told me – and now it seems they may have been a little economical with the truth. Back in November I learned that she had left me a flat in Rosefield, where I'm now living, and this place – Bluebell Lodge. What is this? A farm?'

'You best come with me and I'll show you around. Have you got time for a cuppa?'

'Go on then, a hot drink would be lovely.'

'I'd best take the bike; I don't want to be picking you up off the floor for a third time today.' Tom grinned at me, grabbing the bike from the ground and wheeling it alongside him.

As we turned the corner at the top of the driveway, I gasped. Tom was looking at me, waiting for my response. I blinked, taking in my surroundings. Take deep breaths, Kitty, deep breaths.

'Tom what are those?'

'Those, my friend, are fields and fields of chickens.'

'Bluebell Lodge is a chicken farm?'

'Suppliers of the best free-range eggs in Staffordshire. What you see before you are the finest show chickens and that building over there is the hub of this enterprise.' He pointed to a beautiful old brick building with an old oak door: Bluebell Lodge.

I followed closely on his heels towards the building whilst I admired the view. Tom propped my bike up against the wall and pushed the door open. 'Come on, let's pour that cuppa.'

If I was honest I had never seen so many chickens and I wasn't sure how I felt about owning that many of them. My parents weren't exactly animal lovers and we'd never had any pets when I was a child, not even a fish. Alfie was my first pet and now it seemed I had inherited thousands more.

I didn't know one end of a chicken from the other. Well, technically that wasn't true, I knew one end had a sharp beak and at the other end there appeared to be an awful lot of brown stuff squirting out. I didn't like either end. I had no idea what running a chicken farm entailed but thanks to Agnes Porter it looked like I was about to find out.

CHAPTER 4

Following Tom through the oak door, I found myself standing in an office. There was a desk situated in the middle of the room, with a high-back, brown leather chair pushed underneath. The walls were pinned with what seemed like thousands of winning rosettes that fluttered in the draught when Tom opened the door. There were numerous filing cabinets and piles of papers, and there on the wall, in pride of place, was a portrait of a smiley woman holding a chicken that looked a lot like the chicken I'd run over with my bike on arrival at the Lodge. I wandered over to the photograph to take a proper look. Pausing for a moment in front of it, I squinted to focus my eyes. I recognised that smile. It was the same smile as Mum's. Instantly I knew who this was; there was no denying the fact this woman was the image of Mum. This was the first time I had ever seen her – my grandmother, Agnes Porter.

Tom stood still; he didn't interrupt my thoughts but watched me whilst I studied the photograph. I could feel his eyes on me and he remained silent until I was ready to speak.

'My grandmother?' My voice faltered as I said it. It seemed funny calling her that. Where had she been all my life and why didn't I know she existed? Yet she must have known I did to leave this farm to me.

'Yes, that's Agnes.'

'She's holding a silkie.'

'You're learning fast – I'm impressed. You do have the makings of a chicken farmer; it must be in the blood. That's Dotty in the photo; she was Agnes's pride and joy. Dotty has won competitions for the best breed all over the county, nothing less than first prize every time. They were inseparable; she spoke to that chicken like it was human and they even ate their lunch together, can you believe that?' He laughed.

Usually I felt socially awkward around new people but Tom made me feel at ease.

Glancing up at my grandmother's photograph, a surge of excitement ran through my veins; this was an opportunity to be grasped with both hands – a new beginning for me.

How difficult could running this place be? Granted, I was a little scared to hold a chicken, but one step at a time – I could learn. Plus I had nothing else in my life; nothing else had ever been handed to me on a plate. This was my chance – it couldn't be that hard.

'I'm afraid we've only got apple tea. I've been wanting to nip out all morning to buy some proper teabags, hope you don't mind,' Tom said, handing me a mug while gesturing for me to sit down in the high-back leather chair behind the desk.

Taking the mug from him, I sipped the tea and placed it on the coaster on the desk. Never having tasted apple tea before, I concluded it was an acquired taste.

'The solicitor provided me with some paperwork informing me this place is mine.' The minute I said 'this place is mine' I instantly regretted those words, feeling they were a little forceful. 'I don't want to step on your toes or anything,' I quickly added, placing the letters down on the desk. The thought flashed through my mind that if Tom was suddenly put out by my arrival he may decide to leave the Lodge, which would leave me in a complete and utter mess. I wouldn't have a clue how to run this place.

Perching on the side of the desk, Tom picked up the evidence and glanced over it. 'Yes, this is the same paperwork that was sent through to me here. I knew someone would be coming, I just didn't know who and when.' He gave me a lopsided grin. 'Well, well, well, boss, I will do you the honour of being your right-hand man, if you'll still have me of course, and showing you the ropes. You'll have this place running like clockwork in no time at all.' Tom stood up and, thrusting his arm towards me, shook my hand vigorously. 'Welcome aboard.'

I let out a sigh of relief and had the urge to stand up and hug him. I didn't of course, but I could feel a tingling pulse racing through my body, and knew I was blushing. A handshake would do just fine for now.

'Eek, crikey it looks like I've gone and landed myself a chicken farm!' I laughed, sinking into the leather chair and spinning it around like an excited child.

I quite liked the idea of Tom being my right-hand man, whatever that entailed. I knew I couldn't run before I could walk and I was more than happy to leave Tom managing the farm while I learnt everything there was to know, even if it took a while. I was looking forward to the new challenge, learning the ropes from Tom. At school and college I always seemed to get on well with the opposite sex. I smiled, remembering one of my best friends from school, Jeremy Whiteman. He had been my friend in class five of primary school. He wasn't like the other boys in my class, and he didn't like football. I'd met him in the library. Every lunchtime after we'd eaten we used to browse through hordes and hordes of books. One day I'd tripped over my shoelace in the dinner hall and catapulted my food straight up into the air, and unfortunately it had landed directly on the head of Miranda snooty nose, the most popular girl in the class (though I couldn't work out why). Honestly, you'd have thought someone had died by the sound of her anguished cries. I personally thought the tomato pasta did wonders for her appearance, but the wail drew the attention of the headmaster, who demanded the person responsible for this catastrophe make themselves known immediately. Quaking in my untied shoes, I had just been about to step forward when Jeremy Whiteman's voice had echoed in the suddenly silent hall. 'It was me, sir.' He was marched off to be interrogated in the den of what was the headmaster's office before I could own up. I had the same gut instinct about Tom as I'd had about Jeremy – that he was a genuine person – and I hoped we were going to be good friends.

At that moment the door opened and a girl walked in. She looked at Tom. 'Are you going to introduce us?'

The girl standing before me was wearing olive-green overalls; she was the image of a proper farmer, with the filthiest wellington boots that I had ever seen. Her hair was light brown, piled up loosely on top of her head in a bun with trailing curls, her cheeks were glowing and her face was one of natural beauty. I wasn't sure why but I immediately felt deflated and could feel a pang deep in the pit of my stomach. The pair of them looked like the perfect Hollywood couple standing before me, apart from the attire and the wellies. He was handsome and there was no denying she was exceptionally beautiful.

'Jeannie, meet Kitty. Kitty, meet Jeannie. Kitty is our new boss.'

I took a deep calming breath, and, standing up, I offered my hand.

'Please to meet you, Jeannie.'

Jeannie glanced in Tom's direction; he motioned to her to shake my hand.

'New boss?' Jeannie asked.

'This is Agnes Porter's granddaughter,' Tom relayed.

'Oh I see, delighted, absolutely delighted, to meet you,' said Jeannie, shaking my hand.

Suddenly, I was overwhelmed by the stench.

'Whoa, what's that smell?' I cried, immediately taking a step backwards.

Tom laughed.

Jeannie grinned. 'That, boss, is the smell of the countryside and the sheer hard work of mucking out over a thousand chickens this morning, not forgetting Conker.'

'Conker?'

'The beautiful black Shetland pony – he lives in the field just at the back of the farm. Colourful character he is, to say the least, and quite partial to biting one's bum through the fence if you aren't careful.'

Her aroma didn't leave me enthralled about my new choice of employment; the stench was one of countryside dung. My nose began to twitch so I wrinkled it, then rubbed the end to try and block out the awful smell.

'I've only been here a few weeks myself,' she said, still with a friendly smile.

Phew. I felt a sense of relief run through my body. I must remain professional at all times, I must, I must, were the thoughts racing through my mind. How silly was I being, thanking the Lord that Jeannie and Tom couldn't possibly be a couple after only working together a few weeks. But what was it to me anyway? He was probably in a relationship; men as handsome as he was were not single. I bet he was settled down with a beautiful wife and equally stunning children. The last relationship I'd had was nearly four years ago and a very distant memory.

Tom turned towards Jeannie. 'I suggest if all those coops are scrubbed and fresh bedding laid in all, you deserve an early dart.'

'That was the suggestion I'd been hoping for and one I'm certainly not going to argue with.' Clapping her hands together then giving Tom a cheeky thumbs up, she squealed, 'Fantastic,

I'm going before you change your mind. See you tomorrow, boss, and you too, boss.' And with that she skipped to the door. With a wave above her head, she was gone.

'She's a character that one, like a big kid, and has certainly jollied up the atmosphere around here in the last few weeks.' Then, looking at his watch, he said, 'Kitty, I must dash, how about coming back in the morning and I'll begin to show you the ropes?'

Suddenly I felt disappointed. Maybe he was just late for a meeting or something. I had appeared unexpectedly and no doubt his day would have already been planned out.

'Not a problem, I'll see you bright and early,' I replied, a little saddened. I would have quite liked to have stayed for the rest of the day.

We both headed towards the door; Tom took a huge bunch of keys out of his pocket and locked the office behind us. I watched him amble towards a small cottage situated left of the driveway. It was beautiful. I squinted to read the name – Brambleberry Cottage – etched into the slate sign on the wall next to the door. Tom opened the cottage door then kicked off his boots outside and disappeared indoors. That must be where he lives, I thought – not only handy for work but if he was living on site that would definitely mean I'd be seeing a lot of him.

Heading for home, I began to wheel my bike back along the tarmacked driveway, keeping an eye out for Dotty. I was desperate not to be clumsy and trip over my bike for a third time today or run over any wandering chickens.

I was actually looking forward to tomorrow; it had been a while since I'd had so much to look forward to. There were exciting times ahead and so far my new adventure suited me down to the ground. Well, all except the apple tea and the smell of chicken dung. I wasn't sure I would ever get used to those.

CHAPTER 5

It was Tuesday morning and I was woken by the sound of the milkman clanging his empty bottles into the crates on the back of his float. Peering out from behind the curtains, it seemed the whole world and his wife were already up and bustling about their business in Rosefield. Alfie gave a stretch, jumped down from the bed and followed me into the kitchen for breakfast. I felt an exciting flutter in my stomach; today I was going to learn the ropes of my new successful empire. I could imagine myself sitting in my office at Bluebell Lodge, singing along to the radio whilst completing all the administration duties.

Pouring myself a mug of tea and spreading strawberry jam on a croissant, I could feel myself smiling, wondering what the day ahead had in store for me.

Suspecting Tom and Jeannie would already be at the Lodge by now, I was aiming to arrive as soon as possible and I was sure 9 a.m. would be bright and early enough. I reckoned Jeannie was roughly my age, mid-twenties. I didn't want to cast any aspersions, but apart from her rough-and-ready clothes she really didn't look like a chicken farmer. I could visualise her on the front cover of Vogue, a model in the making, strutting up and down the catwalk in the highest of heels. I didn't anticipate she would stay at the Lodge long; it was probably more like a stopgap in-between jobs until she found something of a more suitable nature.

Once I cleared away the breakfast dishes, I found myself standing in front of my wardrobe, swiping the clothes on the rail backwards and forwards, pondering what to wear. I'd only brought a few changes of clothes with me in my suitcase on the train; I was still waiting for the rest of my belongings to arrive. Finally I settled on a plain duck-egg blue cashmere sweater with a navy pleated skirt that fell just above the knee, opaque tights and black ballet shoes. Swirling around in front of the mirror, I was pleased with my choice. There was no doubt I had dressed to impress. I gave myself a nod of appreciation in the mirror; I looked boss-like and ready for my first day of work at the Lodge. In the past few years I hadn't taken any pride in my appearance whatsoever. I hadn't needed to – I never had anywhere to go or anyone to impress. My hair lacked style – it was dull, boring and scraped back in a ponytail. Oversized sloppy jumpers graced my body and jeans were a must every day of the week, but if I was going to be working in an office every day now I might need to revamp my wardrobe.

With one last twirl and a pat of Alfie's head, I grabbed my coat and threw my lunch into the basket of my bike. I didn't know what the rules for lunchtime would be, so I thought it was best to go prepared; I didn't want to go hungry. The air outside was fresh and crisp. After fastening the buttons on my coat, I bumped my bike down the steps and on the pavement. Closing the front door, I swung my leg over the bike, pushed on the pedal and I was off.

Suddenly I could feel myself beaming as I cycled to work. It had been years since I'd had a purpose, and now I was about to take the chicken world by storm, whatever that involved. In my head I already had the day mapped out. Tom would spend the day at my side in the office, showing me the files, accounts and how to invoice. We would laugh and joke and drink numerous mugs of tea, and I didn't mean the apple variety. Luckily I'd remembered to throw some teabags, milk and sugar into my basket, along with some of the fantastic chocolate flapjack I'd purchased from the baker's the day before.

Arriving at the gate of Bluebell Lodge, the padlock was positioned in the same place on the ground, meaning I wasn't the first person to arrive, which was good because I didn't have any keys to let myself into the office yet. Cycling up the drive, I spotted Dotty; she was pecking about quite happily on the gravel outside the cottage I'd seen Tom disappear into yesterday. His boots were no longer outside his front door so he must be around the Lodge somewhere.

Turning the corner towards the office, I spotted Tom and Jeannie sitting on the picnic bench outside the office, hugging mugs of tea; both were kitted out in overalls and wellies.

Tom raised his hand and waved at me. 'Good morning, boss! Is this what you would call bright and early? Some of us have been up working since 5 a.m.,' he said, winking playfully.

Jeannie was grinning at his joke. Even though she was covered from head to toe in chicken muck already, she still looked gorgeous – sometimes life was so unfair.

'Good morning,' she said. 'Ignore him – he's in one of his wind-up moods today. You'll be fed up with him by lunchtime. I think the smell of chicken poo has gone to his brain.'

The stench of their clothes was already making me splutter and choke. Goodness knows what jobs they had already undertaken this morning to smell like that. I was just thankful I was escaping inside for office duties.

'Good morning to you both. I'll just hang my coat up and pop my lunch in the fridge, and I'll be right back with you.' Propping the bike up against the wall of the office, I disappeared inside with my lunch. Scouting around, I couldn't seem to locate a fridge anywhere, so still grasping my lunch, I slung my coat over the chair and headed back outside.

Both Tom and Jeannie were chuckling when I re-appeared.

Ignoring their slightly annoying behaviour, I piped up, 'I can't seem to locate the fridge?'

'If you walk to the end of that barn and turn right, you'll see the storeroom. Go in through the wooden door and it's in there,' Tom replied, pointing in the direction of the barn whilst winking at Jeannie.

What was it with those two this morning? They seemed hyper and full of mischief. Walking to the end of the barn, not only could I feel their eyes watching me, but I could hear their sniggering. Turning the corner, I was relieved to finally be out of view. This place was huge; there was barn after barn, field after field.

Arriving in front of the door, I pushed it open. Two piercing eyes stared back at me. It was another of those strange chicken breeds but with a completely different appearance to Dotty. I wondered what 'flavour' this one was. My new feathered friend, with its short curved beak and a vibrant red comb on top of its head, had a red flappy beard-type body part hanging down underneath its chin, or whatever the equivalent was on a bird. It had a mahogany body but each feather was also striped with black and tipped with white. The tail was impressive, essentially black and white but with longer feathers displayed beautifully. It was standing on a hay bale looking straight at me.

Taking a few steps towards the bale, I leant over to stroke the magnificent creature. The strange gurgling sound it released from its beak immediately led to the quick retraction of my hand. It stretched its neck and with an almighty crow I was deafened by the loudest cock-a-doodle-do I had ever heard. Stepping backwards in alarm my foot landed on an old rusty watering can and I lost my balance, tossing my packed lunch up into the air as I found myself toppling to the ground once more – only this time I'd landed in something squelchy.

The almighty creature instantly hopped down from the bale of hay and with a Tyrannosaurus-rex-type swagger, it pecked furiously at my home-made granary cheese-and-pickle sandwiches.

Hearing giggles from behind me, I swiftly turned my head to find Tom and Jeannie crouching behind the door, acting like international spies.

'Come on out, I've seen you,' I said wearily.

Tom pushed Jeannie playfully through the doorway, still laughing. 'So you've met Paddy then? He's partial to sandwiches.'

'He's a Speckled Sussex, a rooster. A very handsome fellow, don't you think?' Jeannie added.

I glanced up to find Tom's helping hand stretched out to pull me to my feet yet again.

'Thank you,' were the only words I could muster.

My tights had snagged and my skirt was covered in dung.

'Whoops, very fresh dung, that,' Jeannie said, sniggering.

'I think you may need to change into those,' Tom suggested, nodding towards the far side of the storeroom.

Brushing down my skirt and not forgetting my dented ego, I swivelled my head in the direction of his nod. There, hanging from a peg, was a set of overalls with the name Kitty labelled above the hook. Beneath the overalls, placed on a bench, stood a pair of wellington boots, looking a lot like my size.

'I'm not sitting in the office in them,' I stated. 'I'll wipe my clothes down; I'll be all right thanks very much.'

'You can't stay dressed like that.' Jeannie chuckled, patting my arm.

What did they mean? I didn't see anything wrong with my appearance; in fact this morning it had taken me the best part of an hour to dress well.

'You won't be sitting in any office; this place is an all-hands-on-deck type of place, manual labour at its best. The main task is the welfare of all the birds, and by that I don't mean you two,' Tom teased diplomatically.

'OK, OK, no need for your sarcasm, I get the picture.'

Jeannie's smirk didn't go unnoticed.

'But you did look good,' Tom piped up.

'Very yuppie businesswoman,' Jeannie joined in.

Feeling like an absolute idiot I could feel the fire burning brightly in my cheeks. I'd assumed I would be sat in my nice new office, hugging my warm mug of tea. I didn't actually think I would need to get my hands dirty in any way, shape or form. It wasn't entirely my fault either – neither of them had explained what was expected of me – but I didn't think this was the time to be stamping my foot like a disgruntled toddler. They must think I'd got ideas above my station; cock of the roost, so to speak. Praying I hadn't ruffled their feathers, I unhooked the overalls from the peg.

'Well in that case, I can't wait; point me in the direction of the changing rooms.'

'You can get changed in here. Don't worry about Paddy – he won't look. Oh, and for the record, there is no fridge, your lunch hangs on your peg in a carrier bag of your choice.' Tom sniggered.

'Or on a Friday we treat ourselves to chips and gravy on a tray from Freda's Chippy, the best chip shop around.'

Kicking off my ruined ballet shoes, I irritably waved my hand at them. 'Go on then, get out of here, oh and a mug of tea wouldn't go amiss. And I mean a proper cuppa not that awful apple rubbish.'

They vanished out of sight and the door shut behind them. As they strolled away, I could hear their laughter echoing between the barns.

CHAPTER 6

Looking down at my overalls, I realised there wasn't a cat in hell's chance I carried this look off well. I looked dated and frumpy and resembled nothing more than a sack of spuds – unlike Jeannie who looked like she was modelling the new farmer attire from Gucci. Paddy the rooster was now perched back on the bale after his morning snack and was still following my every move with his watchful eyes. I wasn't sure why, but I got the impression he didn't like me much, and I wasn't sure I liked him after he'd demolished my lunch in record time.

I spotted Tom and Jeannie waiting for me outside the office. Tom was holding a mug of steaming tea.

They peered at me. 'That's more like it – a chicken farmer in the making,' Tom said, laughing.

Clomping towards them in my wellington boots, I grabbed the mug of tea off Tom and plonked my sorry backside down the bench.

'Glad to see it's not that fruity tea and it's not bad, it's actually a decent cuppa,' I said after taking a sip.

Out of the corner of my eye I spotted a small white van being driven by a woman up the tarmac drive towards us.

'Who's this?'

'Oh no, is it that time already?' Tom said, checking his watch. 'Doesn't time fly when you're having fun or, rather, making fun of the new recruit.'

The van pulled up and parked right by where we were sitting. Jumping out and slamming the door, the driver was standing in front of us.

'Good morning, Lucinda, how are you today?'

'Busy, busy, busy, four wedding cakes and what seems like a thousand cupcakes to bake by close of play on Friday. If it's this busy in winter, I'll need to expand my team by summer. I'm run off my feet.'

I recognised Lucinda; she was the lady who had served me in the baker's yesterday, the one who gave me the delicious chocolate flapjack. That flapjack was to die for; even Paddy the rooster could vouch for that.

Lucinda was of average height, not too small and not too tall. Her face was pretty and her blonde hair sported the tightest corkscrew curls I had ever set eyes on. Her fringe was pinned back by a diamanté love-heart clip, which added a touch of glamour. Her make-up was au natural – well, maybe just the hint of black mascara to accentuate her lashes – and I guessed she was in her early-thirties.

'Lucinda, let me introduce you to Kitty.' Tom smiled, turning towards me. 'Kitty is the new boss, started today.'

'Hello, yes, I recognise you; you came into the shop yesterday. How's the first morning going?'

'So far so good, I think.'

'Lucinda bought the cake shop on the high street a couple of years ago; everything is home-made in there, mouth-watering and delightfully delicious. She uses our eggs – the best free-range eggs in Staffordshire,' Tom continued.

'Wow, everything is home-made? You must never sleep.'

'Yep, everything is baked or prepared by me. Every day I'm up at the crack of dawn, all my ovens switched on by 5 a.m. and the first pastries in by 5.20,' she said proudly.

'That's a bit like someone else we know, up at the crack of dawn,' joked Tom, teasing me again. 'They also have a sandwich delivery service – if we remember to ring our lunch orders through by 11.30, the lovely Lucinda will send up one of her assistants with our food. If we forget, we starve,' he continued.

'Where are you staying?' Lucinda enquired.

'I've moved into a little flat just up the road from the baker's.'

'Mother Goose's old place?'

'I believe that's the one,' I said, remembering Tom saying that had been my grandmother's pet name.

'Right, less of this gassing, let's go and get your order, Lucinda, and you pair, meet me in barn two in five minutes.'

Tom had interrupted our conversation quite abruptly and seemed keen to move Lucinda on, or was it just my imagination? I suppose he wanted to get some work underway today and more than likely we had wasted enough time.

Tom and Lucinda marched off up the yard and disappeared around the corner, leaving Jeannie and I to rinse the mugs and make our way to barn two, wherever that may be.

'This way.'

'I'm following. What delights will I find in barn two?'

'Barn two is the hub of the deliveries across the county. When Tom says you're on the early shift that's what we call bright and early – a 5 a.m. start. We take turns, usually a week about. This week it's my week. It's a little scary travelling up the lane in the pitch black of the early morning but once you're the other side of the tarmac drive, Tom has the lights switched on in the yard and there's plenty of light that shines from Brambleberry Cottage. It reminds me of a floodlit football pitch.'

'Is that Tom's place then, Brambleberry Cottage?'

'Yes, that's where he lives.'

'Very handy for work,' I replied.

'Yes, very handy. Here we are – barn two.'

Swinging open the rusty old ramshackle barn door, I stood staring in amazement. I had never seen so many eggs; there were trays and trays stacked up. Not just brown eggs but blue, white, speckled and light brown, an array of magnificent colours. Each table not only contained different coloured eggs but they were also sorted into two piles of medium and large.

'Egg production varies from breed to breed, or flavour to flavour in your case.' She winked. 'All the chickens living on the farm are free-range and each field is divided into sections. We tend to keep the birds that can offer a more prolific return; Rhode Island Red, New Hampshire Red and the Sussex are all breeds that are fantastic, reliable layers.'

My face must have said it all; Jeannie was talking a completely different language to me.

'Don't look so worried – you'll soon get the hang of it all. Each morning we collect the eggs from the coops. We work a section at a time, taking care not to mix up the eggs. We collect the eggs in those wire baskets hanging up over there,' she said, pointing to the far end of the barn, where there were numerous large blue wire baskets hanging from the wall. 'Once your section has been collected, you bring those eggs back here and place them on the correct table. So, for example, if you've collected the eggs from the Rhode Island Reds, take the eggs over to this table and separate them into medium and large and place them on the trays, labelling them with today's date. Then move onto the next section and so on.'

'Gosh, it's like a military operation. I have no idea what a Rhode Island thingy even looks like, except it will have a beak and cluck. You've learnt your stuff quickly, Jeannie,' I joked.

'I've got a brother and we were brought up on a farm, so it's in my blood. At the age of three I bonded with my first pet chicken, Delilah. She clucked around after me all day long. I'm an outdoors kind of a girl; I'd rather be getting my hands mucky than working in a stifling office shuffling paper with the suits.'

'How are you pair getting on?' Tom asked, popping his head round the door.

'Yes, all OK, we're just chatting about the early-morning starts and the weekly rota for egg collection.'

'Did you mention whoever is on the early-morning shift finishes their day at 3 p.m. and the rest of us take care of the locking up of chickens in their houses at night?'

'Chickens have houses?' I began to chuckle, imagining all of the chickens lying down in their beds and switching off their lights.

'Yes, the two most basic requirements for our birds is space and shelter. They need to roost at night, both for their own comfort, away from the wind and rain, and to protect them from predators, which is usually the fox.

'Anyway, after lunch I'll give you a full tour of the farm, but for now I think we can safely declare it's lunchtime.'

'Yay, I'm famished,' shouted Jeannie.

'Here, Kit, catch.'

Looking up, I saw some foil-wrapped sandwiches flying through the air in my direction, thrown by Tom.

'I mentioned to Lucinda your unfortunate introduction to Paddy and your lack of lunch and she's very kindly given you her sandwich. She'll grab something from the bakery when she finishes her rounds.'

'Oh, how very kind and thoughtful, thank you very much,' I said, relieved, hearing my stomach gurgle with hunger.

'OK, I'm off back to the cottage. I'll see you on the bench in an hour.' And with that he strode away and was gone.

Unfolding the foil from my sandwiches, I could feel Jeannie's eyes on me.

'What?' I smiled.

'Cock-a-hoop, nicknames already, Kit, and it's only the first morning. Something tells me you pair are going to get on just fine,' Jeannie joked.

'Shush, stop teasing.' I smiled but could feel myself blushing. I'd immediately noticed that Tom had shortened my name to Kit, and to be honest, I think I quite liked it.

CHAPTER 7

Soon after we finished our lunch, the sky began to darken and within no time at all the heavens opened. It began to bucket down with heavy rainfall. Sheltering under the jutted-out roof of the office, Jeannie and I stood with our backs to the wall, trying to shield ourselves from the rain while we waited for Tom to reappear after lunch.

'Those ballet shoes would have been ruined in no time in this weather.'

'How did you know my shoe size for the wellington boots?' I asked, intrigued.

'That would be a very good guess on my part. Many moons ago I worked a Saturday job in the local shoe shop. I could spot a pair of size-six feet anywhere – oh and the fact you looked about the same size as me, so I brought you a pair from home.' She grinned.

We heard the door of the cottage slam and saw Tom hurrying over towards us. Pulling his raincoat over his head, he was trying to keep the drenching to a minimum whilst splashing through the puddles that had quickly appeared on the ground.

'OK, which one of you pair has been singing this lunchtime?'

'Ha ha, not me, I'm tone-deaf and I wouldn't subject anyone to my appalling voice, not even myself,' I replied.

'Must be you then, Jeannie,' he said, laughing.

Just at that moment, we saw a flash of lightning strike across the dense black clouds, and we all froze to the spot. A boom rolled out across the valley and the trees began to sway in the strengthening gust. The rain became even heavier, sounding like bullets firing onto the roofs of the barns. Another jagged bolt of white split across the sky again; this time the clap of thunder was only a few seconds behind.

'Jeannie, can you return to barn two and start preparing the egg orders that are due for delivery in the morning and remember to take the trays from the back. The orders for tomorrow are pinned on the main board in the office. Also, separate any eggs that are over three days old, pile them up and I can take them to market.'

'No problem.' Jeannie was off straightaway, making a run for barn two.

'You come with me, Kit.'

There he was calling me Kit again. My heart began to flutter and my cheeks flushed instantly. Hoping it wasn't obvious, I enquired what our mission was for this afternoon.

'Mission Conker.'

'Mission Conker, what does that entail?'

'We're going to run in the rain and rescue Conker from the field. He's aging fast now, and even though he's a hardy Shetland, I removed his rug yesterday, and I don't like the thought of him enduring these weather conditions. He'll be getting drenched in this downpour. We can stable him until the storm passes over. Are you ready to make a run for it?' Tom asked.

'Ready as I'll ever be.'

Tom took off up the yard but not before grabbing my hand, his firm grip pulling my flailing legs behind him. Halfway up the path it separated into two. I could make out a black shadow sheltering under the skeleton-like branches of an old oak tree in the field to the right of the path.

The huge drops of water were attacking my body and my clothes were sodden. Focussing on the stable ahead, my wellingtons pounded heavily across the ground, causing the mud to splash up the legs of my overalls. Almost instantly the torrential rain turned the ground to mud, making it slippery, but Tom kept a strong hold of my hand to stop me from sliding.

Finally arriving at the wooden stable, Tom let go of my hand and unbolted the door. Hanging from the hooks inside the stable were all types of pony paraphernalia: a head collar, reins and a saddle. He grabbed the head collar just as another clap of thunder sounded. I squealed, clutching Tom in panic. He smiled down at me, holding my gaze for a split second. All of a sudden I felt very coy, until I looked away.

'Gosh, that was a loud clatter. It'll pass shortly,' Tom said and he headed off straightaway.

I watched Tom stride into the field and lead Conker out of the storm; they began trotting towards me into the warm stable.

'Conker, meet Kitty. Kitty, meet Conker,' Tom said as he swept his wet fringe out of his eyes. 'He'll be safe in here now until the storm passes over. There are blue skies creeping through over there.'

The wet Shetland nuzzled my hand before turning his attention to the hay hanging from the net.

The rain was slowing down and the sun was definitely trying to creep through. I was feeling very unattractive. My hair was limp, my clothes were soaking and this was the first time I had ever had the unfortunate pleasure of wringing-wet feet squelching around inside wellington boots.

Out of the blue Tom slung his arm around my shoulder. 'Well this is an unsuccessful first day. Let's make our way back to the office and grab a hot drink. We can dry off and then head over to Jeannie to see how she's coping with tomorrow's orders,' Tom suggested, guiding me back towards the office.

When we reached the office, the kettle was already boiling and Jeannie was whirling around on the chair. 'Tea is nearly ready,' she called as we entered through the door. 'You pair look a little wet. There are a couple of towels hanging on the back of the door if you need to dry off,' she continued, nodding in the direction of the door.

Placing my boot in the jack, I pulled it off and tipped it upside down.

'There's enough water in there to fill a small fish tank.'

Jeannie, who was now off the chair pouring us both a mug of tea, smirked.

'There weren't many orders today and all are completed. The eggs to be taken to market I've put on the wooden table at the back of the barn, labelled up, and I've locked the barn. If it's OK with you pair, it's fast approaching 3 p.m. so I'll be off.'

'Yes, of course, see you in the morning.'

'Fabulous, see you then, and I hope you've enjoyed your first day, Kit,' she said, throwing me a wink whilst Tom was spooning sugar into his tea, and with that she disappeared through the office door.

Soaked to the skin, I slipped my arms out of my overalls and tied the sleeves around my waist to stop the trousers from falling down. Underneath I was still wearing my cashmere jumper, a jumper which I was very fond of, and there was no way I was risking hanging it on my peg in the storeroom with Paddy the rooster still strutting around in there.

'Tom, is it possible I could have an early dart too?'

'Now you're taking liberties; you've been here two minutes and you're already asking for time off,' he teased.

'Yes, I know, it's just I'm expecting the removal van to arrive in the next couple of hours. I've left all the furniture in the house I sold, but they're bringing my clothes and personal items.'

'Yes, of course you can.'

'Great, thanks.'

'Dare I ask, have you enjoyed your first day?' Tom enquired.

'It wasn't what I was expecting – my dreams of running an office empire dashed, my lunch devoured by a rooster, not to mention dancing in the rain, or more like being dragged along by my wellies to keep me from falling.'

Tom started clapping. 'A huge round of applause for Kitty – she's survived her first day.'

Putting one foot in front of the other, I pretended to hold my make-believe skirt as I bent my knees to curtsy.

'Aha, but the question is will you be back tomorrow?'

'Go on then, if I must,' I teased.

'I'll take that as a complete success then,' Tom said, beaming. 'You may as well get off. Finish your drink first though. I've just got to sort out the order for market tomorrow and I'll lock up the pens later on.'

'There seems to be an awful lot of manual work for just three of us,' I mentioned.

'Usually around March, when springtime is approaching, we have a number of temporary farmhands that come on board for a few months. It's easier if they're on short-term contracts, and it makes the summer months a little easier because that's when egg production is at its maximum.'

I nodded.

'Tom, on a serious note, and if I'm truly honest, I feel a little overwhelmed by it all. OK, I have inherited this place, but can we keep things the way they are for the near future?'

'What do you mean?' Tom answered.

'Would you consider still being the boss and the manager? I'd feel more comfortable until I find my feet.'

'Of course, Kitty, whenever you're ready – it would be a pleasure. This farm is in my blood and I'm going nowhere fast.' Tom smiled.

'Thanks, Tom.'

Despite everything that had gone wrong, I'd thoroughly enjoyed the madness of the day. It had made a change from the lonely existence I'd been leading until now. I felt I was going to like this chicken lark.

Finishing my tea, I headed out the door.

'See you tomorrow.'

Grabbing my bike from underneath the shelter, I swung my leg over the frame and began to pedal down the driveway.

'The combination to the padlock is 1507,' Tom shouted after me. 'Please will you lock the gate on your way out. It'll save me wandering down later.'

'Will do,' I shouted back, waving a hand above my head.

Well, I wouldn't be forgetting that number in a hurry, I thought – that's my birthday, 15 July.

CHAPTER 8

Alfie was sitting on the front doorstep waiting for me to arrive home. I dismounted and bumped the bike up the steps towards him. He was up on his feet, arching his back. Raising a smile, I squatted beside him and stroked his furry body whilst he purred happily. His presence was reassuring and heart-warming.

The removal men were already parked up outside the flat and they jumped out of their van as soon as they spotted me opening the door. Within no time at all they had stacked my worldly possessions in the living room and driven off.

For the next couple of hours while I unpacked the boxes, thoughts of Tom kept creeping into my mind. Feeling fuzzy and warm inside, I whistled to myself as I entered the bathroom and let the water from the taps rush into the bath, swirling the luxury bubble bath into a mass of foam.

I was beginning to feel a little peckish. Teatimes were never adventurous since Mum had died; I barely ever prepared or cooked a meal, unless you counted peeling back the plastic covering on a ready meal for one and placing the white tray on the piping-hot middle shelf of the oven. Tonight was no different; I had mushroom stroganoff to look forward to.

Pouring myself a glass of cool, crisp Pinot from the fridge, I took a sip. Feeling the warm rush of alcohol run through my veins, I relaxed instantly. For the first time in a long time I felt a sense of happiness.

Sinking into the soothing warm waters of the bath, the bubbles glistened in the darkened room from the candles I had lit. I began to feel warm again but felt a sudden tiredness wash over me. Laying my head back, I lapped the water over my body and the scent from the candles began to fill the room. The fragrance of lavender made for the most magnificent peaceful aroma. Closing my eyes, the sound of silence surrounded me.

I must have drifted off for a moment and was suddenly awoken by a soft tapping sound. The water had become rapidly cooler. Reaching for my towel, I dried myself and snuggled deep inside my warm dressing gown, lifting the lapels around my ears. Rubbing my hair dry, there it was again: tap, tap, tap.

Who would that be knocking on my front door?

Pulling my dressing gown tighter around my body, I headed for the front door and held on to the lock. Clearing my throat, I said, 'Hello, who's there?'

'Hi, sorry to bother you, Kitty, it's only Tom,' came the voice from the other side of the door.

My breath caught in my throat; what was Tom doing here?

Opening the door, he was indeed standing on the other side, showered, shaved and dressed in a shirt, with an open top button that revealed a smidgen of chest hair. The scent from his aftershave wafted in my direction. I inhaled and it was more desirable than the farmyard eau de toilette he'd been wearing earlier.

'Good evening. Oh, I'm sorry, did I get you out of the bath?'

I knew I was flushed, bright red to be more precise, and not just from the steamy bathwater. I wanted to come up with a witty reply but all I could manage was, 'Hi, I wasn't expecting you. How did you find me?'

I was standing on the doorstep dressed in a fluffy pink dressing gown, still resembling a drowned rat. I felt nervous and completely tongue-tied.

Tom was grinning. 'Mother Goose's old place.'

'Oh, yes, silly me, I was just taken by surprise.'

Just then a white van drove past and beeped its horn. We both looked up to see Lucinda waving frantically at us; she must have been finishing her rounds for the day. Tom raised his hand and saluted in her direction. Marvellous – this would set tongues wagging. Tom dressed up to the nines and me, well, wearing next to nothing, standing on the doorstep.

'Why are you here?' I quizzed.

'Because I don't have your phone number and it's a six o'clock start in the morning. I'll pick you up, be ready.'

'Six o'clock start, why so early?'

'We are off to market.'

'Market? What are we selling, cows in exchange for magic beans?' I queried, smirking.

'Something like that.'

'OK, I'm game.'

'Be ready. And Kitty?'

'Yes?'

'Make sure you're wearing overalls and wellies.' He winked and his blue eyes sparkled teasingly. I playfully went to shoo him away. Rolling his sleeves up, he brushed his hand against my arm.

'See you bright and early.'

'I'll see you in the morning, cheeky.' I smiled, shutting the front door behind me. My skin tingled; I'd never experienced a feeling like that before. Hearing a constant thud, I realised I was listening to my own heart beating. There was only one thing for it – after throwing my wet overalls on top of the radiator to dry out, I headed straight for the fridge. Reaching for the wine bottle I poured another glass of Pinot to steady my nerves.

CHAPTER 9

I was exhausted when the 5.30 a.m. alarm sounded; snuggling deeper into my duvet, I willed the constant beeping to disappear. Who would actually choose to surface at this ungodly hour? It felt like the middle of the night to me.

Fumbling around in the dark and still half asleep, I clicked the switch; bright spots danced before my eyes, the light dazzling my vision for a spilt second, and then my eyes began to readjust. Alfie stretched his paws and peeped through one eyelid; he was too lazy to open both. He was curled up on top of the warm duvet and promptly closed his eye; he was going nowhere so early in the morning. Peering out of the window, the street was silent. There was no activity; it was in complete darkness with not a soul to be seen.

Still half asleep, I stumbled towards the kitchen. Filling up Alfie's bowl with food, I switched the kettle on and grabbed a quick cuppa. By the time I'd drank my tea, eaten a bowl of cornflakes and was dressed in my dry overalls, I heard a van's engine droning outside on the street.

That must be Tom; no one else was daft enough to be up at this time of the morning, I thought. I heard the engine stop, a van door shut and then footsteps coming up the stairs. Racing towards the front door, I grabbed my wellington boots from the hall on the way.

There it was, the light rap on the door. I opened it to find him standing on the doorstep, rattling the van keys. 'Hey, good morning,' he said cheerfully.

'Hey back, what's so good about it?' I replied not so cheerfully. The gust of outside cold air woke me up instantly. I shivered.

'Grab yourself a hat and a pair of gloves; it can get a bit chilly standing about at the market and there's a lot of waiting around until the auction begins.'

As I climbed into the passenger seat, Tom smiled at me. 'Are you ready for this? Your first ever experience of the market?'

'Ready as I'll ever be,' I grumbled back.

'You don't appear to be a morning person, Kitty.' Tom laughed, patting my shoulder in jest.

Once the engine turned over, the radio in the van kicked in. It mustn't have very good reception because all I could hear was a crackle and it kept switching between stations.

'Do you mind if I switch off the radio?' I enquired. It was too early for pointless noise.

'No, not at all,' he replied, leaning forward and twisting the black knob until there was silence.

'Who does the van belong to?' I asked, trying to make polite conversation.

'It's mine; it's normally parked in barn five out of the way unless we need it to transport the chickens to market.'

'You have chickens in here? We're going to market to sell chickens?'

'Yes, what did you think we'd be selling?' he asked, pulling a comical face in my direction.

I felt myself blush; I wasn't sure whether that was because I'd asked a really stupid question or because every time Tom changed gears his arm brushed against my thigh. I could feel the intense heat radiating from his touch. I wondered if he had noticed it too.

I kept my focus on the road ahead. 'Why are we taking chickens to sell at the market? I thought we were a chicken farm.'

'We are. These hens are old birds; they'll either stop laying eggs soon or they have already. They no longer have a use for us, and they'll be replaced by the POLs.'

'POLs?'

'Point of lay. The laying performance of a hen changes with its age. All will produce the greatest number of eggs in their first year. They begin to lay at approximately five to six months old – this is what we call point of lay. The second and third year's egg production is normally reduced by around twenty per cent, then after the third year it tails off progressively. In the winter months, egg production slows right down and sometimes stops altogether due to the amount of daylight hours. Egg laying is stimulated by daylight.'

'Gosh, it's all very technical stuff. So am I right to assume the birds in the van are over three years old?'

'Got it in one; you are getting the hang of this.' He laughed.

'Who'll buy them if they're no longer producing eggs?'

I hoped the answer would be that the chickens would be acquired by a little old lady with a fondness for hens and they would see their days out pecking around a smallholding, but judging by the sudden silence of Tom it dawned on me that in reality they would probably be purchased by one of the local restaurants.

'We have all day to discuss chickens. Tell me about yourself, Kitty, what's your story?' Tom piped up, changing the subject quickly.

Feeling Tom's eyes burning into the side of my cheek, I found it difficult to talk about myself. There wasn't much to tell – both my parents were dead, I didn't have any friends or a significant other, and I had no social life either.

'I am, I suppose, what you would call an orphan. My mum passed away recently and most of my time was spent caring for her, and

Dad died years ago. I have no brothers, no sisters, and all my life I'd been under the impression my grandparents were dead. I never questioned my parents – why would I? I never had any reason to believe otherwise. It was a shock to discover why I'd been summoned to the solicitors, and I'm still grieving for Mum. It's all very difficult to cope with at the minute. I guess now I'll never find out why I didn't know anything about my grandparents.' My voice began to falter. Every time I spoke of my parents, I missed them. I missed them both deeply. Tears began to fill my eyes. I turned to stare out of the window, hoping Tom wouldn't notice. Taking a deep breath, I swallowed. 'What about you, Tom? What's your story? Have you got a girlfriend?' What a ridiculous question to ask; as soon as the words left my mouth I cringed. So much for playing it cool.

'No girlfriend.' He smirked, shaking his head and meeting my inquisitive stare.

'A wife?' The question seemed to hang in the air. I knew I was staring at him, transfixed.

'No wife either,' he said, laughing, and I couldn't help but smile shyly at him.

'Why ever not, what's wrong with you?' I teased.

'We're here now, cheeky.' Tom grinned.

The market car park was already full to the brim with vehicles, but luckily Tom managed to locate a vacant space towards the back of the car park and swung the van into it. The stillness of the dawn was suddenly replaced by a frenzy of market traders, cars, stalls and crates of animals as far as the eye could see. Opening the van door, the noise became deafening: people talking in all sorts of different languages, constant horns beeping and animals cawing and squawking. There were numerous stalls set out and open, ready for business, and the path between them was lit by lanterns and hanging bulbs. It would be another hour at least until daylight successfully crept through.

A man hollered in Tom's direction. Tom glanced over and waved. I looked round. The man was wearing a blue and white striped apron, a white shirt and grey pants. He was selling fruit – bananas, oranges and apples in particular. I watched him whilst he shouted complete nonsense; well, I couldn't understand him anyway. The customers formed queues, thrusting money into his assistant's hand whilst he filled brown paper bags with fruit, then handed them over.

'Are you OK? You're looking a little dazed,' Tom enquired with concern.

'It's the noise; I've never heard so much noise.'

'It will settle.'

'And it's freezing.' I shivered, thrusting my hands into my gloves and wrapping my arms around my body.

'Let's get the birds unloaded and registered, drop the eggs on the stall and we can have a look around before the auction begins.'

Throwing the van doors open at the back of the vehicle, there were approximately ten crates of chickens stacked up. 'We need to register the birds by our selling number; the number is the same code as the padlock combination back at Bluebell Lodge.'

'1507,' I confirmed.

'Good memory that, my girl.'

Tom seized a trolley, which was more like a noisy contraption on wheels, from the side of the car park; hurling the crates of chickens on top of each other, he began to load them up.

'Are you just going to stand there and watch me hard at work?'

'That sounds like a good plan to me, and you're doing such a fantastic job by yourself.' I beamed, folding my arms and leaning against the van door.

Once the van was empty we made our way over towards a shed that was an excuse for an office. There was a group of farmers huddled outside, laughing and smoking.

'What happens now then?'

'We need to show our identification to the woman behind the desk and inform her how many chickens we're selling and what breed they are. She adds them to the end of the list that's already been registered today and then she'll tag the crates. When the auction starts, the auctioneer will sell the hens by the crate for one price or individually, depending on our preference; today we're selling them by the crate. People bid and the highest bid buys the birds. If they don't sell, they will call out no sale and then at the end of the auction we take them home and try again next week. If they do sell, we collect our money from the office and our empty crates.'

Once the chickens were registered and tagged, we delivered them safely to the auction room. Casting my eyes around the dark, dismal room, I witnessed rows and rows of different 'flavoured' chickens looking subdued in cage after cage; they came in all shapes, sizes and colours. Once the crates were placed in chronological order we transferred the eggs for sale over to a stall in the corner.

'Kitty, I'd like you to meet Bantam Stan; Stan is the owner of the egg stall.'

Looking up I was faced with a stare from a scrawny man; one of his front teeth was missing and the remaining one was not only black and crooked but jabbing into his bottom lip.

Thrusting my hand forward to shake his, I quickly regretted my action. His hands were thick with grime. I gulped and was trying hard to hold on to the contents of my stomach.

Bantam Stan didn't hide the fact he was looking me up and down. 'Well, well, well, who's this hot little newbie?' he leered at Tom.

Feeling my hackles rise, I glared at him before shaking my head and walking off in the opposite direction.

Tom was soon hot on my heels. 'Wow, that was a little frosty,' he exclaimed, waiting for me to calm down.

'Not only am I cold, tired and hungry, but he was a proper idiot. What sort of man ogles a woman like that these days?' I growled.

'I agree, Kitty. I'm sorry, that behaviour was uncalled for but you can't blame the man.' Tom gave a shy smile.

I felt my face heat up a notch and my heart was racing.

'There's never a dull moment with you, Tom,' I murmured, trying to hide my awkwardness.

'Well, it's not hard to find you attractive amongst this lot; you appear to be the only woman for miles,' Tom said, chuckling softly.

Scanning the market, Tom's observation was very true – this place was dominated by men and in fact I couldn't identify another female, unless you counted the woman behind the reception desk or another couple of humans wandering around the market that I wasn't quite sure about.

'I'm sure there's a compliment in there somewhere,' I muttered.

'Come here, silly.' Tom wrapped his arms around me; pulling me in close to him, he gave me a friendly hug. I inhaled; the smell of his oh-so-familiar aftershave sent a tingle through my entire body as he rested his chin on the top of my head.

'Feeling warmer now?'

'Yes, thank you.'

At that very moment a loud bell sounded throughout the market and a further two chimes followed.

'Saved by the bell. Are we ready?'

Pulling away from him, I replied, 'Ready for what?'

'The auction is about to begin.'

Grasping my hand, Tom pulled me to the front of a crowd of jovial farmers that were already gathered behind the silver metal bars of the auction room.

We were facing the rows and rows of chickens in crates, all marked with numbers and breeds. The auctioneer blew into the microphone and suddenly the room fell silent.

Then it began.

Looking up at Tom, I was confused but fascinated. The auctioneer was spouting words and sounds so fast I had no clue what he was saying; it sounded more like a religious chant to me. After every rapid-fire, quick-cadence combination of numbers, words and sounds, he would shout 'sold' then move on to the next crate. I couldn't keep up. There was an excitement in the room, a buzz; hands were flying into the air, noises shouted from the gathered crowd and I was mesmerised by how fast this auctioneer could communicate and keep the auction moving at a steady pace.

Crate after crate was sold and our lot was due up next. Unexpectedly I felt like my personal space had been invaded and was conscious that two men had shoved their way to the front, forcing their uninvited existence next to mine. Luckily Tom's hands stayed firmly in place on the bar, his arms rigid, shielding me from the surge of the crowd.

'Right, these are the lots we want – the next ten crates are ours. Those birds will keep the restaurant equipped with meat at least until the weekend and at a fair profit too,' said the first man who had just pushed past me.

'I'm on it, boss,' replied the second man standing next to me.

I was startled, staring at the men – they were going to bid on my chickens. Dread rose through my entire body and the realisation kicked in that my hens would not be seeing out their days clucking around an old lady's farm but would more than likely be diced and served up on a hot plate in the local Chinese restaurant.

The auctioneer's voice bellowed, I listened intently and the first bid on my chickens was underway. The arm of the restaurant owner was punched in the air and his bid was registered. Hearing a shout from the back of the arena, the next bid was recorded. I strained my neck, trying to witness who the voice belonged to whilst the price was rising steadily.

Both bidders were now against each other.

'Going, going …'

'Yep, boss, we have them.'

'Good lad.'

A wave of dislike rushed through me. I blinked, my stomach churning; I couldn't bear this. Staring with hatred at the two men standing next to me, I acted quickly. There was only one thing for it; swiftly catapulting my own arm upwards, I punched the air, taking Tom by complete surprise.

'Aha.' My bid was noted.

Gasp.

Both men glared at me and one raised his arm again.

I rolled my eyes at them and then in a manic flurry I copied.

We were in direct competition. It was like a game of table tennis. Back and forth we went; there was no way on this earth they would be taking my chickens home tonight.

'For heaven's sake, what are you doing?' Tom hissed in my ear.

I shrugged. 'Saving my birds. This bidding lark is quite easy when you know how,' I replied, glancing up to give him a frosty look.

The entire population of market traders' heads were now locked in my direction and even the birds appeared to be straining their necks through the cage, waiting for their fate to be confirmed.

'You can't get attached to the chickens – they're our livelihood,' Tom said firmly.

'Just you watch me, Tom.'

'You're costing us a fortune!'

'I don't care how much it's costing!'

I had never been more determined in my life. I couldn't let them be drenched in sweet and sour sauce; they deserved to enjoy their finer years of life clucking around the meadow.

'They're over our budget now, boss,' one of the men noted in a disgruntled manner.

My arm was firmly in the air and it wasn't moving.

Tom let out a defeated sigh. 'Kitty, you're a big softy, and OK, you win; we'll take the chickens home and keep the old birds happy.'

'I knew you would see sense.'

'Going, going …'

I stared at the two men with sheer disgust.

'Gone to the lady wearing the overalls in the front row.'

One of the two men stared at me and uttered a loud sigh whilst the other could be heard muttering abuse, but they both skulked off from the front of the crowd with not a chicken between them.

The relief swept over me. Turning round towards Tom, I hugged him. I was ecstatic.

'Bold move, Kit – you've won all ten crates.' Tom's eyes met mine.

'Thank God,' I enthused.

'Look how much you've cost us to buy our own chickens back.'

'I couldn't let them eat our birds, Tom. I know technically you're the boss and I'm sorry I've cost us money, but this livestock deserves a happy ending. Agreed?'

'Agreed,' Tom declared with amusement written all over his face.

'Let's load those crates back the van and get the hell out of here.'

Tom saluted in my direction.

CHAPTER 10

Arriving home that evening after we'd settled the rescued chickens back at Bluebell Lodge, the buoyant mood of the day called for only one thing – a large cool, crisp glass of wine. Glad to be back after such an early start, I felt a sense of achievement and pride. Beginning to daydream, I had a thought: Kitty Lewis, the saver of chickens. I could prance around wearing a pair of red wellies with a matching red cape sporting the capital letters S and C – yes, Super Chick.

What a day.

Balancing on one leg, trying to remove my wellington boots, which appeared to be cemented to my feet, I toppled backwards and landed on my backside. Pulling off the boot after it finally became unstuck, mud flew from the sole and splattered up the wall in the hallway.

'Damn.'

Now feeling too tired, I couldn't be bothered to clean it up. Heading straight towards the fridge, I made a mental note to purchase one of those bootjack thingymebobs and leave it by the front door, especially now this welly malarkey was going to be regular attire.

I heard Alfie in the bedroom, and he soon appeared alongside me, purring gladly.

After a quick bonding session with the cat, I poured a glass of wine and took a well-deserved sip. No sooner had I propped my feet up on the settee and opened my book, than the doorbell rang.

Bugger – who the heck would be ringing the bell at this time of night?

It rang again.

I sat quietly, willing them to go away whilst shushing at Alfie, though he wasn't making a sound.

He stared at me; his eyes widened and then he swiped at my finger, obviously thinking this was some sort of new game.

'Ouch,' I mouthed at him, feeling a short, sharp pain followed by a little trickle of blood running down my finger. That would teach me to shush the cat.

Startled by the loud knock that followed, I tensed up. Surely they have the wrong blooming door and will hopefully go away any moment now, I thought.

Knock, knock, KNOCK.

If nothing else, they were persistent.

'Flipping heck, Alfie, all I wanted was a sit-down.'

He purred back at me like he understood my predicament whilst still watching my finger with a wicked glint in his eye.

I placed my book on the table and reluctantly forced my tired body up and out of the comfort of the settee.

Before I even had a chance to open the door, I heard a voice filter through.

'Kitty, are you in there? Come on, open up, it's only me.'

Recognising the cheerful tones of Jeannie's voice, I flicked the latch and opened the door.

Holding up a thin white plastic carrier before my eyes on her arched finger, the smell of Chinese food wafted in my direction.

'Ta-dah, thought you might be in need of a celebratory meal after today's little escapade. I've heard all about your bidding war.' She smiled, nudging me playfully.

Alfie appeared in the hallway and began to continually wind his way around my legs. I picked him up and held him close; he stretched his nose towards the white carrier bag and purred.

Giving me a quick hug, Jeannie tossed her hair over her shoulder and bounced straight past me in the direction of the living room.

'Where are the plates? I'm famished. I've worked up a right appetite; been up to my eyes in it all day, mucking out.'

However shattered I was, it would seem my plans for an early night snuggled up in my PJs had been wiped out before my very eyes, but that Chinese did smell heavenly and I was in need of some sort of stodge to soak up the wine before I began to talk gibberish.

Placing the plates down on the table alongside the cutlery, I asked, 'Wine? Would you like a glass?'

'Yes, please!'

I poured Jeannie a large glass.

'So,' Jeannie wound the chicken chow mein around her fork, 'a little bird tells me you had the market in uproar today.'

'A little bird?'

'Robin.'

'Who's Robin?'

'Robin is my brother. Full of it today he was when he arrived home. I had a complete rundown of your impressive rescue of Bluebell Lodge's birds.' She was laughing. 'It's kept me amused for the last hour.'

I scrunched my face up. 'I can't believe those horrible men were going to cook up my chickens, the absolute cheek of them.'

Stabbing my fork into the chicken chow mein, I wavered and placed the fork back my plate, making the conscious decision to look into becoming a vegetarian.

Jeannie grinned at me. 'Well done you is all I can say. I think it's a marvellous idea, keeping all the old hens. It's only been a short time, but I've found myself getting attached to my new feathered friends.'

'Me too,' I responded, looking down at the diced chicken on my plate and realising those feathered friends may once have been related to my feathered friends and enjoyed a life clucking around a quaint farmyard until their fate was decided by the highest bidder at a poultry market.

'Are you eating that?' Jeannie asked, giving me a sidelong glance.

'I don't believe I am; I've suddenly lost my appetite,' I confirmed, guiltily remembering every chicken I had ever eaten in my lifetime.

Jeannie smiled. Picking up my plate, she scraped the contents of meat and noodles her own plate and began tucking in.

'Waste not want not.'

'How did Robin know who I was?' I asked, intrigued.

'Tom had mentioned to him that there was a new boss at the Lodge. Those pair have known each other since school, and then they met up at the market – that's how I got the job. Tom mentioned he needed an assistant for the farm and Robin talked him into giving me a shot. I couldn't believe my luck when I landed the job – with such a handsome boss too, what a bonus!' She grinned.

She did like Tom after all; my mood suddenly slumped and now I certainly had no appetite left. What chance did I have if Jeannie was after him?

'More wine?' I offered, suddenly realising we'd drunk our way through one bottle already. 'This is going down too well,' I murmured, gulping mine down like it was water.

'Go on then.'

Retrieving another bottle from the fridge, I poured another two very large glasses.

Jeannie took a sip, then continued. 'Saving the chickens aside, you made quite the impression today. All he's been talking about since he got back was the attractive new boss.' She winked.

Wait a minute. I was busy trying to put two and two together. Did this mean that Tom found me attractive? Would it be too much to let out a huge whoop whoop and dance on the table? Yes it would. Keep your cool, Kitty.

Taking another sip from my glass, there was no denying the fact I was secretly chuffed to bits.

'Well, I'm actually here to try bribing you with this Chinese tonight, fingers crossed.'

Placing my wine glass down on the table, I looked at Jeannie. 'Bribe me? With what? Go on, I'm intrigued.'

'A double date,' she gleefully responded.

'Whaaaa?'

'A double date.'

'With Tom?' My voice was now extending to an excited octave higher and sounded all weird and strangled.

'Of course with Tom, who else?'

My mind was already wandering, flicking along the rail in my wardrobe, mentally trying to choose a desired outfit. Sod it, a new dress was called for – I would need to go shopping.

'Yikes, I'm in! Jeannie, I'm going to need your help – a new dress is in order.' I was grinning ecstatically.

'Not a problem.'

'So who's the fourth person then?'

'Has that wine gone straight to your head? That is four people, silly.' Jeannie, who was also very tipsy by now, giggled.

'I've only counted three,' I responded in a very confused state.

'You, me, Tom and Robin,' Jeannie announced. 'One, two, three, four,' she said, counting on her fingers.

'Very funny, you can't date your brother, that is *so* wrong and I'm sure you'll find it's also against the law.' I giggled.

'I'm not dating Robin, you are!'

My smile suddenly plunged into despair and reality hit. She didn't mean my date was with Tom, which could only mean one thing.

'Then who are you dating?'

'Er, Tom, who else?'

Complete silence.

Coming back down to earth instantly, I gave Jeannie a blank look; what the heck was she talking about?

'Robin couldn't take his eyes off you at the market and begged me to engineer a date! You'll adore him; he's got such a good sense of humour.'

My chest tightened. What a massive disaster.

'Are you OK, Kitty, you've gone kind of white?'

I pretended to be distracted. 'I feel a little faint, to be honest, must be the wine. I'll open the window.'

Once the window was open I began to slowly tidy away the dirty plates while I digested this information. I wasn't sure how I felt about it. Taking another huge gulp of wine, I pondered.

I started speaking slowly, trying to take in the proposal; my natural response was to refuse. I didn't like the thought of seeing Jeannie draped all over Tom. It felt horrible just thinking about it. I'd only known these people a few days, so why was I feeling so crushed? I'd never experienced feelings like this before, and so soon after meeting someone too.

Let's face it, I barely knew Tom, but we seemed to click so well, and he was so easy to be around – not to mention drop-dead gorgeous. There I was admitting it to myself: I liked him, really liked him.

But, in reality why would he ever fall for me anyway? Jeannie was beautiful, stunning; five foot six, with a slim size-eight figure and clear skin to die for. And me, well, I think the words average and ordinary best described me. The only blind date I had ever been on hadn't gone well; he was a trainspotter, and we'd been fixed up by one of my college friends. He liked standing around on station platforms scoring off train numbers in a pocket book. The only thing I fancied that day was a mint choc chip ice cream, but the ice-cream vendor was a no-show due to the excessive downpour of rain. A huge disappointment, just like the company. To say I hadn't enjoyed the date was an understatement, and there was no way I was investing in an anorak; it wasn't cool and it wasn't hip.

I had only really ever been in one serious relationship, with my ex, Luke. I thought we would eventually marry and have the dream, which included a house and two children. However, things began to rapidly fall apart once I gave up my university place. We grew apart and within a term of him starting at university, the relationship had ended. There hadn't been anyone else since Luke.

I settled back onto the seat in the kitchen and thought about explaining my predicament. This was my cue to come clean. Actually now was probably not the time to explain; Jeannie was very much a stranger too and me blurting out after two bottles of wine and a half-eaten chow mein that at my age I had only ever slept with one man seemed like too much too soon.

'So what do you think? Is it a yes?' urged Jeannie, waiting for an answer.

'What's Tom's take on it all?' I asked, my stomach churning, not really wanting to know the answer.

'He's definitely up for a night out, said he would look forward to it if you were game.'

My heart sank to a new depth; if he was willing to go on a double date and I wasn't his date then I needed to face facts – we were never going to be more than friends.

Take a deep breath, Kitty.

What was I thinking anyway? I couldn't date an employee; I was technically Tom's boss – it could never work!

I stifled a yawn. 'Time for bed for me, Jeannie. I was up early, and I mean early.'

'Well, come on, I'm dying here, what's your answer? Robin thinks you're really attractive. I'm not leaving until I have an answer.'

I laughed but then suddenly realised she wasn't kidding.

'Come on – tell me for heaven's sake!'

'OK, it's a night out. You can show me the nightlife around these parts.'

This was going to be torture.

'Excellent.' Jeannie clapped her hands in excitement.

There was nothing excellent about it; it was most definitely on a par with the trainspotting date. It was probably for the best that I didn't mix business with pleasure; well that's what people say, don't they? So why wasn't I convinced?

CHAPTER 11

At the ridiculous time of 4 a.m., I turned on the bedside lamp and propped myself up against my pillows. Reaching for my book, I began to read. Usually within no time, I would feel myself dropping off to sleep, but after five minutes I gave up. It was no use; I couldn't concentrate on the words and my mind began to wander. I was wide awake. Thoughts of Tom filtered through my head. The double date was already playing on my mind. I kept trying to tell myself that he was going on a date with Jeannie and it wasn't a big deal, but who was I trying to kid?

It was a very big deal.

What could I do about it anyway? Absolutely nothing, so why was I losing sleep over it? I never lost a wink of sleep over Clive Ramsbottom, the obsessed trainspotter.

I tried to read again and before I knew it, it was 6 a.m. I found myself dragging on my overalls and pushing my feet into my wellington boots. Wheeling the bike through the hallway, I'd decided I might as well be up at the Lodge. It was pointless hanging around here with nothing to do for another few hours and Alfie was still curled up fast asleep. Trying to block all romantic nonsense from invading my head, I cycled along the quiet street in the darkened morning sky.

The air was a little nippy so I pedalled faster, trying to keep warm. Arriving at the Lodge, the padlock was flung on the ground in its usual place, which could only mean one thing: Tom was up and already moseying about.

Riding past the cottage, I could see the outside light was shining up the yard and his boots were no longer sitting outside the front door. Hearing a distant shout of my name from the barn, I pretended I hadn't heard him. I carried on until I got to the office, where I dropped off my bike. My stomach was twisting in knots; the feeling of gloom lay in the pit of my stomach. I just needed to forget about Tom and Jeannie and get on with my job.

'Good morning, Kitty, I've been shouting you!' Tom smiled excitedly when he reached me.

How could anyone be so smiley at such an early hour and how could anyone look that handsome?

'What are you doing up at this time?' he queried.

'I couldn't sleep, had a bit of a restless night.'

'Ooo, excited for your date with Robin?' He grinned warmly.

That was the last thing I needed to hear. There was nothing like rubbing my nose in it.

'Ooo, excited for your date with Jeannie?' I blurted out, mimicking him and then feeling totally shitty.

My lips started to quiver; damn, I was going to cry. Tom was silent and I risked a glance. He looked upset.

'I'm feeling a little sad this morning, Kitty. I've been up since the crack of dawn scouring every barn, every hay bale, but I still can't find her.'

'Who?'

'Dotty – she's disappeared.'

'Granny's favourite chicken?'

'Yes, she vanished yesterday from the yard and no one has seen hide nor feather of her. I'll be deeply upset if the fox has got her.'

I nodded. 'I'll have a look about for her.'

I felt so despondent about the double-date situation that it was good to have a distraction, though I didn't like the thought that Dotty was missing. I began to hurry over to the furthest barn in search of her.

'Hang on. Before you go …'

My heart lifted. This was the second he would look deep into my eyes and tell me he'd made a mistake – he didn't really want to wine and dine supermodel Jeannie but preferred average Kitty; it was me he wanted to whisk off on a date.

'Yes?'

'Can you feed the chickens in the bottom paddock? The food's in the stable. Fill up all the red feeders then let the chickens out of the coop to roam around the field.'

My eyes were now blurred with the ambush of tears. Trying to ignore the queasy feeling in my stomach, I turned and walked away from Tom, up the yard. He still wanted to date supermodel Jeannie. Of course he did.

Trudging towards the field, I wiped the tears from my eyes. Kitty Lewis, you need to get a grip of yourself – whatever will be will be. Concentrate on your work and throw yourself into the business. Do not fling yourself at the first man you have a crush on. It didn't matter how many times I gave myself a good talking to, I still felt devastated.

Arriving at the bottom paddock, there was a right old racket sounding out from every henhouse.

'Bwok, bwok, bwok, bwok.'

Swiftly climbing over the rickety old fence, I moved towards the houses, panic beginning to take over. The chickens sounded like they were distressed.

Feeling flustered, I decided I would free the chickens first then locate the food from the stables, as per Tom's instructions.

Wrapping my fingers around the chains, I pulled. The doors to the coops were unleashed, flinging them wide open. Peering back at me were hundreds of alert orange eyes, sitting above light coloured beaks. Collectively those beaks looked lethal. All the hens were identical, each with a smooth rosy face, small red earlobes and an attractive mixture of browns and blacks with a beetle-green sheen to their feathers.

In a synchronised hop from their perches, the chickens were soon happily foraging around outside in the grass.

Mission chicken was so far successful.

Hurrying towards the stables, I found the huge sacks of chicken pellets leaning against the back wall. Inside each sack was a scoop. If I was going to wander back and forth with a small scoop it would take me forever to load up the trays with their food. Using my initiative, I hunted around the stable for a bucket. Finding one, I filled it to the brim with pellets and sauntered back out to the field.

Crouching down and squeezing myself between the slats of the wooden fence, I swung my bucket of feed and headed for the red feeding trays.

All of a sudden there was an eerie silence around me, not one bwok, not one cluck and not one cock-a-doodle-doo.

Swiftly swinging my head around to look, I saw thousands of chickens standing still, their beady orange eyes locked in my direction. An uneasy feeling swept through my entire body.

I took a step forward.

The chickens also shunted forward in my direction.

I took another step forward.

They copied.

I picked up my pace and then began to run like hell towards the feeders whilst glancing backwards over my shoulder.

In a Jurassic Park-style moment, a thought flashed through my mind: I was stranded on a tropical island in an isolated Central American location populated with cloned dinosaurs, or to be more precise, cloned chickens.

Willing my legs to move faster, the chickens were now thundering towards me with a certain type of determination.

My mouth opened and I let out a high-pitched scream that echoed all around the fields.

Suddenly I was in the middle of a chicken stampede. Hundreds of squawking chickens ran at me, their wings flapping and feathers flying. In a complete frenzy, they launched themselves in my direction with their eyes locked on the bucket of feed. Still screaming, I catapulted the bucket up into the air and my body hit the ground hard. Hundreds of chickens appeared to be scuttling all over me whilst they pecked at their food. Lying on the ground, I played dead. I didn't dare move or make a sound in case they realised I was still there.

'For heaven's sake, Kit, what are you doing down there?'

'Tom, help me,' I squealed indignantly.

Tom extended his hand to yank me up.

I blinked up at him, clutching at my clattering heart; I gasped for breath then grabbed his hand.

Hauling me up with his firm grip, I was back on my feet. I felt embarrassed; once again there I was lying on the ground in front of Tom. No wonder he wanted to go out with Jeannie, who made all this look like child's play. She seemed to manage to do all the farm jobs without even breaking a sweat and never ended up on her back in a field, having to be rescued.

'Are you OK?'

'Do I look OK?' I stared at him thunderously.

Ignoring my outburst, he took a handful of corn from the tossed bucket lying on the ground and scattered it in the opposite direction. The chickens bounded away.

'They could have killed me,' I blurted.

'A little overdramatic, don't you think? They were just hungry.'

'Hungry? Hungry? They would have eaten me alive if I'd given them half the chance.'

'Kitty, before you open the door ...'

'Oh back to the full Sunday name now, are we?' I interrupted, knowing that I was being rude, but it just wasn't turning into a great day.

Tom looked at me incredulously.

'Kit, before you open up the doors or the hatches, the food needs to be placed in the trays first, otherwise they'll eat you alive.' He laughed.

'I'm glad you find it funny because I certainly don't.'

'It's just a little setback and one you won't forget in a hurry. Fill the food trays up then let the chickens out – simple.'

I cleared my throat and was about to throw a sarcastic comment in his direction then thought better of it, just in case he was a chicken charmer and could entice them to fly at me once more.

'Do you want to talk about it?' Tom asked.

'Talk about what?' I barked back.

'Your bad mood today.'

Great.

'No, I'm not in a bad mood; there's nothing to talk about.'

Leaning forward, he gently plucked a chicken feather from my hair.

'A bit of mud suits you – gives you a country appearance,' he stated, changing the subject quickly.

Looking down at my overalls, I cringed; they were splattered with mud and squirted with chicken mess.

'You are doing a grand job,' he encouraged.

I glowed.

'Pink suits you – you're blushing.' He nudged me and gave me a mischievous grin.

'Oh shut up, Tom. Stop teasing me.'

Folding my arms, I stomped off, muttering something about making myself a cuppa. I felt sure that if I had turned round, I would've seen Tom grinning.

CHAPTER 12

Friday night was upon us and not just any Friday night but the night of the so-called double date.

With much teasing from Tom and Jeannie all throughout the week, I'd made it clear to them on numerous occasions that my only involvement would be to attend and enjoy a night out with friends after a hard working week. They, of course, completely ignored my protests and, with their juvenile behaviour, took it upon themselves to chant, 'Kitty and Robin sitting in the tree, K I S S I N G,' every time I had the unfortunate pleasure of passing them in the yard.

My stomach had been churning the whole day and I was hoping to have been struck down by a deadly disease, but it seemed luck was not on my side and it just wasn't meant to be.

Choosing an unassuming outfit of white skinny jeans accompanied by a pale blue tunic – bluebell white to be precise, according to the label – I completed the look with my old tatty grey pumps. Inconspicuous and comfortable was the only way to go on a night out of this nature, and the thought of tottering around in high heels filled me with dread. This was a night for keeping my feet firmly on the ground. Giving myself a quick twirl in the mirror, I had to admit the outfit might have been simple but it was indeed striking.

The next hour flew by; my hair was blow-dried, my nails painted and I sat in front of the mirror applying my make-up. Keeping to the au-natural look, wands of black mascara complemented by a nude shiny lip gloss completed my look and with a few squirts of perfume I declared myself ready.

Hearing the taxi beeping outside, I grabbed my coat and bag from the table in the hallway. Reluctantly shouting 'goodbye' to Alfie, I closed the front door and walked down the stone steps towards the car. I spotted Jeannie and Tom straightaway; they were already settled in the back seat sharing a giddy moment of laughter. I immediately felt deflated.

Right, focus Kitty – remember you agreed to do this, oh and he's Jeannie's date for the evening not yours.

It was time to get this night over and done with.

Taking a deep breath and wearing a smile, I clambered in beside the pair of them. I was hit with the scent from Tom's aftershave, which suddenly made me go weak at the knees as I slumped down into the seat of the taxi.

'You scrub up well,' Tom commented.

I gazed up at him and thanked him politely with a smile.

'You look lovely too, Jeannie,' I managed to say, which wasn't difficult for Jeannie; she was one of those lucky people who could wear a black bin bag and it would automatically look like a stunning fashion creation straight from the catwalk.

'Thanks, Kitty. Robin's going to meet us in the pub because he finished work late. He won't be long.'

I nodded.

On arrival at the pub we wandered through the double swinging doors and started to nudge our way through the crowds, with Jeannie leading the way. In contrast to the quietness of the street outside, we were suddenly deafened by noisy chatter and music blaring from massive speakers that surrounded the square dance floor I'd spotted in the corner of the room. It was already jam-packed with Friday-night drinkers and dancers who were enjoying their freedom from work with a whole weekend to look forward to.

My goodness it was warm. Engulfed by the sweltering heat, I immediately began unzipping my coat and threw it over my arm whilst following Jeannie and Tom like a lost sheep.

A confident Jeannie had already miraculously strolled ahead, bypassed the masses and pushed her way through the thirsty revellers and was now in deep conversation with the barman.

Tom had stopped in a space. I lingered behind him and we waited patiently for Jeannie's return. Watching her across the room, a smile crept across my face, remembering Mum's favourite saying: 'Kitty, you only need three friends in life: a lawyer, a policeman and a barman!' Well, from where we were standing, it certainly looked like Jeannie had mastered the third.

She hollered in our direction over the heads of the noisy crowd.

'What are you pair having to drink?'

'A pint for me, oh and get one for Robin too, he won't be long. What about you, Kitty, what would you like to drink?'

I'd thought about this dilemma for the whole afternoon. My options were limited: wine – the root of all evil, which without a shadow of a doubt would flow through my body in five seconds flat, leaving me talking gibberish all night long and with the hangover from hell in the morning – and beer, which left me forever frequenting the facilities. Oh gosh, I didn't know.

'Come on, we're dying of thirst here, Kitty.'

'Gin and tonic please,' I piped up.

'Nice choice!' Tom said.

I had no idea where that request had come from.

If the truth be known, never having tasted gin and tonic in my life, I thought it sounded classy. I'd watched many a late-night movie where the sophisticated woman snapped her fingers to the passing waiter and ordered one.

'With a slice?' Jeannie shouted over.

'A slice of what?' For a moment there I was confused; why would I want a slice of cake with a drink in the pub?

Giving the impression I couldn't hear properly due to the racket of the drinkers, I cupped my hand around my ear, mouthing, 'I can't hear you.'

'Lime, do you want lime in your drink?' Tom whispered quickly. He'd suddenly realised I wasn't at all a social butterfly and didn't have a clue what she meant.

'Yes please,' I shouted, giving Jeannie a thumbs up. However, she had taken it upon herself to answer for me and was already facing the barman, with the drinks lined up in front of her.

Heads turned whilst Jeannie squeezed back through the muttering, disgruntled crowd, who were not impressed with her rapid serving of beverages.

'It's not what you know, it's who you know!' She giggled, handing us our drinks.

'Who's that then?' I asked, genuinely intrigued.

'Danny,' Jeannie responded whilst glancing back in his direction. 'He's worked here for years.'

Danny proceeded to serve a rowdy stag party that had surged towards the bar after building up a sweat on the dance floor.

Suddenly we were interrupted by the double doors of the pub flying open, and then I saw him, the man with the warm smile, making his way over to where we were standing.

'Aha, here he is!' Tom waved him over.

Luckily for me he didn't resemble my last blind date in any way, shape or form but why would he? I should have figured any brother of Jeannie's was surely going to be beautiful. His dark curly hair fell across his golden skin, his hazel eyes flashed instant warmth, and his jaw was firm and strong. His beauty could take anyone's breath away. My eyes travelled up the length of his body.

He was the kind of guy who belonged on the cover of a romance novel, not in the local pub of Rosefield.

Tom heartily shook Robin's hand.

'Kitty, I would like you to meet Robin. Robin, meet Kitty.'

My eyes met his shyly. Leaning forward, he slipped a kiss on both of my cheeks, taking me by surprise.

'Hi, Kitty,' he said in a lovely low, soothing voice.

Oh my.

Feeling socially awkward, with a nervous smile, I managed to say, 'Hi,' and then I quickly averted my eyes from his and took a sip of my drink.

Trying to keep the smile on my face was a challenge in itself as the gin and tonic slid down my throat, leaving a very bitter aftertaste. Staring down at the glass, I wasn't impressed with the sophisticated drink and was rather regretting my choice; I should have dived straight into a bottle of Pinot.

Looking up, I could feel Tom's eyes upon me; his amused face was watching my every move. Taking another sip, I raised my eyebrows in his direction and mouthed, 'What?' He threw his head back and chuckled loudly after probably guessing it was the first time I'd ever tasted gin.

How did that man read me like a book?

Robin and Jeannie observed us both with a quizzical glance.

'Shall we grab that table over there?' Tom nodded towards a vacant table in the corner, situated away from the now rapturous stag party who'd been reunited with the dance floor and were currently jumping around on invisible pogo sticks and singing at the tops of their voices.

'Yep, let's go – it beats getting pushed from pillar to post standing here, and then we've also got a base for the evening.'

Robin patted Tom on the back whilst moving towards the table. Jeannie hung back and gave my hand a quick squeeze whilst no one was looking. 'Well come on, spill the beans, what do you think of my brother?' She winked.

'I don't know,' I whispered back. 'I only met him two minutes ago.'

Jeannie tucked her arm through mine and led me in the direction of the awaiting dates at the table. 'Come on, you'll love him. He's so charming.'

Approaching the lads, I actually felt the colour drain from my face and wasn't sure whether that was down to the heat, the gin or the fact any minute now I was going to have to make conversation with a complete stranger. Dutch courage was needed. Taking another large sip of gin, I held tightly my smile whilst the awful drink slithered down my throat.

Pulling out a chair like a true gentleman, Robin looked at me with those amazing eyes.

'Take a seat, madam.' He slipped into the chair next to mine.

'So, Kitty, what kinds of things do you like to do?' Robin asked softly.

All eyes were on me.

What sort of question was that? My mind went completely blank.

I tensed up; I didn't like to be put on the spot and I began to drum my fingers on the sticky wooden tabletop, suddenly feeling a little bit teary.

'Our Kitty loves rescuing old birds from the clutches of restaurant owners at the market,' Tom said, lightening the mood. I could have kissed him for changing the subject and freeing me from the scrutiny.

'Tut, tut, Kitty. But that was rather hilarious,' Jeannie hooted. 'I couldn't believe it when you brought the chickens home to roost, so to speak.'

Blinking the teary mist away from my eyes, I giggled too.

'That was the best decision I've ever made,' I said, remembering the look of horror on Tom's face when I thrust my hand into the air and bid on our own chickens.

Jeannie held her glass in the air. 'I propose a toast to Kitty for rescuing those hens.'

'To Kitty,' the rest of them echoed.

'I was sorry to hear about your mum; Jeannie filled me in. Do you have any other family in these parts?' Robin enquired.

I braced myself and took another sip of my drink.

'Not that I'm aware of, but who knows? I only found out my grandmother died a few months back after believing she'd been dead for years,' I blurted out.

Robin's mouth fell open and the look of surprise on his face said it all.

'That must be a shock to your system,' he said.

'It's OK; there isn't a lot I can do about it. The truth is, Robin, I've been the sole carer of my mum for the last few years and all I like to do is read. It wasn't until the last couple of weeks – when I met these two lovely people – that I actually started thinking about my future.'

Tom smiled warmly. 'I'm glad we're good for something.'

'Mum passed away not so long ago, and Dad was killed in a car accident when I was ten. I have no brothers or sisters and it was a strange situation when I was summoned to the local solicitors' office and informed I was now the proud owner of a flat and Bluebell Lodge in a place I'd never heard of, left to me by Agnes Porter.'

My voice was shaky; I still found it extremely difficult to talk about. I loved my parents deeply and it was a lonely existence without them.

'Gosh, it must be such a difficult time,' Robin said.

I was filled with an intense yearning to dispose of this topic of conversation as quickly as possible.

'It's fine, what can I do about it?' I answered, avoiding all eye contact and swigging the last of the gin from glass. It wasn't fine though, was it? It wasn't that simple. I wanted answers; I wanted to know why I never knew my grandparents. Why had I never met them? I wanted to know why my parents kept the truth from me. I had all these questions I needed to ask and no one to answer them. One thing was for certain though: tonight was the first and last time I would ever be drinking gin. Sophisticated or not, it wasn't for me.

I rubbed my eyes. Feeling a lonely tear slide down my cheek, I brushed it away. I was aware all three of my new friends were watching me intently.

Eager to change the subject, I smiled. 'Next time I'm invited out remind me not to blubber like an idiot.'

Tom took my cue and moved the conversation on.

The next hour or so flew by. Still feeling nervous, I let the others dominate the conversation. All four of us laughed at Tom's silly stories of scrumping apples from the orchards at the back of the Lodge and Robin admitted to being a keen fisherman as a child – well, for one summer only it seemed, until he discovered Amy, the blonde girl whose father owned the local fish-and-chip shop.

'My round next. Are we all having the same again?' Tom asked, throwing me a sly grin.

'A glass of wine would be perfect for me this time, thanks.'

Tom swigged the last of the beer from his glass. 'I thought so. The hard stuff didn't take your fancy then?'

I managed a sarcastic smile in return. I liked Tom's sense of humour. I liked Tom full stop.

'Tequila please,' Jeannie insisted.

'Er no! Once she starts asking for tequila that means only one thing – she's forgotten her limits and it all goes downhill from there.'

'Argh go on, please.' Jeannie dropped her gaze to her empty glass. 'You are such a spoilsport, Robin,' she joked.

'Same again for us both,' Robin confirmed, sliding their empty glasses towards Tom. Standing up, he grabbed the empty glasses and manoeuvred his way towards the crowded bar. Glancing over my shoulder, I watched him until he disappeared.

'How's your night going so far?'

Turning around instantly, the rest of us looked up to find Danny the barman had appeared at the side of the table, smiling down at Jeannie.

'Not so bad, how about you? It's busy in here tonight.'

'Always is on a Friday. I've been run off my feet, but luckily for me I was on the early shift so I'm off to meet the lads on the other side of town for a few beers.'

'Aren't you sick of the sight of beer after serving it all the time?' Jeannie joked.

'Ha ha, that would be a no!' He grinned. 'Anyway, I'll catch you later. I hope you all have a good evening.' And with that he disappeared through the door.

'He seemed a nice chap,' I said.

'Yes, he is. I've known him for years; he comes from a lovely family too,' Jeannie replied.

'Looks like Tom may be a while – the queue at the bar is moving slowly. I'll nip to the Ladies before he's back. I won't be long.'

I coughed to grab Jeannie's attention. Staring at her wide-eyed, I hoped she would understand the telepathic message I was trying to transfer between our two brains: *Please do not go to the toilet and leave me alone with Robin*. I knew he wasn't a mass murderer or anything, but I hadn't a clue what to chat to him about. I was completely new to this situation. It was one thing listening to funny stories in a group, but faced with a one-to-one, panic gripped my stomach. It soon became apparent that Jeannie was no psychic. Swiftly standing up and pushing her chair under the table, I was left alone, facing Robin, wondering what to say.

'Do you come here often?' I asked nervously.

As soon as the words left my mouth, I felt like an utter idiot. How cliché.

Robin smiled then laughed.

Every time he smiled he exposed the most perfect white teeth that I had ever seen.

'Aha! Are you trying to chat me up?' he joked, his eyes glinting at me. Leaning in towards the table, he cupped his hands around mine.

I held my breath.

'Seriously, before the others come back, I'd like to apologise for putting you on the spot earlier. I didn't mean to upset you, talking about your parents.' Robin's voice was soft and soothing.

I smiled at him.

'Apology accepted, but honestly there's nothing to feel sorry about. It's still very raw for me. I take one day at a time and hopefully some day I'll be able to speak about my parents without bursting into tears. At this point in time, light-hearted fun is the way forward for me until I discover who I am and what I like to do, because, quite honestly, I have no idea about anything at the moment.'

Robin nodded. I could see from the kindness in his eyes he got it and understood I wasn't in any way ready for a relationship, and certainly not a casual fling with a bloke I'd only just met in the pub.

'Tom and Jeannie are good people and being surrounded by them will hopefully carry you through such a difficult time. And me, well I'm always around as a drinking buddy, taxi driver or someone to sit with you on a night in watching a film. You just give me a call, no pressure.'

I thanked him. It was a kind offer and I would definitely think about it.

'Well you pair look pretty cosy,' Tom exclaimed as he carefully placed four drinks on the tabletop without spilling a drop of liquid.

I jumped in my chair and quickly removed my hand away from Robin's and grabbed the wine glass, taking a gulp.

The white wine instantly warmed my stomach; a taste I knew and loved so well.

'Don't be daft, I was just about to go and find Jeannie; she's been gone awhile.'

'You're right; she has been gone a while. I think I'll visit the little boy's room too,' Tom replied, darting towards the toilet door before I even had time to reply.

Turning towards Robin, I smiled. 'I won't be a minute; I'll go and locate that sister of yours. She seems to have forgotten the way back to the table.'

'Do you fancy grabbing some food after we've finished our drinks or maybe going to a club?' Robin asked.

'That would be lovely, but I've not budgeted for a huge night out. I've not really worked out my financial situation properly yet, but no doubt we'll all have another night out soon.'

'I'd like that, even though going out with my sister can be annoying at times.'

'Jeannie's lovely. She probably says the same about you.' I laughed.

'I doubt that. When she comes out with me she has a canny knack of talking me into buying her drinks. It always costs me a fortune.'

We both laughed.

'Right, excuse me for a second, the Ladies is calling.' And with that I weaved in and out of the gathered groups of drinkers and headed towards the toilet.

Pushing open the door of the Ladies, I was greeted by a dusty green velour fringed curtain hanging lopsided over the cracked windowpane in front of me. To the left of the window there was a row of empty cubicles. It seemed all the door locks were broken except the one at the far end of the row, which was evidently in use, as the door was tightly shut and the engaged indicator on the lock confirming it was occupied.

The interior of the powder room was clearly more powder than room. The threadbare, flea-bitten carpet had a grubby sheen from lack of vacuuming; it had definitely seen better days and there was less room than on jam-packed London Underground trains during rush hour.

It was just about functional but clearly the design vision of an individual who'd spent many years at Her Majesty's pleasure. I shuddered when I spotted the dusty old dried-flower arrangement that was propped up by the corner basin. Without a doubt it had been present since the 1950s.

Then I heard a sound, a muffled giggle.

I stood still.

I heard it again, followed by a thud and a shuffle of feet.

'Shhh, get off, there's someone there, be quiet.' I heard Jeannie's voice.

Frozen to the spot, I couldn't believe it.

There must be some kind of mistake.

'Who's there?' I heard Jeannie whisper from the other side of the door, followed by another chuckle.

My jaw dropped open.

Then I heard 'Shhh' – it was definitely said by a man.

I stood perfectly still, not daring to make a sound. I didn't want them to know it was me. I felt very sad suddenly. I wanted to be wrong but the dread rose up through my body. I recognised Jeannie's voice instantly and she was sharing a moment with ... I didn't want to bring myself to think about it, but it had to be him, it definitely had to be Tom; who else could it be? He had gone to the bathroom only moments before me – he was inside the cubicle with her.

Quietly gliding out of the room and back into the pub, I noticed that Robin was now propping up the bar. The queue had started to dwindle and the pub was beginning to empty. The partygoers were moving on to the clubs. Before he noticed me I slipped silently out of the double doors and hailed a taxi; there was only one place I wanted to be right now and that was home.

CHAPTER 13

Safely within my flat, I kicked off my pumps and threw my coat over the hook in the hallway, heading straight for the fridge to pour myself a large glass of wine.

Loyal, reliable Alfie appeared in the doorway to the kitchen; he was purring merrily, glad that I had finally returned home so he could snuggle down on the duvet and fall asleep next to me. Scooping him up in my arms, I buried my tear-stained face deep in his fur; I didn't know what I would do without him.

Carrying him to the living room, I placed him gently down on the settee and then grabbed my wine from the kitchen. Taking a huge gulp, I picked up my book to read. I read the same paragraph over and over again and, defeated, placed the book back on the table. I switched on the television and settled back down beside Alfie. Flicking through the channels, the images on the screen were nothing but a blur. I couldn't focus; my mind was racing, replaying the night's events on a loop in my head.

Soon enough, my tired, battered body was calling out for the comfort of my bed.

'Come on. Bedtime, you,' I murmured softly towards Alfie. 'It'll all look better in the morning, I'm sure.' I wasn't certain who I was trying to convince. He immediately jumped down from the settee and padded across the room towards the hallway. I followed him.

Unexpectedly, I heard the woody echo of knuckles rapping on the front door.

'Kitty, are you there? It's me, Tom, please let me know if you're there!' He sounded worried. What was he doing here at this time of night? Maybe he thought I'd overheard him and Jeannie in the loos …

I turned the key in the lock and held the door open to find Tom's concerned eyes gazing back at me. The cold air hit me instantly and I shivered.

Tom's hands were dug deep down in his pockets to shield them from the frosty temperature of the night air. His shoulders were hunched up and his neck was scrunched down inside the upward-turned lapels of his coat as he struggled to keep warm.

'What happened tonight? I was worried. One minute you were there, next you were gone. I didn't want to wait until morning to ring you. I'm sorry if I've startled you; I needed to make sure you were OK.'

This was my chance to tell him, my chance to set the record straight, my chance to come clean about why I had scurried off into the night.

But I was too scared of his reaction; I couldn't face his rejection.

'I've never had a girl disappear on me before.'

Jeannie was his girl; he wasn't interested in me.

I didn't answer him; my voice was suffocating from the large lump that was stuck in the back of my throat.

'Are you OK? I was worried – you vanished.'

I swallowed the emotion in my throat, but still no words would come out.

'Can I come in? It's freezing out here.'

'Yes,' I breathed, against my better judgement.

'You've been crying.'

He leant in towards me. Studying my face closely, he lifted my chin with his hand; his beautiful eyes met mine – again.

I only managed a nod. Conscious of the lump still in my throat, I didn't dare speak.

Pulling a tissue from his pocket, he gently dabbed the tears away from my eyes.

'Don't cry,' he murmured softly.

He reached for my hand. Entwining his fingers around mine, he squeezed them tightly then pulled me in close. Resting my head on his chest, it spun with alcohol. Hearing the constant thud of his heartbeat, more tears slipped from my eyes. He kissed the top of my head; his arms were wrapped tightly around my body. I wanted to stay there; I wanted to stay draped in his arms forever.

Gradually releasing me, he tilted my head towards his. 'Go and get some sleep now. I won't keep you up, I just needed to know you were safe.'

I managed a nod.

'I know this is all so difficult for you, the passing of your parents, living in a strange place, but remember I'm your friend; I'm here for you.'

With one last peck on the cheek, he disappeared down the steps into the whirls of fog that had descended from the winter sky.

I couldn't deny my feelings. I didn't want his friendship – I wanted him, full stop.

CHAPTER 14

Leaning my head against the carriage window, I closed my eyes for a moment whilst my body jolted along in time to the motion of the train. As the train swayed around the bend, I did my very best to stop the contents of my stomach rising towards my throat; the hangover from hell was battling against me at every twist and turn. I watched the rows and rows of terraced houses overlooking small concrete yards roll past.

I was exhausted – shattered, to say the least. I'd tossed and turned the entire night, the room in a spin from the alcohol consumption and my body in turmoil from the tears that rolled. Luckily the weekend was stretched out in front of me; I had forty-eight hours to recover and pull myself together until I came face to face with Tom and Jeannie again.

The cry of a baby sounded out behind me and the gentleman sat opposite peered over the top of his newspaper and sighed with frustration.

The train trundled on past power stations, canals, bridges and fields, with the token abandoned trainer dangling from the power line above. Embankments were littered with rusty old cans and crisp packets and the odd item of clothing that had been dumped and forgotten.

This journey wasn't familiar to me. I'd only ever travelled it once before, but that had been in the opposite direction, the day my new adventure began. Now I was travelling back, back home to Cheshire: there was somewhere I needed to be today. Already out on her early-morning deliveries, Lucinda had spotted me and stopped her van outside the stone archway to the station. She was delivering a christening cake. I smiled but wasn't in the mood for polite conversation. I made my excuses – I'd miss my train if I stopped to chat.

'Where are you going?' she asked.

'Home, I'm going home,' I replied before disappearing through the stone archway that led down to the station platform.

For the next twenty minutes or so I dozed in and out of consciousness. Feeling a light tapping on my shoulder, I raised my head to find the guard standing in front of me, his hand stretched out, waiting to stamp my ticket. Once he was satisfied, he moved quickly onto the man with the newspaper before exiting the compartment and moving on to the next.

Now I'd been travelling for almost an hour, my surroundings were becoming more familiar, and I recognised the outskirts of the town I used to live in, the place where I grew up. I spotted Lucy's semi-detached Victorian house, with its long, narrow, well-tended garden. Lucy had been my best friend at school for a short while. She'd lived a few streets away from me and we were alike in so many ways. Our love of books brought us together. Unlike most children we knew, we preferred the company of a good book to playing outside in the street. We would sit side by side for hours on the floral-covered ottoman in her bedroom reading until her mother called her for tea.

I never knew what happened to Lucy; my last memory of her was watching in despair whilst she waved frantically from the back window of her father's Fiat Strada as it followed a removal van out of the street. I never saw her again. She'd left a forwarding address and we wrote letters to each other for awhile, but as time went on those soon dwindled.

Finally arriving at the station, I hung back, waiting for the passengers to file out of the carriage. Through the window, I could see the station was busy with the hustle and bustle of the weekend travellers. Everyone seemed to be in a hurry, striding fast, weaving in and out of the crowds of people. Stepping the platform, I clutched my bag tight against my body and followed the masses towards the exit sign.

There was a lengthy queue in front of the booking window; an irate passenger was shaking his fist, arguing with the assistant who was safely tucked away behind the toughened glass. There were groups of commuters huddled together, chatting and smoking, whilst others sat on the benches reading newspapers or books. Onlookers eagerly waited, with continued glances at their watches, the arrival of their trains. There was commotion and noise everywhere and stampedes of late passengers running towards the doors of train carriages.

Pushing the turnstile, I was relieved to be away from the disorder of the platform. Breathing in the fresh, cold air, I began to walk briskly along the street. I'd only walked about 100 yards when I began to feel nervous; I felt an unsettled presence behind me, but weirdly there was no one there. The street was unusually quiet and I continued walking up the crest of the hill. Taking in the view, I saw the old church was directly in front of me.

Pushing open the weathered wrought-iron gates, the grand entrance to the graveyard, I noticed one of the ornamental statues was broken and had toppled to the side; it was now lying on the ground, in desperate need of restoration. There were gravestones that were forgotten and lacked attention, overrun with dense weeds, whilst others were immaculate, dotted with flowers that had been strategically arranged in the silver aluminium pots standing in front of the stones.

Feeling the tears well up, I crouched before my parents' stone, running my fingers over the chiselled words.

In Loving Memory of Julian Lewis and his beloved Wife
Alice Lewis
Reunited
Treasured parents of Kitty Lewis

They had finally been reunited; my mother and father laid to rest side by side. The emotion was surging through my body, the free flow of tears rushing down my cheeks. This was the first time I'd set eyes on my mum's name chiselled into the headstone. It all seemed so final, seeing the words carved out in stone. I felt empty and alone. Wiping away my tears, I rearranged the pretty fresh flowers standing in the vase on their grave.

I smiled gratefully at the flowers.

It was comforting to know that one of my parents' many friends or neighbours hadn't forgotten them.

I plucked the card from the posy and squinted through my blurry-eyed tears. It read: Forever in your debt, thank you xx

Staring down at the card, I reread it. I was puzzled; it didn't mean anything to me, of course, but it meant something to someone.

There were no other words.

I flipped the card over, looking for clues but there was nothing, nothing at all; it was blank.

My heart began thudding inside my chest, my hair stood on end and my skin prickled with fear. What did that mean? Who was forever in their debt and why? Who had placed the fresh flowers on the grave? How was I going to find out the answers? I stared at the card for a couple more seconds. The chilly wind in the air whistled all around me and the ground began to feel damp below my knees.

Today was my mum's birthday, the first year in my lifetime I couldn't actually see her or speak to her. I needed to visit her today; I needed to feel close. She was here; I could sense her all around me.

Dad's death was like a kick in the stomach. His was the first bereavement I had ever experienced. For months after his death, my feelings catapulted between disbelief, anger and confusion. By contrast, Mum's death was expected but still excruciatingly painful. One parent dying was shattering, but with both gone, I felt alone, my roots hacked away from underneath me, leaving me with a very vulnerable existence.

I wandered over to the wooden bench that sat next to the path, not far from the grave. It wasn't time for me to leave yet. I settled on the bench and pulled out my book from my bag. I began to read. Sometimes reading was the only comfort for me.

It was nearly an hour later when I looked up from my book. I noticed a couple at the far end of the graveyard; they were wrapped in each other's arms.

Standing up, I placed my book back into my bag. I glanced at my parents' grave for one last time and a few seconds later I walked back through the deserted churchyard towards the wrought-iron gates at the entrance.

I cupped my hands together and rubbed my fingers vigorously in an attempt to warm them up. It was a short walk from the graveyard to my old family home. I stood on the pavement opposite the place where I used to live and looked on while a small child merrily played in the front garden. She was bundled up in a warm winter's coat, with a stripy multicoloured scarf and matching hat. I watched her push a pram up and down the front path, singing with joy.

There was an aching familiarity about the place; the memories crowded my head. I could visualise racing around the garden with my dad, while my mum brought us glasses of lemonade to quench our thirst in the heat of a summer day.

I observed the mother wandering out of the house onto the lawn with a beaming smile. I could hear the exchange of excited chatter, the little girl relaying all of her afternoon games to her mother. I watched them skip inside, hand in hand.

This was no longer my home. I needed to face facts; those times were long gone, but I was thankful my memories kept them very much alive, even if at this moment in time the pain of remembering was unbearable.

The journey home was one of calm and peace. I'd done what I'd needed to do. Even though I felt weary, I rested my head against the windowpane and read for the whole journey. The train ride seemed quicker on the way back to Staffordshire and in no time at all I'd arrived back at the station and caught a bus back to my flat.

I let out a breath and was glad to finally be home.

This was my home now, and standing in my hallway with Alfie at my side I felt a real sense of belonging.

CHAPTER 15

Sitting in the small yard at the back of my flat, I perched on an rotten wooden chair that had definitely seen better days while I sipped my morning cuppa. Last night I'd slept for nine hours solid, the most uninterrupted sleep I'd had in a long time. I glanced around the yard. There was no denying it lacked attention; it was dull and boring, grey flagstones with nothing more, the lack of colour and imagination apparent. A few potted plants accompanied by brand new patio chairs would certainly help to bring my little space of tranquillity to life. I might even push the boat out and plant some vibrant climbers that would give a new lease of life to the wooden fences that separated the spaces between the ground-floor flats. I pictured Alfie curled up on a cushion by my side whilst I drank tea. Once transformed this would be a fantastic haven to indulge in my favourite pastime of reading books. I had hopes and dreams for this space and was ready to grasp this new day with both hands. With a spring in my step, I ventured back indoors. I scooped Alfie up into my arms; he butted his head lovingly against my face.

Hearing a knock on the front door, I opened the door with Alfie in my arms to find Lucinda beaming back at us.

'Good morning, Kitty, sorry to call on you unexpectedly. I was just passing in the van and thought I'd pop in to see how you are. You've been on my mind since I saw you at the station. I just wanted to make sure you were OK.'

'Yes, I'm fine, sorry if I didn't seem with it; it was my mother's birthday and I was travelling home to visit my parents' grave.'

Lucinda touched my arm and smiled.

'Who's this?' She leant forward and gave Alfie a playful ruffle on the top of his head; he promptly took a spirited swipe at her and we both laughed.

'He's full of character,' she said, grinning.

'This is Alfie, my inherited cat. He was waiting for me in the kitchen when I arrived and we've been best friends ever since.' I smiled at him.

'Very cute. They always say a dog is man's best friend but I'm a cat person too.'

'Well that's something we have in common. Have you got time to come in?' I asked.

'I don't want to be a nuisance.'

'Don't be daft.'

'Well, in that case, yes please,' Lucinda answered, squeezing into the hallway beside us.

'Come on, let's go and switch that kettle on.'

I didn't know Lucinda very well but she seemed friendly.

'What are your plans for today?' she enquired.

Stirring the sugar into my tea, I sat down opposite her at the kitchen table and chit-chatted about my hopes and dreams of transforming my outdoor living space into something a little more spectacular, which wouldn't be difficult considering its current state.

'There is a major flaw in my plan though,' I said, sighing. 'The only transport I have is the old bike with the basket on the front. I'm not sure I'm up to making numerous trips to and from the garden centre on that thing; the basket won't hold much and I have no idea where the garden centre is.'

'I have a plan,' Lucinda said.

'I'm listening.'

'Who is the owner of a small white sandwich van? That would be me.' She smiled. 'We could pile the plant pots and the flowers in the back of the van. I'd be delighted to help you. We could transform your yard in no time at all.'

'That's extremely kind of you.' I was beginning to feel a surge of excitement; this was just what the doctor ordered, keeping me focussed and busy on a Sunday morning. 'Are you sure?'

'It would be an absolute pleasure. I'm on my way to the garden-centre cafe now. I need to deliver their cakes. It's a beautiful day, so why not; there's no time like the present and I'm up for it if you are?'

'There's no time like the present,' I repeated.

'You may want to change from your PJs first though,' Lucinda said, laughing.

Patting her arm, I chuckled. 'Give me five minutes and I'll be right with you.'

Flinging my T-shirt over my head, I sprayed some deodorant, slipped my legs into my scruffy old jersey tracksuit bottoms and with a quick brush of my hair and teeth, in less than five minutes flat I was ready and raring to go.

I sat alongside Lucinda in the van as she pulled off to join the oncoming traffic. The aroma of the freshly baked cakes from the back of the van was heavenly.

'Well it's safe to say those cakes smell simply delicious.'

'Victoria sponge, cupcakes, lemon drizzle cakes, home-made brownies, meringues and carrot cake – you name it, it's stacked up in the back.' She smiled.

'What's your story, Lucinda? How did you end up owning the cake shop?'

Lucinda ran her hand through her curls and started up the engine.

'Now there's a question that involves a bloke called Simon. It's been a while since I thought about him.'

'Just tell me if I'm being too nosey,' I said.

'No, not at all, it's no secret. Simon was an ordinary bloke, a bloke I'd met in the local pub one summer evening when I was nineteen. After a whirlwind romance we were married at twenty, with an exciting future to look forward to. Simon worked as a delivery driver and I was a catering student at the local college. I was happy at first but changes in our marriage had crept in – so slowly I didn't notice them at first.'

'What changes?' I asked.

'Sex had become infrequent and there were never any kisses or cuddles unless he actually wanted sex; he was never ever spontaneous and never bought me gifts of any kind. At Christmas there wasn't even a small present waiting for me under the tree, just the excuse 'we're saving money'. I never had a clue what we were saving for. He no longer provided any mental stimulation for me either. Our relationship had been one-way traffic for a while. I would continuously clean up after him, wait on him hand and foot and all I usually got in return was a grunt, then he would doze off in the armchair in front of the television. Simon became lazy; he lacked ambition and like a bolt out of the blue it hit me – I couldn't waste any more time on this man. He never ever said he was unhappy, but I was. I knew I didn't love him any longer; I was bored rigid with the relationship and we'd grown apart. I left him. Our marriage lasted just two years.'

'Wow! That was a brave move.'

Lucinda nodded. 'It was a decision I didn't take lightly, but I knew I couldn't carry on. I did, however, have the decency to leave him his toothbrush, a towel and the distasteful clock on the mantelpiece, a wedding present that his mother had kindly given us.'

I chuckled.

'My passion for baking spurred me on and after selling our marital home, the small shop with living quarters above in the high street came up for sale. I think it was just meant to be.'

I nodded. 'It certainly sounds that way.'

'I went for it! I decided owning my own shop with a home above would be far better for me in the long run than renting. I'd have the best of both worlds: a place to live and a business to run.'

I could see Lucinda was driven not only by ambition but enthusiasm to match.

'I bought the shop and put my heart and soul into my business, and I've never been happier.'

'So is Simon a distant memory then?'

'Ha yes, very distant,' she replied, manoeuvring the van into a parking space outside the garden centre.

'That's enough about me!' Lucinda smiled, flinging the back doors of the van open. Glancing into the back of the van, I saw boxes and boxes of delicious-looking, mouth-watering cakes.

'Wow, look at all those.'

'That, my friend, is only today's orders. By the time 4 p.m. comes and goes these will all be demolished and the only thing to show for all my hard work will be a few crumbs stranded on the customers' plates. Sunday afternoon tea is one of their busiest times,' Lucinda stated proudly.

Entering through the revolving doors of the garden centre, I followed Lucinda into the cafe area.

'Good morning, Lucinda, perfect timing,' the waitress called.

Lucinda shouted a good morning back as she went by and headed straight towards the door marked 'staff only'.

Loading the cakes the aluminium kitchen counter, we were back through the door as quickly as we'd entered it.

'I'll see you tomorrow.' She waved her hand in the direction of the assistant who was suddenly busy fighting off customers whilst she laid the cakes out in the display cabinet next to the drinks.

Ambling into the main hub of the garden centre, I saw the shelves were packed, and I was amazed by all the garden paraphernalia. I gathered I needed a trowel, a watering can, plant pots and plants, and maybe a little compost, but there were hundreds of implements and instruments, every gardening tool known to man. My mind boggled.

'OK, so what look are you trying to achieve?' Lucinda asked.

I didn't have a specific idea in my mind at all; I just wanted to put my own stamp on my little patch, make it more homely, inviting, and brighten it up a touch.

'Look at those,' Lucinda squealed. 'They're in the sale – bargain price.'

My eyes darted over to where Lucinda was pointing; there before us was a wrought-iron bench with a table to match wrapped up and draped with a large red sale sign.

'Very shabby chic – they would fit perfectly in the yard against the back wall. You could brighten them up with some soft furnishings and they could probably be left out in the winter. Oh and it would look perfect with a candle flickering away in the middle of the table on those warm summer nights.'

'I like those and such a fantastic price too. I think they've sold!' I laughed.

'What's your favourite colour?' Lucinda queried.

'I love all shades of blue and purple.'

'Let's head outside to the plant section. I can already see there's a large selection of geraniums, campanula and lavender.' Lucinda pointed towards the far aisle. 'They'll look perfect combined with a purple and blue flowering clematis climbing up the walls. Grab yourself a trolley.'

'Isn't it the wrong time of year to plant them?'

'Maybe, yes, but they're in the sale and hopefully, if there isn't a heavy frost, by spring they'll be bursting with colour.'

Pushing the small silver trolley up and down the various aisles, I saw rows and rows of potted plants, flowers and shrubs. I was overwhelmed with the beauty that surrounded me, the vibrant colours and the fragrance. Lucinda picked up various plants, checking the roots and holding them next to each other, ensuring the colours complemented one another. Only once she was satisfied did she place them onto the trolley.

I had a fantastic morning; it was the first time I wasn't dwelling on my parents or Tom in the back of my mind. Chit-chatting away to Lucinda, I felt very at ease and was grateful she'd taken the time to see how I was settling in.

An assistant was kind enough to help us load the bench and table into the back of Lucinda's van and alongside my watering can, trowel and various ceramic pots, we placed all the plants in cardboard boxes which we found next to the tills. I was very happy with my purchases.

'Hold on, one more thing I've forgotten, don't move,' I shouted at Lucinda and quickly ran off back inside the garden centre.

Lucinda stood there looking puzzled, waiting patiently for my return.

Five minutes later I came out with a huge grin on my face, holding a white cardboard box bound together by a green gingham ribbon. 'We need supplies and your Victoria sponge cake looked too delicious to leave behind,' I said.

We grinned at each other.

After a short drive we arrived back at my flat. Balancing the table and bench between us, we managed to manoeuvre them through the hall and living room and finally towards the back door.

Once outside we removed the tatty rotten chairs and positioned the new shabby-chic furniture against the wall.

Standing back, we admired them. 'It certainly looks better already.'

'I agree – it brings the space to life. Do you fancy a drink and some of your delicious cake before we begin potting those plants?'

'You read my mind,' Lucinda said, sitting herself down on the new bench with Alfie, who'd now wandered outside and immediately jumped onto Lucinda's lap to see what all the fuss was about, before curling up on the bench next to her.

'I think he approves,' Lucinda said, smiling.

Shortly after, I came through the back door juggling a pot of tea and two slices of Victoria sponge. Setting the tray down on the table, the china teapot didn't match the cup and saucers but they were the only ones in the cupboard. Call me old-fashioned but I always think tea tastes better when drunk out of proper china cups, especially when accompanied by cake.

I couldn't help but make lots of ooos and ahhs as I tasted the delicious sponge cake.

'Is it nice then?' Lucinda giggled.

'Nice? It's amazing! You are one very talented lady. That was just what I needed. I've never tasted cake like this – it is scrumptious,' I replied with a beaming smile. 'I wish I'd bought more!'

'Thank you kindly. All my cakes are made with the finest eggs from the best chicken farm in the whole of Staffordshire,' Lucinda said, and chuckled.

Even though the air was chilly and we were wrapped up in our coats, there was a lovely atmosphere. We could have sat there all afternoon drinking tea and chatting. I was really glad of Lucinda's company. I was interested to hear about her daily routine: she was up at the crack of dawn every day baking cakes.

She was a marvel and passionate about the business she had started from scratch.

'We best start the repotting,' Lucinda suggested, laying all the ceramic pots in a long line in front of the wall. 'If we water every plant first and then place a small amount of compost in each of the pots, turn the plant upside down carefully, like this, and jiggle them out of their existing pots, then place them on top of the compost and pat more soil around them, we'll be done in no time! I'll jiggle – you trowel the compost in.'

This was definitely a job for two people.

I hummed happily while we worked alongside each other.

'We'll have this space transformed in the blink of an eye,' I said, amazed.

'I was just thinking the same thing,' Lucinda said, smiling warmly.

Once all the plants were potted, the climbers planted in the large wooden barrels and the shoots tacked to the fence, we stood back and admired our work.

'Drumroll please. I now declare Kitty Lewis's yard fit for purpose,' Lucinda joked.

'It looks perfect.'

'It will do once spring arrives; the overall effect will be truly magical.

'We need a toast, a small tipple to mark the occasion.'

Hearing clapping behind us, startled, we both jumped out of our skins. Spinning around, we came face to face with Tom and Robin peering over the back fence like naughty schoolboys.

'Not bad at all, ladies. Looks like you've both been busy,' Tom mused.

I caught Robin's eye. I hadn't seen him since I ran out of the pub, leaving him stranded by the bar. He seemed fine and not at all put out.

'Looks very inviting,' Robin hinted. 'I think we should christen all your hard work with a beer.' He tilted his head, smiling, and as luck would have it … he lifted a carrier bag full of beers up over the fence.

'This is definitely how Sunday afternoons should be spent, drinking beer with friends,' Tom said.

'OK, if we must!' Lucinda and I answered at the same time, laughing and holding up our hands for a high five.

CHAPTER 16

A few weeks later my daily routine was more established and I usually left the house for the Lodge at 8.30 each morning. Tom and Jeannie were extremely kind and took care of the early mornings and late shifts between them until I felt a little more confident around my new feathered friends.

Springtime was creeping in fast. The sugar-coated, frosted grass had now been replaced by green shoots swaying in the morning breeze. The daffodils nodded their heads in delight, bees surfed from flower to flower and the flute-throated dawn chorus of birds erupted into song every morning as I cycled up the long path towards the Lodge.

I began to appreciate why it was named Bluebell Lodge – either side of the driveway, bluebells had burst from the earth, covering every spare piece of ground. The outstanding beauty was breathtaking and the scenery all around was truly idyllic.

Glancing over in the direction of Brambleberry Cottage, I saw that too had burst into colour. It was so beautiful with the champagne and pink climbers already in full bloom, twisting their vines around the old wooden arched doorway of the 1850s cottage.

Suddenly pulling my brakes, I dragged my feet along the ground and stopped pedalling. Placing both feet firmly on the ground, I watched the window. I was sure I'd spotted a shadowy figure lingering behind the curtain. I watched for another minute and then realised there was nothing unusual about this; Tom had probably nipped home for something he'd forgotten. I stared for a moment longer and there it was again. The curtain twitched – there was a small gap between the draperies – but I couldn't see anymore. I was certain there was someone standing there.

Suddenly I could hear the sound of Tom whistling from the courtyard outside the office. I knew it wasn't him inside the cottage now.

'Good morning, Kitty,' an enthusiastic Tom shouted over in my direction.

'Shhh,' I hissed back, not taking my eyes off the cottage.

Tom wandered over to me. 'Whatever are you doing?' He raised his eyebrows in wonder.

'I could have sworn I spotted a shadow hunched behind your curtain; it moved and the curtains twitched. There's someone in your house.'

'Don't be so melodramatic. I suspect it's more likely to be the faulty catch on the upstairs bathroom window blowing a draught through the cottage.'

We stared at each other.

At that very moment the office phone rang. Tom hurried to answer it. I followed him and leant my bike against the stone wall.

'Don't worry, Jeannie, we hope you feel better soon,' I heard him say.

I wandered inside the office to see Tom hanging up the receiver.

'Is everything OK?' I asked.

'It's Jeannie, she won't be in today – she's been struck down with a stomach bug.'

'Poor thing, I hope she feels better soon.'

Tom walked towards the back of the office.

'Aren't you at least going to take a look at what's going on in the cottage?' I asked, jerking my head back towards the door.

'No, I'm going to switch the kettle on and then you're going to help me bath and prune Paddy for the upcoming show,' Tom said firmly.

'You're going to do what to Paddy?'

'*We* are going to bath him.' He looked sideways and smirked at me.

'There have been many firsts in my life over the last six months, but bathing a rooster has to top the lot,' I said, laughing nervously.

Grabbing a mug of tea off Tom, I strolled towards the barn to find Paddy. Sneakily I glanced back over my shoulder towards the cottage, but there was no movement. I felt uneasy, but there was nothing to see – the curtains hung still.

CHAPTER 17

I was trapped in the barn with a beady-eyed rooster who was constantly clacking at me. Despite being here a while now, neither of us had really warmed to the other.

There were only two thoughts running through my head: either I was going to be eaten for his lunch or seriously injured in the next five minutes. My money was on both.

Tom had asked me to retrieve Paddy from the barn with a simple set of instructions. However, things were proving rather tricky. I'd already failed the first instruction: keep your voice soft and calm in order for the chicken to feel secure in your presence.

My heart was pounding against my chest and I was petrified, rooted to the spot. My feet suddenly weighed heavily inside my wellington boots. My educated guess would be that the chicken show would be well and truly finished by the time this rooster had been caught, never mind bathed. Shaking my head in disbelief, I wasn't sure whether this was a wind-up – who baths chickens? Apparently, according to Tom, it was a very competitive arena out there. I was yet to be convinced – and trust Jeannie to be sick today of all days!

There was a good chance this was going to end in a fight. I had visions of the local news showing pictures of a poultry farmer in combat with a rooster. Biting down on my bottom lip, I decided I needed to set some ground rules with Paddy.

I hesitated.

Do not attack me was the first rule for him.

By the look in his eye, we were not singing from the same hymn sheet.

I swallowed.

I needed to be assertive and show him who was boss. Namely me – or so I had to convince him.

'I'm warning you, Paddy, play nice.'

I couldn't believe I was actually conversing with a chicken, but needs must – my life was hanging in the balance.

Perhaps I should turn around and pretend he wasn't in the barn. Tom could go and fetch him later.

Paddy flapped his wings.

There was one door – the only way in was the only way out and Paddy was patrolling it like the best of guard dogs.

I flinched; there was no escaping this.

I can do this, I can do this, I repeated over and over again in my head.

Softening my voice, I began calling his name. I wasn't sure whether he actually knew his name, but anything was worth a try.

Edging forward slowly, one step at a time, I made a tentative approach towards my great feathered friend, who was still not particularly friendly.

He stood up.

'Come on, Paddy, let's go and win some prizes.' I continued to talk in a low, soft voice.

He didn't look like he was enjoying our chat as he stretched his neck and didn't take his eyes off me.

I was so close to him now, another few steps.

I remembered Tom's instructions. 'Once you've caught the chicken, gently but firmly grab him with both hands and place each hand over each wing, so he can't flap.'

That instruction was simple enough to follow; it was the catching of the chicken I was having difficulty with.

Taking a deep breath, I realised it was now or never.

Reaching forward, slowly looking Paddy directly in the eye, I leant towards him and cupped my hands around his feathered body.

With an almighty squawk, he jumped up in the air, flapping his wings with manic force. Taking me by surprise, I fell forward and landed on top of a hay bale. Picking myself up and brushing myself down, I turned towards him and prepared myself for round two.

With a shake of his tail feathers, he hopped across the room, still watching my every move.

I followed.

Walking slowly towards him, I was even more determined not to be made a fool of. Slowly I backed him into a corner – he had nowhere to go. Crouching down, I gradually stretched my arms out wide, ready to cup his wings in my hands, when the barn door suddenly flew open.

'Hey, what the heck is keeping you?' Tom hollered.

His sudden arrival startled me and I fell back on my heels, my hands thrust to the floor to steady myself and now they were caked with dirt from the ground. Paddy leapt into the air with speed and perched comfortably back on the hay bales at the far end of the room.

I let out a huge sigh. 'Calm and steady you said and you come thundering into the barn frightening the life out of the pair of us.'

Tom began to laugh.

'It's not funny,' I muttered, standing up and wiping my dirty hands on my overalls.

'You forgot to manipulate Paddy so he was facing the opposite direction to you!'

Scooping a handful of chicken corn from the open sack by the door, Tom threw it down towards the corner of the room. Without hesitation Paddy hopped from the bales and began pecking away. Very carefully, Tom bent down and picked up Paddy without a flap or a cluck. Tucking the rooster between his ribs and upper arm, he held his legs between the fingers of the hand that was pinning him to his body. With his other hand, Tom was gently petting Paddy's feathers.

With a wide grin, Tom smiled in my direction. 'All very simple when you know how.'

'Everyone dislikes a show-off,' I muttered crossly.

CHAPTER 18

The weather was warming up and it was a very sunny end to the week. With Paddy bathed, clipped and pruned, we would rise the following day at the crack of dawn, like Paddy himself, to register him in the annual poultry show in a nearby village. This was all a revelation to me.

'Morning, Kitty,' called Tom from the open window of the van that had just pulled up alongside me.

I had awoken at first light and was currently standing on my tiptoes outside my front door, watering my new hanging basket.

I waved.

'I'll just grab my coat, give me two minutes,' I shouted before dashing inside. With a quick ruffle of Alfie's fur, I closed the front door and plonked myself down next to Tom in the front of his van.

'Are you ready?'

'I can't think of a better way to spend my Saturday than at a poultry fair. What a lucky girl I am!'

'OK quit the sarcasm, otherwise we're in for a long day,' Tom said, grinning.

'How's Jeannie, have you heard from her?' I was genuinely concerned for her health. She had been off work all week now but a part of me was enjoying my time alone with Tom.

'According to Robin, she won't make today either; she's still tucked up in bed and very much under the weather. Even her dad's home-made chicken soup isn't agreeing with her. I'll call in on her later to see how she's doing.'

Wide-eyed with horror, I looked at Tom. 'You don't mean actual home-made chicken soup?'

Tom sniggered. 'Of course I don't. Jeannie's father, Ted, he's a lovely man, has always been a keen gardener and grows all kinds of fruit and veg on his land. It'll more likely be vegetable soup if I'm honest.'

'That's a relief! What about Jeannie's mum, does she work at their farm too?'

Tom looked stricken. 'That's another story.'

'What do you mean?' I asked.

Tom hesitated.

'Jeannie and Robin's mum died during her third pregnancy. I can't remember what the condition is called, but Bea, their mum, and the baby didn't make it. They never really knew their mum.'

I was so shocked by the story. How awful for Robin and Jeannie. At least I had known my mum; Jeannie and Robin had never even had that opportunity.

'Did Ted ever remarry?'

'No, his children were his main priority, and after Bea died he was never the same again.'

We spent the next few moments in silence; Jeannie and Robin were on my mind. I felt saddened by such a tragedy – their mother taken away without any warning. I was unsure what I would say to either of them. I knew the circumstances were different with my father; I'd built a relationship with him, I had memories to treasure, but Jeannie and Robin had nothing.

'Look, here we are,' Tom said, following the arrows from the cardboard signs hammered into the ground, leading us to a makeshift car park in a field. The grass was already unrecognisable under all of the mud that had been churned up by the cars, tractors and vans that had arrived at the fair.

'Wow, it's certainly busy,' I exclaimed.

'This event is huge; it's important for everyone, villagers, farmers and suchlike. There isn't much to do around here and this type of fair is a massive event – people feel proud showing their livestock and the kids love it.'

Tom retrieved Paddy, who was sat inside his show cage waiting patiently, from the back of the van.

'I'm just going to fill in the paperwork for Paddy and notify the judges of the categories we want to enter him in. I need to check the times too.'

'What do you do with Paddy now?'

'I leave him in the show tent. It can be very noisy in there with a large number of birds gathered in one room until they settle down,' Tom replied. 'The chicken show is usually first. I'll be two minutes. You have a wander about and I'll catch you up.'

Whilst I waited for Tom to come back, I studied the fair. It was full of activity everywhere I looked. Despite the crowds and the hustle and bustle, good humour prevailed.

Over at the far end of the field, there was a live band playing, villagers dressed in gaudy clothes dancing to the beat of the drums. They merrily weaved in and out of each other, skipping and laughing. There was a great stir and excitement all around them.

There were all kinds of different stalls, ranging from sweets and candyfloss to toys and books. Children were crowded around the old-fashioned sweet stall, anxious to swap their money for a white paper bag full of penny chews. A group of excitable toddlers were running and squealing. They were being herded along by their mothers whilst grasping tightly at their colourful balloons, which were bouncing along in the air. I spotted jugglers and stilt walkers who amused the villagers with their tricks and acts. In the opposite corner was a small funfair, including a helter-skelter, the children giggling whilst they slid down the winding slide on their hessian mats. Merry-go-rounds twirled and whirled with delighted riders. The words 'faster, faster' could be heard being screamed hysterically from the waltzers and teenagers could be seen stumbling over their own feet with dizziness once the ride was over. Donkeys were also in on the act, plodding up and down, providing rides for the youngsters. The whole field was a medley of sights and sounds.

I was beginning to feel hungry and blamed the tantalizing wafts pouring out from the hotdog stalls and burger vans. Digging deep, I turned out my pocket hoping to discover enough loose change to purchase either.

At that moment I spotted Lucinda; her stall was abundant with the most delicious-looking cakes laid out on a very pretty duck-egg-blue floral tablecloth. Standing in front of the stall was a queue a mile long, excited children tugging on their parents' arms, pointing at the scrumptious cakes, all eagerly waiting for a taste. I gave her a friendly wave and she looked over in my direction, relief flooding her face whilst she mouthed 'help' at me.

'I'm coming!' Walking briskly, I headed over to her, rolling my sleeves up; I was ready to give a hand.

'Am I happy to see you! It's been bedlam.'

'Would you like some help by any chance?'

'Right at this moment, Kitty Lewis, I could kiss you, thank you so much.'

We spent the next five minutes slicing cakes, popping them into paper bags and handing them over to the waiting customers. Within no time, the entire stall was nearly empty.

'You're running out of cake,' I exclaimed.

'Extra supplies will arrive any minute now. I've sent the cavalry back to the shop. I've been up all night baking but I left the rest of the cakes in the fridges at the bakery. I didn't think I would sell out so soon.'

'I'm hoping you have more of those flapjacks; I'm partial to a bit of flapjack.' I swore Lucinda's flapjacks could win awards. It also amazed me how slim Lucinda was. I knew for a fact if I was in her profession I would be nibbling away all day, and as for the licking of the chocolate bowl, I wouldn't delegate that job to anyone else.

'Where's Jeannie? Is she with you?' Lucinda asked.

I shook my head. 'No, not today. She's under the weather and still in bed.'

'I hope it's not too serious?'

'I think it's some sort of food poisoning. Hopefully she'll be as right as rain very soon. On our way here, Tom briefly filled me in on Jeannie and Robin's mum – what an awful situation.'

Lucinda nodded. 'Awful doesn't come close; it was absolutely tragic. Robin told me the circumstances. Do you know the full story?'

'Tom just gave me the gist, that their mum died during her pregnancy.'

'Yes, it's true. Soon after Jeannie was born, Bea, her mother, was pregnant with another child. Ted was overjoyed with the news. He'd always yearned for a large family; he was one of five children. But things didn't go smoothly – during the late stages of the pregnancy, Bea was suffering with severe headaches, blurred vision and an acute pain below the ribs. It happened in the middle of the night during the lambing season. Ted was helping to deliver the lambs in one of the fields furthest away from the farmhouse. In the distance he heard muffled shouting, and in the dark of the night he spotted a torchlight meandering towards him across the field. Then it suddenly stopped dead and the light lay still on the ground. He thought it was strange and his gut instinct told him something was wrong. He abandoned the lambs and ran towards the light and found Bea lying collapsed on the ground, her arms and legs, neck and jaw jerking. She'd lost consciousness. There was nothing he could do except race back to the house, where he phoned for an ambulance, but by the time he got back to her it was too late. He held her tight, his arms wrapped round her body, praying. The doctor at the hospital confirmed that Bea had suffered from eclampsia, but her fit was so severe that their baby suffocated during the seizure and also didn't make it.'

'That is absolutely heartbreaking,' I managed to say, blinking back the tears.

'Jeannie and Robin never knew their mother – Ted brought them both up as a single parent. It's been a struggle for him, but he's dedicated his life to that pair.'

It was so sad that I couldn't find any words to say.

'Let's change the subject quick.' Lucinda nodded in Robin's direction. 'Here he is now, my knight in shining armour.'

All eyes were fixed on Robin; he was staggering towards us, peering over the umpteen white cardboard cake boxes he was carrying with a huge grin on his face.

'Hello, Kitty, how are you? Come on, you two, grab these boxes from me.'

'All's fine with me; let me give you a hand.'

Taking the top two boxes off the pile, I'd no sooner placed the lemon drizzle cake onto the cake stand sitting on the floral tablecloth than it was snapped up.

'Your cakes are in high demand, lady!' Robin exclaimed.

'I could murder a drink. How about a free cupcake for the person who goes and fetches me one?' Lucinda gave a pleading smile.

'No need, look who's coming over with a tray of teas. Tom must have read your mind!' I said.

'I'd just spotted you, so I thought I'd get the drinks in. Come on, you lot, grab a tea,' Tom offered, holding out four polystyrene cups. 'There are two cups with sugar and two without; I couldn't remember what everyone had.'

Tom had registered Paddy in his categories and after filling up his water drinker had hurried back over to us via the tea stand.

Lucinda finished arranging her cakes on the table and after serving a couple more customers declared herself on a much deserved five-minute break.

'Here you go, choose yourself a cupcake; there are three left on the cake stand.'

'No, there's only two left now,' I corrected.

'There were three,' she said, puzzled.

'Who's pinched a cupcake?'

We all looked at each other and then turned back to Tom immediately.

Guilt flickered in his eyes.

'It wasn't me, your honour!' Tom began laughing.

'Stop right there! I think the white coating around your lips is very much a giveaway,' I said, laughing.

'Busted!' Robin grinned.

Lucinda tutted and wagged her finger playfully towards him.

'You're terrible!' I said.

There's no denying at that very moment in time I felt like I belonged. So far it had been a grand morning; I was really enjoying myself. If only my parents could see how far I'd come, they would be proud.

'Robin, how's Jeannie?' I asked.

'Not too good to be honest. Every time she moves, she's sick. We suspect she has a severe case of food poisoning.'

Suddenly I felt a little guilty. There was my friend lying in bed, too sick to move, and I'd been busy flirting with Tom.

Our conversation was interrupted by a voice that boomed out over the crackling tannoy. 'The chicken show is about to begin.

Please make your way over to the show tent. The judging will commence in exactly five minutes' time.'

Immediately the footsteps of the exhibitors could be heard thundering across the field towards the tent.

'Lucinda, we'll catch you after the show,' I called before being dragged along with the crowd and herded towards the tent.

'Good luck, everyone,' she shouted after us.

'Are you ready for this?' Robin grinned at me.

'As ready as I ever will be.'

All around the edge of the tent there were metal cages, perching on top of trestle tables, enclosing magnificent birds of all different breeds that were more pruned and better looked after than I was!

The cages had been separated into different categories, and there was Paddy peering back at us from behind the bars alongside all the other chickens that were entered in the 'best in show' category.

There was already a group of eagerly awaiting exhibitors sitting on the rows and rows of wooden church-like pews laid out in the middle of the tent.

At the front of the tent was the judges' table covered in a crisp white tablecloth, with three chairs in a line behind it. Three glasses of water mirrored the chairs, placed next to the judges' names.

We all scanned the crowd and then Tom pointed to a spare bench slap bang in the middle of everyone. We dashed towards the empty seats and settled ourselves down, waiting in anticipation for the results to be revealed. The judges were dressed in white coats and resembled the staff at the local hospital; it all seemed very serious and official.

Inside the tent the poultry farmers were all of a certain age and calibre, with the exception of Tom and Robin, who were miles younger than the rest. A group of them were standing in a huddle at the rear of the tent, poised with their hands clasped behind their backs, waiting for the judges to begin. They all appeared to be wearing the same attire: nattily unkempt tweed jackets, flat caps and green wellington boots.

Abruptly, one of the judges hammered on the table with his fist to attract everyone's attention. One and all in the tent stopped talking and looked up towards where the judges were sitting. Several shushes could be heard all around us. The judges went through numerous categories, announcing the winners, and applause rang out from the onlookers. There was a prize for each winner along with a hefty handshake from the judges, which was followed by the proud pinning of rosettes onto their clothing; each one was worn with pride.

The final category was upon us, the one we had been sitting there waiting for all this time. It was time for the cream of the crop to be revealed. Whose rooster would be crowned the ultimate bird? The time had come to announce the 'best in show'.

It was at this moment I glanced towards the front of the tent. 'Wow! Look at that rooster – he's stunning! What type of breed is he?' I enquired, pointing to a cage that was situated very near to the judges' table.

'That would be a Norfolk Grey and that would also be Bert, direct competition for Paddy.' Robin winked at me.

'He's yours?'

'He certainly is,' he replied smugly.

'May the best bird win!' Tom chipped in.

'What are our chances next to Bert?' I whispered in Tom's ear.

'Very good. Relax, it'll be fine.'

The judge stood up behind the table; the tent was now in complete silence. My heart was beating in double time. Slowly opening the envelope, the judge pulled out the card and paused.

The gentleman sitting directly in front seemed very agitated; he was shuffling in his seat and could be heard muttering 'hurry up.' I watched another farmer frantically pacing up and down in front of the cages.

Scrunching my eyes closed, I waited for the result.

'And the winner of the best in show goes to Kitty Lewis and her Buff Orpington rooster Paddy.'

Tom sprang to his feet cheering and whooping.

I opened my eyes and blinked. 'Did he just say Kitty Lewis?' I needed clarification.

'You've won, you've won!' Tom's lovely smile lit up his face.

'Kitty Lewis, if you are in the show tent please come up and collect your prize,' the judge requested.

I was dumbfounded.

Tom had done all the hard work, pampering Paddy, getting him in tip-top condition for the show; I couldn't even catch him, and there was Tom registering me as the owner.

Wide-eyed in amazement, I looked to Tom for guidance – he was beaming with pride.

'Congratulations! Go on, go and retrieve your prize.' He gestured in the direction of the judges.

Stumbling towards the front of the tent, I stepped over numerous feet and felt plentiful pats on the back whilst I made my way through the crowd. Pinning a rosette with the words 'first prize' to my coat, I couldn't help but beam at the judges as they shook my hand one by one. Paddy too had a first-prize rosette pinned to the front of the cage; he appeared to be taking it all in his stride. 'That's a champion you have there, Kitty – make sure you look after him.'

I was so overwhelmed, I was speechless, but I could feel the wide smile stretching out across my face. Returning to my seat clasping a bottle of wine and a voucher for a year's free supply of chicken food for Paddy, I sat back down.

'Well done you! I've been beaten by a novice,' Robin said, laughing.

'I feel like a fraud – I didn't do anything, you did it all,' I whispered to Tom.

'We all have to start somewhere – don't worry about it. Now speech, speech,' Tom insisted, smiling.

Theatrically, I dabbed my eyes, laughing. 'Thank you to all those who have supported me.'

'Stop there! Stop rubbing my nose in it!' Robin grinned.

'Ahhh, look at you beaming with pride.' Lucinda came strolling towards us and gave me a rib-crushing hug. 'Your very first rosette, congratulations! Where are you going to pin it?'

Pausing for a moment, I took a breath. 'I think I'm going to pin it next to all Dotty's rosettes in Grandma Agnes's office.'

'That sounds like a fantastic idea. Talking of Dotty, has she turned up yet? She's always been a familiar fixture, pecking around the Lodge. It's not the same without her.'

'No she hasn't.' Tom sighed. 'It's been twenty-one days now and counting.'

'Do you think it's down to the fox?' asked Robin.

'More than likely,' he replied sadly.

'Let's go and release Paddy back at the yard and then who's for a quick celebration drink down the pub?' I asked, attempting to lift the mood back up.

'Me, me, me!' That was a resounding yes.

'And no gin and tonic for you,' Tom said, and grinned in my direction.

'Sounds like an excellent plan. I just need to pack up the table at the cake stall. I've sold every last crumb,' Lucinda proudly declared. 'It won't take me two minutes to load up the car. I'll meet you all back at the pub.'

'Yes, OK, we'll just go and drop off the champion and see you there.'

Travelling back to the Lodge with Tom, I was feeling happy. Granted, I knew deep down I wasn't a worthy winner; I hadn't done a thing, but it was lovely of Tom to let me take the credit. As he drove the van towards the Lodge, he pulled up and waited in front of the gate and left the engine revving.

'I'll undo the lock,' I said, jumping out of the van and bounding towards the gate.

'1507,' Tom called after me.

I waved my hand above my head. Yes, I know, I thought. I'm not going to forget my own birthday in a hurry.

Swinging the gate open so Tom could drive the van through, I wasn't sure how I was going to cope on my birthday this year. For as long as I could remember I'd spent it with Mum, but in a way I was looking forward to the summer months at the Lodge with my new friends. It would keep me busy.

There was no denying I had had the most enjoyable day yet, but there were sporadic moments when my thoughts flicked to Jeannie and Tom and the night of the date. I'd had so much fun with Tom and every time I thought of them together, waves of emotion flooded through my body. Why did I feel such envy and sadness? I needed to control these feelings and fast. If I wasn't careful, the way I felt could affect all of my new friendships, not to mention potentially placing a massive strain on the professional working relationship at the Lodge. The Lodge was my new lifeline, and if I didn't have that I would be left with nothing. If Jeannie and Tom felt an attraction towards each other, there was nothing I could do about it except try and learn to accept it, however difficult that may be.

Glancing up towards the top of the drive, I froze.

'Tom, Tom, look,' I squealed at the top of my voice, pointing towards the grass verge. Immediately Tom looked up. A wide grin spread across his face.

'Well would you believe it?' he shouted back to me. There, waddling in front of us, was Dotty, with six little chicks following their mother hen.

'Dotty's a mum!' I squealed in delight.

'She certainly is and that's why she's been missing. She must have been sitting on her eggs. What a lovely surprise!'

CHAPTER 19

Spring was certainly a busy time down at the Lodge – the work seemed to have doubled overnight. Not only was Dotty a new mother but so were half of the other chickens. The older chickens needed to be rehoused into the bottom paddocks, the point-of-lay chickens moved up to the next fields and all the new mother hens with their chicks needed to be segregated into their own little coops.

Egg production was at full capacity. I'd never seen so many eggs. They were all different shapes and sizes and the range of colours was truly spectacular.

The activity within the yard at the Lodge had also increased. The accounts were certainly showing that there had been a surge in profits and this was the ideal opportunity to hire more staff. So Tom had taken on a number of temporary farmhands to help us with the everyday running of the place. One of the barns had been converted into a makeshift shop that sold free-range eggs and fresh grown produce from the farm during the warmer months. Lucinda kindly baked scones and flapjacks, which she dropped off early in the morning, and her scrumptious baking always sold out within a matter of minutes. Visitors arrived at what seemed like every minute of the day. I couldn't believe how much this place had come alive in a matter of weeks.

Each year for as long as Tom could remember there had always been an annual Easter-egg hunt held at the Lodge for all the local families. It was an occasion everyone looked forward to. Bluebell Lodge was perfect with its stunning backdrop and was certainly an ideal place for Easter fun and games. Lucinda in recent years had offered to make all the mouth-watering chocolate eggs for the children single-handedly. Whilst chatting one morning on her early-morning delivery, she explained to me it was essential to temper the chocolate. I didn't have a clue what she was talking about until she enlightened me to the fact that this was a method of heating and cooling the chocolate for moulding. The heating and cooling separated the cocoa solids and ensured the set chocolate would have a high gloss and smooth finish. It all sounded very complicated to me. I was relieved my only job would be to write the clues for the Easter-egg hunt.

Everyone was hoping for a clear spring day. Amongst the famous bluebells there was also an opportunity for the visitors to handle the newborn chicks. Conker the Shetland pony was also on hand to provide rides around the field. He was always a firm favourite amongst the children. Tom would also be revving the tractor's engine, and for the adults there was always the Pimm's tent. Hours of fun could still be had after all the chocolate had been found. I was really looking forward to it, although as this was my first proper event at the Lodge, it was all a little daunting, but I knew I could do it. Tom was fantastic, encouraging me every step of the way. This was an ideal opportunity to introduce myself to more of the locals and the ones I'd met so far had made me feel so welcome, I was settling in well.

I was grateful that the Lodge had come into my life when it did because I hadn't a clue what I would be doing right now or where I would have ended up otherwise. I'd begun to learn all the ropes at the Lodge and there was only one thing left on my agenda to improve and that was my social life. Since Jeannie had been ill from her episode of food poisoning, she had never seemed to fully recover. She'd promised me on numerous occasions we would enjoy a bite to eat together or travel to the next town to watch a film at the picture house, but always at the very last minute she would cancel. Usually it was due to tiredness, and Robin confirmed that she would indeed take herself off to bed at every opportunity. Before Jeannie went off sick, her job was very manual and some days I wasn't sure how she managed to shift all those bales of hay; she made it look so easy. I couldn't even lift one on my own, never mind haul it onto my shoulders and carry it to the bottom fields. Maybe she was working too hard. Since her return Tom had been fussing around her all the time, making sure she was OK. The temporary farmhands were worth their weight in gold and until Jeannie was fully back on her feet, Tom put a ban on her lifting anything, unless it was a mug of tea.

On Saturday morning at 8 a.m., Bluebell Lodge was beginning to be crammed with all things Easter. Easter bunting hung from every corner of the yard and trestle tables lined the outskirts of the long driveway, which was adorned with bluebells dancing in the light breeze. The Pimm's tent had been erected in the first field.

Conker looked dapper. Not only had Jeannie hosed him down and brushed every scrap of mud from his body, she had entwined fabric daisies around his headband.

'You look nice, Kitty!' Jeannie said, bustling past me, placing a tray of home-made scones down on one of the tables before she wandered back over in Tom's direction.

'Thank you,' I said, smiling.

It had taken me nearly an hour this morning to decide on my outfit; it was such a difficult choice. The weather was in that in-between stage: it wasn't quite warm enough to mill about in just a T-shirt, but on the other hand it was too warm to wear a thick jumper or coat. I wasn't sure a dress would be a roaring success if I had to plod around the fields leading Conker whilst the children rode on his back. In the end I plumped for a floral blouse with blue jeans and my new pair of wellington boots.

I caught sight of Tom up the ladder, pinning bunting across the front of the office. Jeannie was holding the long stream of flags for him and passing them up in stages. Robin had just arrived in his van and waved over in my direction. All hands were on deck.

Tom looked completely at ease, taking everything in his stride. He always seemed happy; I could see him laughing with Jeannie as he threw his head back. His hair was a little longer, his fringe flopping in front of his eyes and he would often push it to one side. He had the beginnings of a beard and his face was a little tanned in the springtime sun. He was simply gorgeous. Feeling my pulse quicken and goosebumps rising to the surface of my skin, I felt myself blush. Since that night in the pub, I'd tried to block any feelings I'd had for Tom out of mind. I valued the friendship of both him and Jeannie and I really didn't need to complicate matters any further.

I'd thought about blurting it out on many occasions, but what was I thinking? I'd been hurt enough in the last year and I knew the feeling of grief wasn't quite the same, but I didn't want the risk of rejection too. Tom had made it obvious that he was attracted to Jeannie so there was no need to embarrass any of us. At that moment, Tom looked over in my direction and smiled. I smiled back and went about hiding the chocolate eggs all around the Lodge. Once the bunting was firmly attached, Tom climbed down the ladder and he and Jeannie bounded across in my direction.

'The Easter-egg hunt will begin at 10 a.m. Will you be OK to say a few words, Kitty?'

'You want me to say a few words?'

'It'll be over quickly, it's nothing to worry about.'

'But you're still running the place,' I insisted.

'Yes, I know, but you're the owner, and with most of the village coming over today, it'll be the ideal opportunity to introduce yourself to everyone.'

I wasn't feeling very confident. I'd never addressed an audience before, but I was sure I could manage a quick introduction and declare the Easter-egg hunt well and truly open. Jeannie squeezed my arm and gave me a sympathetic look. 'You'll be absolutely fine.'

Robin touched my shoulder and poked his head between us. 'Sorry to interrupt but people are already starting to arrive.'

Looking up the long driveway, I saw Robin was right; there were numerous families already here, browsing at the various tables, purchasing cups of tea and slabs of cake. The children were full of beans, playing tag, laughing and skipping straight towards the bouncy castle.

I decided to take one last stroll around the Lodge and the fields to make sure everything was in place. I was determined to make today a success. And by the time I got back to the yard, it seemed like the whole village was there.

'I think it's time, Kitty. Are you ready?' Tom asked.

Nervous butterflies were beginning to flutter around my stomach at a rate of knots. I let out a nervous sigh and smoothed my blouse down then strolled towards the front of the gathering crowd.

Standing on top of a strategically placed crate, I glanced over the sea of people. Unless anyone looked closely enough I doubted they'd see my legs trembling. Clearing my throat, I was ready.

I stole a furtive glance at Tom; he raised his eyebrows and nodded in my direction to give me some encouragement. I blew into the microphone that Jeannie had quickly handed to me from the nearby table.

'Good morning, everyone.'

I paused for a minute, waiting for the babble to calm down and for everyone to look in my direction. I stood smiling whilst people settled and waited for me to carry on with my speech. There were what seemed like hundreds of eyes looking back at me.

'Hello! I would love to take this opportunity to welcome you all to Bluebell Lodge's annual Easter-egg hunt. It's great to see so many people here this morning. For those of you who don't know me, I'm Kitty Lewis, and I'm the new owner down here at the Lodge. If you spot me wandering about this morning, please feel free to come and say hello. I'm looking forward to meeting you all. But in the meantime, without further ado, I declare the Easter-egg hunt open.'

There was a loud cheer from the excited children standing in front of me and they soon scarpered off on the trail to discover the delicious chocolate eggs. Stepping down from the crate, something caught my eye. I glanced over towards Brambleberry Cottage. Squinting in the direction of the downstairs room, I was sure I saw the curtain twitch again. Maybe it was down to the faulty catch on the upstairs window blowing a draught through the cottage like Tom had suggested. I watched carefully, waiting for some sort of movement but was disturbed by a gentleman called Willard Jones, who introduced himself to me as the local butcher.

I was just about to engage in conversation with Willard when a small child stomped fiercely over to him and yanked hard on his tweed coat. We both looked down at the little boy who was very disgruntled that Eleanor Winterbotham, another child from the same class as him at school, had just pushed him away from the hay bales he was searching in for eggs. She point-blank refused to let anyone else inside the barn until she discovered a chocolate egg. Leaving Willard to console his son, I glanced back at the curtains one last time, but they hung still. I wandered over towards Tom, who was selling raffle tickets.

On seeing me approach, he punched the air. 'You smashed that.'

'Don't be so dramatic. It was nothing! But thank you anyway!'

His eyes sparkled playfully in my direction.

I wished he wouldn't look at me like that. It was all very confusing. I'd already witnessed the closeness between Tom and Jeannie when they were hanging up the bunting, yet he always had the knack of making me feel so at ease.

The yard was busy with local children running in every direction, searching every nook and cranny, and then we heard the first shout. 'I have one, I have one!' The joyful look on the little girl's face said it all as she clutched her chocolate egg.

I noticed Conker was already plodding around the field with a small child hanging on for dear life to the handle on his saddle, and even more children were queuing, patiently waiting for their turn.

The adults were beginning to huddle around the Pimm's tent, chatting away. I nipped behind the trestle table and grabbed a couple of glasses for Jeannie and me after I'd spotted Jeannie hurrying across the yard and into the office. She was probably just having five minutes to herself. Following her lead, I weaved my way through the crowd, being careful not to spill the drinks. Leaning down on the door handle with my elbow, I pushed the door open with my foot.

Jeannie turned round whilst pinning an invoice the noticeboard.

'Ta-dah!' I said, holding up the two glasses of Pimm's. 'Look what I've got.'

Jeannie grabbed my arm. 'I'm so glad you're here, I've got something to tell you.'

'Go on,' I said, placing the drinks down onto the office desk.

'But first you have to promise not to share it with anyone.' She grinned nervously.

'Of course, I promise.'

'I'm pregnant.'

I covered my mouth to stop myself from gasping. I was stunned. 'So it wasn't food poisoning?'

'No, I've been suffering with a very bad bout of morning sickness.'

I felt suddenly guilty; I didn't feel very ecstatic. I knew I was being completely selfish. There was my friend standing nervously in front of me, her eyes watching my every move, waiting for a reaction.

'Are you pleased?' I asked.

'At first I was a little shocked but I've come to terms with it now, and I really can't wait,' Jeannie answered.

'Well in that case – congratulations!' I managed to say whilst Jeannie launched herself into my arms and hugged me tightly.

'I don't suppose you'll be wanting this then?' I said, holding up the glass of Pimm's.

'Not for me,' she replied. 'But you can have both!'

I didn't need to think twice about it. Picking up both glasses, I instantly swilled them down my throat, hoping it would dull the pain that was festering in the pit of my stomach. I was trying to be happy for Jeannie, but it was just so difficult.

'I best get back to the chick-handling; everyone will be wondering where we've got to.'

'Have you told Tom yet?' I asked.

'No, not yet, so I'm asking for absolute discretion in the meantime, Aunty Kitty!'

'That's not a problem, of course. I understand.'

Walking out of the office, my mind wandered back to the night in the pub. I flicked my eyes in the direction of Tom. Every time I looked at him my heart melted, but that was it now – it was game over.

The direction of Tom's life was about to change dramatically. He had new responsibilities, lifetime responsibilities, and I needed to get over my crush. Glancing over at the cottage, I pictured Jeannie at some point moving in with Tom. It wouldn't be long before their child would be tottering around the yard. Biting down hard on my bottom lip, I prayed hard that the tears wouldn't roll down my face.

'Are you OK?'

I whirled round to find Tom standing in front of me.

Gosh, it was all so complicated.

'Yes, of course I'm OK, I just needed a minute. I was feeling a little overwhelmed with everyone being so kind to me today.' I nodded sheepishly, swallowing the lump in my throat. 'Will you excuse me? I promised to lead Conker around the field next,' I continued.

Now it was too late to even mention my feelings towards him – it would be cruel to throw them into the mix, and Jeannie was my friend. What sort of friend was I if I couldn't be happy for them both?

Any last hope I ever had of Tom even noticing that I existed had just evaporated before my very eyes. Jeannie was pregnant with his baby. They would become a family. There was no doubt about it – both of them would be terrific parents.

How things changed in such a small space of time.

Even though the next few hours flew by, I carried on in a trance. Numerous people introduced themselves to me; I smiled in the right places and nodded when it was needed, but I didn't remember any of their names.

The hordes of people were now dispersing rapidly. Tired children clutching their chocolate eggs and balloons could be seen trailing down the long driveway, heading home, behind their parents.

Tom, Robin and Lucinda were gathered in a huddle outside the office.

'What next?' I asked.

'A huge tidy-up,' said Robin, wiping his hand across his brow. 'That was a busy day.'

'Then as far as I'm concerned it's wine o'clock,' chipped in Lucinda.

I hadn't even managed to catch up with Lucinda. She had been flat out, decorating cupcakes and gingerbread men with the children at one of the tables near the bottom of the driveway.

I saluted Lucinda. 'Wine o'clock definitely sounds like a plan to me.'

I spotted Jeannie heading in our direction. I smiled but scurried past her, shouting that I'd untack Conker who was currently tied up by his lead rope to the fence in the bottom field. Usually I was up for a bit of company– after all, I spent enough time on my own – but right at this very minute my head was whirling, and I needed time to gather my thoughts.

Nipping into the far stable to grab a handful of carrots for Conker, I stopped dead in my tracks. The entire stable was swathed with twinkly fairy lights draped around the walls. In the middle were two chairs facing each other on either side of a small table. A white linen cloth adorned the table, decorated skilfully with scattered sugar-pink rose petals. Dozens of tea lights were dotted over the floor, yet to be lit. It was plain to see a romantic meal was on the cards. Jeannie must have been up at the crack of dawn, getting this prepared. She was obviously planning on telling Tom the wonderful news that he was about to become a father.

Collecting my thoughts, I flung my arms around myself whilst I shivered. My whole body was trembling. My heart was pounding. Regardless of what my thoughts were on the situation, Jeannie had gone to great lengths to set the scene and she had achieved it perfectly.

Turning around, I closed the stable door behind me. Putting on a brave face, my eyes pricked with tears.

My feet stumbling in front of each other, I reached Conker. Throwing my arms around his neck, I buried my face deep into his neck. I felt so sad.

Startled, I felt a warm hand being placed on my arm.

'Well, that's a sigh and a half.'

I looked up to find Robin holding out a can of beer towards me.

'I thought you might like one of these. Everyone's been working so hard and today's been a resounding success.'

I took the can from him and nodded my appreciation. Robin was a total sweetheart; he was a kind man and most definitely handsome. Maybe I should give it a go – I didn't have anything to lose. Pulling back the ring pull, Robin chinked his can against mine.

'Here's to us,' he whispered softly whilst looking into my eyes. We both took a swig. Gently his fingers reached for mine. Taking the can from my hand, he bent down and placed it on the ground with his. Pulling me close, he wrapped his arms around me and hugged me. Resting his chin on top of my head, he spoke softly.

'I really like you, Kitty.'

Gulping, I felt I was being watched. Looking up over his shoulder, I saw Tom further up the field staring at us. I felt myself blush; hotness burnt in my cheeks. Our eyes met but he shifted his gaze to the ground and quickly turned and walked away. Robin still had his arms tightly wrapped around my body.

I hesitated and then looked up at him.

He was waiting for me to speak. He was waiting for me to say something. His expression was earnest, but his eyes sparkled with anticipation. I faltered at first, but before I'd made up my mind about anything, I heard the words leave my lips: 'I like you too.'

I had no idea what I was doing.

CHAPTER 20

I spent the rest of Easter in something of a daze. Truth be known, I was a bit of a mess. I didn't even bother to change out of my pyjamas for a couple of days and spent most of the time curled up on the sofa, reading, with Alfie by my side. I continually glanced down at the page of my book and found myself rereading the same sentences over and over again. The day of the Easter-egg hunt had been an emotional journey. At the start I had been overjoyed, ecstatic, looking forward to the day ahead, then my mood had turned sombre. I felt battered and bruised. It had hit me hard when Jeannie had shared the news that she was expecting a baby. It wasn't something I was expecting to hear. The setting in the stable was truly romantic and Tom would be celebrating by now. I knew I should feel happy for them both, but it didn't stop me feeling incredibly sad. I wasn't ready to speak to anyone. Looking up at the blue sky through the living-room window, my thoughts turned to my parents. I could hear my mother's voice shouting down at me, telling me to pull myself together. I smiled; sometimes she nagged way too much for my liking.

Before Mum became ill she'd been a very calming influence in my life. One of our favourite things to do had been to flick through an old suitcase of photographs that was full to the brim of my childhood memories. Mum would take each photograph out of the case and relay when and where the picture had been taken. The oldest photograph of me was with my parents, standing outside our home whilst they clutched their new bundle of joy; I was wrapped up tightly in a white crocheted blanket. My mum used to keep the suitcase on the top shelf of her wardrobe; I always needed to ask her permission to look at the photographs because I was too small to reach the shelf. That suitcase was one of the things I kept from my old family home. It held special memories, and in fact all my memories of my mother and father were secured inside that case.

Thinking about the case and its treasures, I wondered once more why my parents had never mentioned my grandparents to me and why I had never seen a photo. Why had I never met them? My mum was a kind, decent person and I wasn't aware she had any deep, dark family secrets to hide. I was very surprised that she'd kept this information from me. It was all a mystery and a mystery that no doubt would be difficult to solve, yet I was determined that someone somewhere must know something.

Pulling myself to my feet, I wandered into the kitchen to make a fresh drink. When I'd got up, Alfie had peeped from one of his eyes, but had soon closed it again; he was as lazy as me this weekend. Settling back down on the settee, I rested my head on the arm. Slowly my eyes closed and I must have dozed off into a deep sleep because I was woken by the paperboy posting the free paper through the letter box. Glancing over to the clock, I realised I'd been asleep for nearly three hours. I picked up my untouched cold mug of tea and walked into the kitchen.

A microwave meal for one was on the cards for tonight's tea; either that or beans on toast made with stale bread. I sighed and glanced out into my little yard at the back of the house; the climbers were certainly doing their job, and it was amazing how much surface the new green shoots could cover in such a short space of time. After making a fresh cuppa I pulled the kitchen chair out from underneath the table and plonked myself down. Taking a sip of my tea, I knew what I needed to do. I needed to get on with it. This was about the happiness of Jeannie and Tom and their unborn child. It wasn't about me; it was about what was right for them. Luckily for me it had been the Easter holidays and up at the Lodge Tom and the farmhands had it under control. Tomorrow I was due back in work and I would embrace the situation. I wanted to be a part of their lives and if that meant this was the only way, then I would grasp it with both hands. They were my friends, the closest thing I had to family. The wallowing in self-pity stopped right here.

There was only one thing for it: a long soak in the bath accompanied by a large glass of wine. I knew after I'd washed my hair and climbed into a clean set of PJs that everything would feel a whole lot better.

The following morning, cycling up the long driveway, I couldn't help but smile – there was Dotty with her army of fluffy chicks foraging around in the flower beds outside the cottage. Tom's boots were missing from the doorway, which meant he was up and about and more than likely feeding the chickens in the bottom field. At that moment, I spotted him walking up the yard towards me, swinging the baskets of eggs, which were full to the brim.

'Morning, Kitty, how are you?' He appeared quite chirpy. He must be happy with the news then, I thought.

It was one thing having a secret crush on Tom, but I was so relieved I hadn't acted on it.

'Absolutely fine, thank you. How about you?'

I waited for Tom to gush with his news, but there was nothing, not even a hint he was about to become a dad.

I stared at him, waiting.

'Why are you staring at me like that?'

'Like what?'

'Like that,' he said, laughing and imitating my expression.

Shaking my head, I said, 'No particular reason. Did you have a good Easter?' I asked, managing to change the subject quickly.

'Very quiet to be honest. I moseyed around the farm and tidied up the clutter inside one of the barns, oh and I made a list of jobs that need to be carried out this week.'

'It sounds like you had a ball!' I joked.

'There wasn't much left to do once the Easter-egg hunt had finished, so I made the most of the quiet time.'

I bet he did, I thought. Soon Tom would have no idea what quiet time was when he was cradling a baby that was crying morning, noon and night.

'Anyway, so come on, what's going on between you and Robin? Is there romance on the cards? Come and tell me all about it,' Tom said, plonking himself down on the bench and patting the space next to him.

There were a million and one things I could have said but I didn't. A surge of emotion rushed through my body.

'There's nothing to tell,' I said, sitting next to him, flexing my wellington boots and avoiding eye contact with him at all costs.

Silence.

Gazing up at him, I saw he was grinning at me and I met his inquisitive stare. 'Now, Kitty Lewis, do you want to tell me the truth?'

'Honestly, there's nothing to tell.' There wasn't actually anything to tell. I hadn't clapped eyes on Robin since he wrapped his arms around me in the field. I had spoken to him on the phone a couple of times but I told him I was a little unwell and I'd catch up with him soon.

'Well, if that's the way you want to play it, then so be it.' He scrunched his face up teasingly at me and patted my knee. I felt myself blush. 'Come on, you; I have a different kind of job for you to do today.'

'Hang on a minute, I thought I was the boss!' I joked. 'Shouldn't I be the one giving out the orders?'

'You delegated that job to me! No doubt you'll be giving out orders very soon, but in the meantime …' He laughed.

Following him into the office, I stared around the room. It most definitely looked like a bomb had exploded. Every drawer in the filing cabinet was ajar and there were piles and piles of papers stacked up, covering the desk. I had no idea what any of them were for.

'What's going on in here?'

'It's that time of year when not only the coops receive an extra spring clean but the paperwork needs a thorough sort out too.'

'There's a lot of paperwork to sort out,' I commented.

'It's not too bad. Those piles over there are for shredding – the shredder is just behind the desk on the floor. Those invoices are over five years old so we can destroy those and then move the remaining ones in the filing cabinet up a year and so on. To be honest, anything you think we don't need anymore just destroy it. Let's reshuffle this filing system so each and every one of us will know exactly where everything is.'

'Yes, I can do that. I'll make a start now,' I offered, removing my jacket and throwing it over the back of the chair. Obviously I hadn't a clue what I was doing, but sitting in the office for most of the day suited me down to the ground.

'Once you've worked your way through this little lot, there's also that cupboard over there that's bursting with paperwork. Could you possibly see what you could do with that lot as well?'

'Not a problem. What's in that safe there?' I asked, pointing to another cupboard-like feature with a combination keypad on the front.

Tom looked up to where I was pointing. 'I've no idea what's in there; that was Agnes's cupboard. I don't even know what the combination is for the lock,' he said, shrugging.

'OK, I'll work my way through these papers first.' Walking over to the radio, I switched it on and sank down into the office chair.

Suddenly the office door opened and in walked Jeannie. 'Good morning, you pair. I was wondering where you were,' she said and smiled.

This morning Jeannie looked radiant. Her skin was clear and her cheeks a little flushed. Standing at the door, she cupped one of her hands underneath her stomach. It was an instinctive reaction, but there was nothing to see as yet. Her overalls were still baggy, but no doubt that would soon change as the months rolled on.

'Good morning, Jeannie,' Tom replied. I watched with curiosity; there was nothing, nothing at all – not even a hint that they were in a relationship, never mind having a baby together. If I hadn't known, there was no way I would've guessed. I was impressed that they weren't letting their private life impinge on their professional life, so to speak.

'Perfect timing, Jeannie. Please will you pass me those bin bags and switch that kettle on? I may as well have a cuppa whilst I sort through this paperwork,' I said.

Jeannie scrunched her face up at me. 'Cheeky, what did your last slave die of?' she joked.

'Huh?' I pretended to be insulted.

'I'll leave you girls to it. I'm heading down to the barn to pack the eggs for the deliveries. I'll see you later.' And with that Tom was gone and the door closed behind him.

Perching on the desk, Jeannie swung her legs back and forth waiting for the kettle to boil. I was tempted to ask how Tom had taken the news of the baby but something held me back. I didn't want to pry. Jeannie would tell me in her own good time, and unless Tom mentioned the baby I wouldn't say a word. They didn't need me interfering. I was sure Tom would be shocked but delighted, and maybe the pair of them had decided to keep their news quiet until after their first scan. Wasn't that what most couples did?

'How are you feeling, Jeannie?'

'Absolutely great this morning. I've nibbled on a couple of ginger biscuits, which seemed to curb my sickness a little.'

'Any mad cravings? Pickled onions, roast beef monster munch or eating ice?'

Jeannie looked up at me like I had gone mad. 'Eating ice?'

'Yes, eating ice! Honestly, I saw it on a TV programme once. There was a pregnant woman who would just order a glass of ice at the bar. Then she would sit there and quite happily chew her way through it!'

'Ewww … no ice chewing for me, but I am a little partial to chocolate though. Chocolate for breakfast seems to be the norm at the moment.'

'By any pregnant woman's reckoning that's probably the most wonderful craving to have.'

After a quick drink, Jeannie disappeared out of the office door to carry on with her chores. Glancing around the room, I didn't know which mound of paperwork to start on first. Grabbing the pile nearest to me, I thought I might as well start with the desk because once that was clear it would be easier to work from the uncluttered space.

Sitting on the floor, I fed each sheet through the chrome teeth of the shredder. To tell the truth, I hadn't really got a clue how important any of it was. But I was sure we didn't need to know that Willard Jones ordered ten dozen boxes of eggs to sell in his butcher's shop over half a decade ago. It was a very therapeutic job though, and it certainly wasn't taxing. The piles were soon diminishing.

Nearly two hours and several bin bags of shredded paper later, I was near the end. Sipping on a glass of water, I scanned the room – only two smaller piles left to shred, then I'd have a look to see what was inside the cupboard. Dragging the bursting bin bags across the office floor and out the door, I piled them up outside. Out of the corner of my eye, I noticed Tom striding up the path towards Brambleberry Cottage. He always returned home for his lunch. Since beginning work at the Lodge I could never remember Tom spending his lunchtime with Jeannie and me. He paused outside the door – he must have sensed me watching him. Turning around, he waved his hand above his head in my direction then disappeared through the front door.

Going back inside the office, I stared at the cupboard. I'd skipped breakfast this morning and now my stomach was beginning to gurgle and hunger pains were slowly creeping in. I decided to break for lunch before I started to clear out the final cupboard.

Jeannie popped her head around the door. 'Are you ready to eat?'

'You read my mind! Yes, come on, let's eat before I start on the rest of this clearance.'

'How's it going in here? Are you able to sort it into some sort of order?'

'It's not been too difficult. If in doubt I feed it through the shredder!' I laughed.

'That sounds like the best way.'

'I've got that one left,' I nodded in the direction of the cupboard, 'and then I'll reorganise the filing system.'

'What's in there?' Jeannie pointed over to the safe.

'Tom said that belonged to my grandmother. He doesn't know the code to open it, so I'm not entirely sure.'

Grabbing the carrier bag containing my lunch from the top of the filing cabinet, I followed Jeannie outside and we sank down onto the bench. She stretched her legs straight out in front of her then sighed. For a split second I had forgotten she was pregnant.

'I'm feeling really tired. My mind is active but my body just won't move. If I'm like this now what's it going to be like after six months? I'm dreading it when I become huge.'

'They always say you bloom in your last trimester.'

'Well I'm hoping so, because I feel blooming awful right now.' She laughed, sinking her teeth into a cheese sandwich and then went pale and placed the sandwich back inside the tinfoil wrapping.

'I can't eat that,' she said. 'I don't fancy it at all.'

Glancing at Jeannie, I saw she did look a little peaky. 'What do you fancy then?'

'I feel like chips and gravy with lashings of vinegar!'

'Ha ha, this could be your first craving. Right, I'm on it – your wish is my command! You put your feet up, I'll take the bike and I'll be back in ten minutes.'

Tossing my purse into the basket of my bike, I put one foot on the pedal and pushed off. Suddenly a thought crossed my mind and I placed both feet back on the ground. 'I'd best check if Tom would like some chips.'

Leaning the bike against the stone wall, I strolled towards the front door and knocked on the door to Brambleberry Cottage. I stood on the herringbone doormat and waited. I heard a scraping of a chair across the floor and talking. I strained to listen; I recognised Tom's voice. A couple of seconds later it was silent and then I heard the sound of his footsteps approaching the door. The door opened slightly and Tom peered around the edge of the door.

'Is everything OK?'

'Yes of course. We're treating ourselves to some chips for lunch, would you like some?'

'No thanks, I'm fine.'

I'm not sure whether it was my imagination but Tom looked shifty and seemed to be in a hurry to close the door.

'Are you OK? Did I interrupt you?' I knew I was prying but I was convinced I'd heard Tom's voice. He had definitely been talking to someone.

'Yes, of course I'm OK. Ted's popped in the back door; we're just catching up on some farm stuff while I'm eating my lunch. I'll see you in an hour.'

'Working lunch, no rest for the wicked.' I smiled and turned around towards my bike.

I quickly glanced back over my shoulder to see a shadow shift behind the closed curtains – Tom must have been watching me walk back up the path.

Cycling down the path and towards the chip shop, something was beginning to bug me and it wasn't just Tom's odd behaviour. Instantly my thoughts turned to the safe, the unopened safe of Grandma Agnes. I was feeling a little anxious and couldn't quite put my finger on why. The harder I cycled, the more my mind whirled. Placing two bags of steaming hot chips in the basket, I furiously pedalled back towards the Lodge. I was now completely breathless.

Jeannie hadn't moved a muscle except for the fact she'd slid down the bench and her eyes were closed, her face tilted towards the afternoon sun.

'Here you go: chips and gravy with lashings of vinegar.'

Looking up, she smiled. 'Mmmm, they smell divine, just what I needed.' Before I'd even propped the bike up against the wall of the office, she was stabbing her fork into a chip and swirling it around in the gravy at the bottom of the white polystyrene tray. Jeannie began chatting whilst we sat there eating, but my mind was wandering. I wasn't listening to a word she was saying. Curiosity was beginning to eat me up; I only had one thing on my mind. I wanted to know what was inside that safe.

How was I going to work out the code? There could be hundreds, maybe thousands of different combinations. In addition,

I was also feeling pretty bad about the prospect of going through the safe, but to be honest, Grandma Agnes was dead now and the safe would have to be sorted at some point. As I was now the boss and, as far as I knew, her only surviving relative, wasn't I the best person to do it?

'Are you listening to a word I'm saying?' Jeannie was watching me with an amused look on her face.

'Oh no, I'm sorry, Jeannie. I was daydreaming.'

Patting my knee, she stood up and laughed. 'Don't worry about it, I was only babbling on about absolutely nothing! Thank you for the chips. I'd best wander back down to the bottom field.' I watched her slim figure walk down the yard. I couldn't imagine her with a baby bump, but no doubt it wouldn't be long before it started to show through her baggy overalls.

Strolling back into the office, I threw the chip wrappers into the bin and turned my attention to the locked safe.

Scooping my hair up in my hands, I tied it back with the bobble that was wrapped around my wrist. Bending down, I looked closely at the lock. There was a keypad and four spaces followed by a green enter button. Next to the enter button was a red LED light. I chewed on my lip and stared. I was tempted to try and crack the code. I wasn't sure why I was even so intrigued. The safe could easily be empty. But curiosity got the better of me and I leant forward. Pressing the numbers one, two, three, four, the light still stayed red. It appeared Grandma Agnes was a little more adventurous with her choice of combination numbers.

Randomly, I began to press numbers: zero, three, seven, six. Nothing.

I tried again: nine, eight, seven, six.

Still nothing.

After a few more attempts I got up and slumped into the office chair.

I don't know what I was expecting. Did I really think that I'd work out the code so easily and the safe would suddenly ping open and reveal all of Agnes's secrets?

Now I was chewing on the inside of my cheek, a habit I'd acquired as a little girl; I always did this when I was deep in thought.

Pausing, I swung the chair around and stared at the lock again.

I went over to examine the keypad thoroughly.

Hovering nervously over the door I scrutinised it closely. I'd seen detectives do this in the movies. The numbers zero, one, five and seven were more worn than the other numbers on the keypad. My heart was thumping, my hands were sweating and my skin began to prickle. Taking a deep breath, I punched in the numbers in that exact order.

The light remained red.

Sighing, I crossed my legs and sat directly in front of the safe. Leaning my elbows on my knees, I cupped my hands around my face. The last time I could remember sitting like this was in primary school.

I typed in the numbers backwards.

The light still remained red.

Closing my eyes I thought hard.

Come on, Kitty, you must know.

It hit me like a bolt out of the blue.

Rubbing my sweaty hands together I pressed the numbers one, five, zero, seven. I was praying the numbers were the same as the combination code for the gate at the end of the driveway, the numbers of my birthday, 15 July.

Please open, I urged silently.

There was a little pause then a click.

Staring at the lock, the red light changed to green.

There were two things I was absolutely sure about before I rifled through the safe: that the numbers were no coincidence and that there were a lot of questions that needed answering. I was beginning to think more and more about Agnes and why my parents had pretended she was dead.

CHAPTER 21

Curled up on my bed, I yanked the duvet up to my chin. Clasped in my hand was a fabric-bound journal held together by an elastic band. This afternoon when I had peered inside the safe my heart had lurched; it appeared to be empty. Frantically I thrust my hand inside, feeling every nook and cranny. Lying right at the back, I felt an object, and, pulling it out, I found it was some kind of journal. I had hidden it from prying eyes and closed the safe again, making a huge effort not to read it at work. Now that I was back in the flat, on my own, in peace and quiet, it was time.

I made myself comfy. Alfie jumped onto the bed next to me. He arched his back and I stroked his soft fur. He paddled the covers gently, his claws lifting the fabric of the duvet before he settled down and curled up in a ball.

Staring at the journal, I knew I was about to invade someone's privacy. My head was telling me it was wrong to trespass into someone else's life, but my heart was telling me to open the book.

What was I going to do? The fact was this book was in my grandma's safe and it might help me to uncover more about my family. If I returned the book back to the safe unread, it would always be on my mind.

Taking a deep breath, I removed the elastic band. Opening the front cover I was met with the words 'Violet Porter' in bold capital letters.

I had no idea who Violet Porter was. I didn't recognise the first name at all, only the surname, which was the same as my mother's maiden name.

I was curious about this book. Why was it the only thing in the safe? My heart was racing; the pulse in the side of my head was throbbing. My hands began to sweat as I turned the first page.

'Violet Porter, aged sixteen, 1960.'

Whoever Violet Porter was, her handwriting was small, neat and joined up, and as I flicked through the book there appeared to be an entry for most days of the year.

I settled down and returned to the first page. It was dated 21 October.

21 October 1960

Mum and Dad have been rowing downstairs. It was something to do with Christmas but I couldn't quite hear. They must have known I was trying to listen because I heard Dad tell Mum to shut the door. The house is not the same now Alice has left.

I know she's older than me at 27, but she's always kind to me, looks after me and sticks up for me when I'm in trouble with my parents. Mum and Dad seem to have less patience with me; they don't seem to like my quirky ways or my friends. Mum always niggles at me. Alice just tells me it's because they aren't as young as they used to be. It feels different, kind of empty, now Alice has left. Mum wept for hours after she finally moved out and started her new married life with Julian. I did too. I feel kind of abandoned, but Alice has promised I can go and stay with them anytime I want, because they have a spare room. Though when Alice suggested I could stay, Mum was very adamant that one day they would need that room for a nursery and they shouldn't make me promises. They haven't moved that far way, maybe about an hour or so, but Alice has moved nearer to Julian's family now. I think Mum and Dad were arguing over Christmas dinner, which is a little ridiculous as we're only near the end of October. Maybe Alice wanted to spend it with Julian's family. It will be strange if that happens; it will be the first year without my sister at home.

Staring at the words on the page, my mind was in overdrive; this didn't make any sort of sense to me at all. I reread the entry again. Sister? I racked my brains but I came up with nothing. My parents had told me my grandparents were dead, and now, even more surprisingly, it seemed my mum had a sister. Which would mean I might have an aunt somewhere.

There was only one thing for it – I carried on reading.

22 October 1960

This morning Mum confirmed that Alice will be spending the day with Julian's family at Christmas. Christmas won't mean anything to me this year without spending time with the ones who mean so much to me. I am deeply disappointed. I can picture myself sitting around the table with turkey and all the trimmings alongside my parents and no one will speak. Alice was always the one that made the conversation. I don't mind admitting I cried into my pillow, not just because of Alice but because T will be spending it with his parents too. We talked about trying to meet, but I think it will be too difficult for him.

23 October 1960

T waved at me this morning on his way to work. He's handsome and his smile is simply gorgeous.

24 October 1960

It's Monday-night madness and tonight Ethel and I have our dancing shoes at the ready. I'm quite envious of her new shoes; they have a small heel. I am not allowed a shoe with a heel. We have matching skirts and there's a live band playing at the memorial hall. I am excited. I love music; I can lose myself to the rhythm and dance all night. Fingers crossed T and George will be able to make it. My mum gave us the usual lecture about maintaining our good reputation in public. My mum should be grateful we don't have the same standards as Tricia Lowe, because that girl certainly has a reputation. My mum worries too much. I doubt she was ever young and knew how to enjoy herself.

25 October 1960

T was a no-show last night. I was disappointed but something must have come up. I looked over my shoulder all night, watching the door, hoping he would show up, but he didn't. I'm just having a few minutes upstairs by myself because Alice and Julian are due over very soon for afternoon tea. I've missed Alice. I hope I can go and stay with her soon.

27 October 1960

Yesterday dragged on and on. This morning couldn't come soon enough. I waited for five minutes around the corner for T to drive past in his van. I couldn't believe it when I saw him indicate and pull over. He doesn't usually pull over. What a lovely surprise. He winked and handed me a small letter. My heart flipped. This is my third letter from T now. Ripping open the envelope, I stood on the edge of the street and read it. 'One day, one day soon xx' was all it said, but that was enough, for now. I was on cloud nine today. Today was a good day.

I was so engrossed in Violet's writing that I was startled by the
sudden ringing of the phone in the hallway. Rushing towards it,
I picked up the receiver to find Robin on the other end. He and
Lucinda were going to the pub for an hour and they asked me to
join them. I politely declined. All I wanted to do this evening was
to read more about Violet Porter. I hurriedly returned to the diary.

28 October 1960

*Mum and Dad are trying to arrange a dinner party with
the Smithells from Green Park. Green Park, I say! Everyone
knows those houses are worth an absolute fortune. Mum was
nearly hyperventilating when Mrs Smithells informed her she
would check her diary and get back to her with a date at the
earliest opportunity. She's been pacing up and down the living
room now for nearly fifteen minutes waiting for a date to be
confirmed. She's been hinting for a while that their son is a
perfect gentleman and he would like to escort me to the exquisite
Christmas party at Handover Place. I'm sure Winston Smithells
is just as embarrassed as me regarding my mum's matchmaking
attempts. He may be what they call a 'good catch', but he's not
my catch. Handover Place is too posh; I would have to mind
my Ps and Qs. And me in a posh dress ... please! Mum told
me I needed to grab this opportunity and if Winston became
a permanent fixture in my life I wouldn't want for anything.
I thought about it for a minute, only a minute mind. Surely
you needed to marry someone for love?*

29 October 1960

*During my lunch break today the inevitable happened. I'd
nipped out from the farm on the sandwich run whilst Mum
and Dad were tending to the livestock. T's van was parked*

outside the bakery. I checked the registration a dozen times to make sure I wasn't hallucinating. Glancing through the window, I saw it was him. He looked gorgeous; the sleeves of his overalls were rolled up, revealing his strong tanned forearms – a perk of always working outdoors. He turned around and spotted me; immediately he flashed a beautiful grin. I felt my knees tremble. I blushed and looked at the ground in a coy manner. T opened the door and I got in.

Mum and Dad questioned me on my return – how had it taken nearly an hour and a half to buy sandwiches from the shop? Mum appeared angry, but I think that was more down to me missing Winston Smithells, who'd turned up unexpectedly at the farm to purchase some eggs. I, on the other hand, was relieved, more than relieved, that I'd missed him.

30 October 1960

I think my mum is being unreasonable. Tomorrow night I have been invited to a party at Ethel's house; my mother has ordered me to refuse the invitation. I AM SIXTEEN. How can she order me to refuse such an invitation? She asked my dad to support her in this matter, but as usual he sloped off to the snug, clutching his newspaper – anything for a quiet life. I tried to talk to her but she reminded me this was her house and I lived under her roof. If Alice were here she'd have stuck up for me and persuaded Mum to let me go. Mum thinks Ethel is a bad influence; she thinks the girl will lead me astray. I am determined to go to the party. Ethel is my best friend; she's fun, and just because she doesn't live on Green Park that doesn't mean she's a criminal in any way, shape or form. I reminded my mum we do not live on Green Park either. My mum reminded me not to backchat my elders. I stomped out of the room.

I found myself smiling down at the diary after reading the last entry. It was clear that Violet Porter was a determined character. Rubbing my eyes, I yawned and stared through the open curtains of my bedroom window; the streetlight was shining outside. It must be getting late; the blue sky had already darkened. Glancing at my watch, I saw I'd been reading for nearly an hour and my eyes were beginning to droop. I wanted to read more; I wanted to discover more about Violet, but it would have to wait until tomorrow. I hadn't told a soul what was in the safe, not even Jeannie. I felt a little bad about that because I was privy to her secret about the baby, but that's the way I wanted it for now.

Shutting the book, I immediately opened it again.

I'd changed my mind. I was hooked; I couldn't put the journal down. I promised myself I would only read a couple more entries then I must go to sleep.

I read on.

31 October 1960

Tonight Mum is watching me like a hawk. You would think I'm a child, not sixteen years old. Retiring to my bedroom at approximately 9 p.m., I muttered goodnight to my parents. Noticing my mum's smug smile, she nodded in my dad's direction, he mumbled goodnight and dropped his head back down in the direction of his newspaper. I'd already packed a small bag of party clothes and hidden it at the bottom of the wardrobe. Ethel was expecting me; we'd arranged it at lunchtime. T is involved in the plan.

1 November 1960

I got back home but it was the worst journey ever. It must have been after 2 a.m. There was a storm and the wind was so strong. A tree had been uprooted and was lying across the road. T had to drive me the long way home in his van. The party was fantastic; Ethel and George are finally an item. I wish it were that easy for T and me. One day, he always says, one day.

Sneaking out of the house was easy. Once Mum and Dad were in bed they were out for the count. Mum plugs her ears to block out the noise of Dad's snores and he's such a heavy sleeper even an earthquake wouldn't wake him. I crept downstairs and quietly closed the front door behind me.

I could see the headlights of T's van waiting for me at the bottom of the track; the engine was running. I opened the doors to the back of his van and climbed in. The makeshift bed was still set up.

I began to change my outfit and I stripped my jumper over the top of my head. I noticed T's eyes were transfixed; he was watching my every move in the mirror. We locked eyes and foolishly grinned at each other. Kneeling down, I playfully put my hands on my hips and gave him a cheeky smile. He whistled. Emptying my bag, I quickly changed my clothes then joined him in the front of the van.

He placed his hand on my knee; his touch was electric and sent shivers up and down my spine.

He moved his hand up my thigh.

I chastised him and moved it back to my knee. He kept it there all the way to the party.

When I got back home that night, I sneaked back in through the side door, which I'd unlocked before I left. The door leads through the boot run where the laundry is kept then into the kitchen.

There was silence.

My parents were still asleep.

I'd done it – they were none the wiser.

I think I love T.

Closing the diary, I bound it with the elastic band and placed it safely in the top drawer of my bedside cabinet. I couldn't keep my eyes open any longer. Alfie was still fast asleep. I wandered across the room to draw the curtains. Before shutting them I looked up into the night sky. I liked Aunt Violet; she had character, but why had my mum never told me she had a sister?

CHAPTER 22

Next morning, after quite a restless sleep, I cycled up the path towards the Lodge. The air was nippy and all the trees that adorned the track were swaying in the brisk wind. The sky was dull and the clouds threatened rain. I wasn't sure how I felt this morning. My mind was a whirl with unanswered questions. All I knew was that I had gained an unknown aunty overnight. Truth be known, I was wishing the day away; it couldn't go quick enough. All I wanted to do was to stay tucked up under the duvet and read, but I knew with Jeannie not being able to do as much now that she was pregnant that this wasn't possible, and we had such a lot to do today. Violet Porter's diary would just have to wait.

Tom was shutting the front door of the cottage behind him as I arrived and he looked over in my direction.

'Good morning,' he shouted and waved his hand above his head.

I screeched to a halt right in front of him and placed both my feet on the ground to steady the bike.

'I've been meaning to ask …' I looked up at him.

'Ooo, this sounds ominous!' Tom joked.

'Do you own Brambleberry Cottage?'

In truth, it had crossed my mind before, but I'd never asked the question. If the cottage was in the grounds of Bluebell Lodge, wouldn't it be part of the estate?

I was intrigued.

Tom stretched his arms out in front of him and then glanced down at his watch.

I tilted my head, waiting for a response.

'Lucinda will be here in around half an hour, but before then do you want to come inside for a chat?' he asked, nodding towards the cottage.

'Yes, I think I do,' I answered, swinging my leg over my bike then resting it against the cottage wall.

Walking towards the cottage door, I tightened the band of my ponytail and tucked the escaped, windswept hair around my ears. I was conscious my heart was pounding and a feeling of trepidation ran through my entire body. We kicked off our boots at the front door, Tom twisted the door handle and I followed him inside,.

Walking on the quarry-tiled floor of the hallway, it felt cold underfoot. I'd never been inside before and the cottage oozed character with the exposed beams that ran the whole length of the ceiling. A wooden staircase adorned the hallway with a regal-looking burgundy carpet that disappeared out of sight. On the small round mahogany table sat a bottle-green telephone with its large disc dial and curled cable dangling from the receiver. Hanging all around on the bare stone walls were numerous time-worn embroidered samplers. Glancing into the sitting room, the furniture appeared sparse and simple. Everything seemed to be in its original state, like the cottage itself.

Grasping at the latch on the solid oak door to the kitchen, Tom pushed open the door and bent his head down under the low archway.

The kitchen was homely; an oversized pine farmer's table was situated in the middle of the room. There were dirty breakfast dishes spilling over in the white Belfast sink and a newspaper that lay open on the granite worktop. Freshly baked crusty bread was sitting on the table, sliced, on a chunky wooden board with the knife lying next to it. The kitchen window was framed with floral curtains that looked out over fields and fields – the view was spectacular.

I could hear the noisy hum of an old refrigerator and I noticed a pile of Tom's work clothes draped over the racing green Aga, probably drying.

'Take a seat,' Tom said, gesturing towards the kitchen table.

He reached above his head and grabbed a couple of mugs from the cupboard and placed them next to the kettle.

'Tea?' he asked.

'Yes, please.'

After switching the kettle on, he sat himself down at the table opposite me.

This would have been the ideal time to tell Tom about Violet's diary but I didn't want to tell him yet. I was shocked to find out I had an aunty I knew nothing about and I wanted to read a little bit more before I confided in anyone about my find.

Cutting to the chase, I asked, 'So the cottage, who does it belong to?'

Tom stood up and threw a couple of teabags into the teapot then poured the water in. He placed a tray on the table in front of me, which included mugs, sugar, milk and biscuits.

'Help yourself,' he said.

'Thank you, that's very kind,' I said, pouring the milk into my mug.

'The cottage belonged to your grandmother,' Tom continued.

Sipping my tea, I listened in silence.

'I don't know the ins and outs of it all and I don't think this is my story to tell, but all I know is Agnes couldn't live here anymore.'

My heart was beating in double time waiting to hear what Tom was about to reveal.

'Brambleberry Cottage has been in her family for years; this was her family home and she told me she spent her married life here. Agnes was a private person; she never meddled in anyone's business. She worked hard and Arthur was her life; they ran the farm together. When he died her world changed. She threw herself into the Lodge and worked hard, probably to occupy her mind. I started to work here when I was a young man. Arthur had already died. Agnes took me under her wing. I failed all my exams at school and wasn't what you would call academic. Agnes gave me a chance. I can remember her words: "School isn't everything, lad. It's a good attitude and hard graft that will get you far in life." '

I laughed as Tom mimicked my grandmother.

'She told me she didn't have a son to help her with the farm and I was the next best thing.'

'So how long have you lived here?'

'Once Arthur had passed away, Agnes carried on living here for another few years. They had always owned the flat on the high street and had rented it out to different couples. It was only in the last few years that she moved into it herself.'

'Why would she want to move out of here?' I asked, glancing around. 'Look at this place. It's so homely and those views are amazing.'

'The circumstances were all very peculiar, to say the least.'

'Go on.'

'One morning Agnes failed to turn up for work. I waited for another hour and thought maybe she was feeling unwell. The yard was busy, so once all the orders had been sorted I wandered over to the cottage. I knocked on the door, but she didn't answer. I had an uneasy feeling; it wasn't like her, so I let myself in. I found Agnes sobbing her heart out at this kitchen table, holding a letter with a photograph.'

'Sobbing? Did you find out why?'

'No, just at that moment Ted walked in through the back door, muttering something about borrowing Agnes's tractor to plough his fields.'

'Robin and Jeannie's father?'

'Yes, Robin and Jeannie's father. His tractor was in for repair.'

'What happened then?'

'Agnes stood up and brushed herself down and disappeared with Ted to fetch the keys to the tractor.'

I could sense there was more to this story.

Tom pushed the plate of biscuits in my direction.

'Biscuit?'

'Oh go on then,' I answered. 'I may as well live dangerously.'

'It was that evening; Agnes came and found me in the barn. I was tinkering about; I can't even remember what I was doing. She dangled a bunch of keys before my eyes and placed them in the palm of my hand. She told me that they were for me.'

'What were the keys for?'

'The keys were to Brambleberry Cottage; Agnes left that night and went to the flat, and never ever came back. She suggested I become the new live-in manager; in fact she was adamant. She made me promise I would be on hand to take care of the Lodge. I thought it was a little strange because she was getting older and it would've been ideal for her to be living on the doorstep of the farm instead of travelling in on her bike each day, but she convinced me it was for the best. I didn't argue with her, to be fair. There was never a chance I would've been able to afford to move out of home without Agnes's help – she gave me a fantastic opportunity and I grabbed it.'

Unexpectedly, Tom's face saddened.

'You want the cottage don't you, Kitty?'

Suddenly realising Tom thought I was here to take the cottage from him, I said, 'No, I don't want the cottage. Don't be daft – it's your home. I'm quite happy at the flat. Honestly, don't worry.'

He let out a sigh of relief. 'Are you sure?'

'Yes, I'm absolutely sure. If Agnes wanted you to have the cottage, then who am I to argue?' I told him.

Leaning across the table, he moved my mug to one side and took both of my hands in his. Our eyes met.

I smiled at him.

'For a minute there I thought you were asking about the cottage because you wanted to evict me.'

'Of course I don't, I love living in my flat and Alfie is very settled too.'

It was moments like this that Tom confused me. The warmth of his eyes as he smiled at me and the feel of his touch gave me mixed signals. Maybe he was grateful that I wasn't about to evict him, but it felt like more than that, at least to me. In my mind the connection was there.

He let go of my hand, and we both stood up. 'Come on, we best get back to work.' Pushing the chair under the table, I followed him back into the hallway.

Tom paused outside the open door of the living room.

'That photograph that Agnes was holding the morning she was upset is over there.' He gestured by nodding in the direction of the mantelpiece.

I spun around and followed Tom's gaze.

'Do you remember the date? When was it that Agnes was upset?' I asked, going into the living room after him.

'Yes, it was last year, near the end of July.'

'That was around the time Mum passed.' I stood next to him. He lifted up the photo and handed it to me.

Taking the photo from his hand, I stared at it.

My jaw dropped and I gasped.

Immediately I flipped the photograph over, looking for clues.

I took a deep breath and looked at Tom.

'Are you OK, Kitty? You've gone kind of pale.'

'I'm not entirely sure,' were the only words I could muster up, and I really wasn't sure.

I sank into the plush velvet sofa, still staring at the photo.

'The thing is, Tom, that's me in the photo.'

'What? Sorry, I don't follow.'

He stepped towards me, his eyes boring into mine, and he took the photo from my grasp.

The picture was of a young girl standing on the steps of Brambleberry Cottage. There was no mistaking the cottage and there was no mistaking me either. It was me as a baby, wrapped up in the same white crocheted blanket as the photo that had been taken when my parents took me home from the hospital. The woman holding me in the photo was not my mother.

Tom flipped the picture over.

He read, 'Violet and Kitty, 16 July.'

My mind was in overdrive. 16 July, the day after my birthday, which meant Violet knew about me; she had held me the day after my mum had given birth, but why didn't I know who she was? And given the fact that the photograph was taken at Brambleberry Cottage my grandma must have met me too. I scrutinised the photograph, but it wasn't the best quality. It had been taken from a distance, so I couldn't even see if Violet resembled my mum.

'Who's Violet?' Tom asked.

'My mother's sister.'

'Your aunty,' he said simply.

I swallowed. 'Yes, my aunty.'

Bleary-eyed, I gazed up wearily at Tom. He wrapped his arm around my shoulder and I lay my head there and wept. The tears wouldn't stop.

'What's going on?' he asked gently.

My voice cracked. 'I have no idea.' And that was the honest truth – I didn't have a clue. I couldn't find any more words to say; I didn't understand any of it.

My heart ached for answers.

CHAPTER 23

Jeannie had collared me coming out of the cottage. She'd just finished loading the egg orders into the back of Lucinda's van. Lucinda waved at me and shouted out of her open window, 'I'll catch you later – I've got a huge cake order to bake.' She seemed in a jolly mood today, unlike me. I forced a smile and waved back.

'Morning, how are you?' Jeannie chirped. 'Have you seen Dotty's chicks? They're growing so fast,' she said, pointing in the direction of Dotty, who was strutting up the yard with her fluffy little army following her.

Act natural, I said to myself but I couldn't answer her. I wasn't sure why but I could feel my lips starting to tremble again and tears began to cascade down my cheeks.

Jeannie looked up, startled. 'Kitty, what's up? Are you OK?'

I shook my head.

'Why are you crying?' She took my arm and ushered me to the bench outside the office.

'Sit here.' I could see the concern in Jeannie's face as she sat down next to me; she didn't take her eyes off me.

I wiped my eyes.

'I'm OK.' My voice was shaky. I knew I was being daft but I couldn't help myself. Everything was getting on top of me and the emotion was flooding out. It wasn't just the photograph that had set me off; today was my dad's birthday, and even after all these years it still felt like it was yesterday.

'Well you don't look OK to me. Come on, it can't be that bad,' Jeannie said.

Hearing the approach of footsteps, I looked up through my tears and saw Tom bending down in front of me. He placed his hand on my knee.

'Kitty, you can't work like this today. Honestly, Jeannie and I will manage. You get yourself home and rest, and come back when you feel up to it,' he said softly.

I hesitated for a second, but then before Tom changed his mind I stood up and brushed myself down. They were both being so kind, which made me even more tearful. Dabbing my nose with the tissue, I looked at Tom. 'Thank you,' I managed to say.

I could feel them watching me whilst I cycled down the drive. Being sent home suited me. To be honest it was a blessing in disguise; my heart wasn't in work today.

Pedalling along the track towards the road, I stared across the fields. I desperately wanted to speak to my mum. The pain that ripped through my body was sometimes unbearable when I realised no matter how much I wished to hear her voice again it would never happen. Glancing up at the sky, I said softly, 'Mum, what's going on? Why did I never know you had a sister and why didn't I ever know my grandparents?' Of course there was no reply.

Arriving home, I walked into the kitchen and was greeted by the unwashed leftover dinner dishes from the night before, which were currently keeping my dirty breakfast dishes company.

I shrugged at Alfie, who was winding his body in and out of my legs. 'I'm sure they can wait.'

I poured myself a glass of water then scooped him up and wandered into the bedroom. I hadn't even bothered to make my bed this morning; the duvet was still crumpled, my PJs tossed on top of it. Placing the glass of water on the bedside table, I snuggled under the bedcovers. Alfie purred contentedly then jumped up onto the duvet and soon settled down next to me.

There was only one thing I was going to do for the rest of the day and that was to try and discover any clues about Violet Porter.

Reaching for the diary, I turned the pages.

2 November 1960

I would do anything for T. Last night was simply the best. It felt like we were a proper couple at the party. He made me feel so special and he held my hand all night – he never left my side. One day, I just know, one day we will be together – we are destined. I am prepared to go through anything for T. Without a question of a doubt I will wait for him; when he's ready I will be there. There will be nothing that stands in our way. I feel so happy.

3 November 1960

Last night I dreamt about T. It was so real. I know it sounds daft but when I woke up I could smell him. We lived in one of the posh houses in Green Park; we owned a garage and a garden with roses trailing all around the door. Our two children were squealing with excitement, running around the garden with our new puppy. One day I will live with T and one day I will have children with him. We will have the perfect family and even if we don't live in Green Park it doesn't matter as long as we are together.

4 November 1960

There's something going on downstairs. Julian has arrived without Alice and has been ushered into the living room, and as usual I've been shooed to my room. Mum said I'm too young to listen to their adult conversations. I am sixteen years of age! I am not a child! T doesn't treat me like a child; he listens to everything I say. I'm so lucky to have him. I am sitting at the top of the stairs trying to listen to what's going on, but Dad's popped his head around the door and caught me. He's ordered me to my room. It's so unfair. I can hear my mum crying. Why is my mum crying? Now it's gone silent. I can't hear anything else.

I'm sitting on my bed and I've just written a letter to T. I'll pass it to him in the morning. I wonder where he hides my letters; I will have to remember to ask him.

I've just heard the front door close. I looked out of the window and watched Julian walk off down the long driveway. Where was Alice? Why wasn't she with him?

I'm so fed up in my room. I'm going to brave my dad and ask him what's going on. Wish me luck.

5 November 1960

I'm sorry I didn't come back to you yesterday, diary, but I was so upset. I plucked up the courage to go into the front room and my dad was standing with his arms wrapped around my mum. I've never seen my dad show that much emotion before.

Mum spoke through her tears and told him I had a right to know. I didn't like the sound of that and I was right not to.

My mum sat me down on the settee; she sat next to me and placed her hand on my knee. My dad sat himself down in his armchair opposite and remained quiet.

Then she told me.

Alice was in hospital.

She was admitted late last night to the Royal General.

Alice had woken up with a severe pain on the right side of her abdomen. She had staggered to the bathroom to fill up her glass with water and then she had collapsed.

Julian rang for an ambulance. At first he thought she might have appendicitis but Alice told him she'd already had her appendix removed when she was ten years old.

On arrival at the hospital they admitted Alice and gave her a bed for the night. The nurse issued Alice with a pregnancy test and the test was positive – she was expecting her first baby. The pain was increasing and becoming more severe and they took Alice for an emergency scan. The scan revealed there was a fertilised egg that had implanted itself outside of her womb, in one of her fallopian tubes. She began to feel dizzy and vomited. They took her down to the operating theatre. Alice needed surgery to remove the egg. They inserted a tiny camera and instruments through small cuts in her stomach under a general anaesthetic. Mum explained it's what's called an ectopic pregnancy and now it has been removed. Alice is no longer pregnant.

Gazing at the handwritten words on the page, I couldn't believe what I was reading. Mum had been pregnant before she was carrying me. How awful for her to go through such a traumatic experience. I'd been really close to Mum and not once had she ever hinted she was pregnant with another child. I couldn't even imagine the emotional impact it had had on her or my dad. Why had she never told me?

I read on.

6 November 1960

I was allowed to accompany my parents to the hospital to visit Alice. I was under strict instructions to behave and not to upset Alice is any way. This is another example of my mother treating me like a child; I do actually know how to behave. I shook my head at her in disbelief that she even had to say that to me. We arrived at the hospital and travelled towards the maternity wing. I thought this was strange because Alice no longer had a baby – how must she feel being surrounded by newborn babies after losing hers.

Alice wasn't in good spirits; it was only to be expected. She looked so pale and tired. Julian was at her side, and as soon as she spotted us walking through the double doors she broke down into uncontrollable sobs. Julian placed his arm around her shoulder and handed her a pile of tissues.

We sat by her bedside for nearly twenty minutes in silence just watching her. I didn't know what to do so I asked her what she'd had for lunch to try and make conversation. Mum shushed me and gave me the death stare. I remained quiet after that. Soon after, the ward bell sounded and the nurse shouted a five-minute warning for all visitors to leave. Just as we stood up to leave, Alice spoke. She looked at Mum and the only words to leave her mouth the whole time we were there were 'I'm sorry'.

I felt like I'd been kicked in the stomach reading Violet's diary. I was a little confused as to why my mum would be apologising for losing her baby – she didn't have anything to say sorry for. I felt for her, knowing how upset she must have been at the time. The grief would have been immense. I wondered if she knew she was pregnant or whether it had only been discovered when they issued the pregnancy test at the hospital. I supposed I would never know. I read on.

Alice wasn't the only one lost for words today. After we left her bedside and walked towards the door of the maternity ward,

I heard a voice, a voice I recognised. I stopped dead in my tracks and listened again. Mum shouted 'What now?' at me and Dad tried to hurry me along, but I remained rooted to the spot. I made an excuse that I needed the toilet and assured them I would hurry up and meet them both back outside the entrance. I waited until they were out of sight and followed the sound of the voice to the doorway of another maternity room. I was paralysed. I watched on whilst a woman in a bed cradled her newborn baby. It was a girl; I could tell that by her pink hand-knitted booties. I heard the nurse congratulate the father. He was ecstatic; you could see the joy in his face and hear it in his voice. His arm was wrapped around the woman and he kissed her cheek. I heard him tell her he was the happiest man alive and that he was so lucky to have a wife like her and a new baby daughter. I felt sick; I wanted to scream and shout but nothing came out. I must have caught his eye, standing in the doorway. He looked up at me. He removed his arm from around his wife's shoulder and instantly the colour drained from his face.

Our eyes locked.

I stared at T and he stared back at me. As the hurt stabbed through my body, the realisation kicked in. He had a family.

I turned and ran down the corridor, tears streaming down my face.

I cried the whole car journey home. My parents thought I was crying for Alice. I didn't tell them any different. My whole world had just fallen apart all around me.

Never mind Violet feeling like she was on an emotional rollercoaster, I was too. I needed some air. I began to have gripping pains in my stomach and it was beginning to rumble. Flinging the bedcovers off me, I wandered into the bathroom and splashed some tepid water onto my face. Patting it dry with the towel, I felt Alfie nudging me, meaning he was hungry, and I was too. I bent down and carried him into the kitchen. After I gave him his lunch, I threw a bottle of water and my purse into the basket on my bike and cycled off towards Lucinda's bakery.

The street was busy with lunchtime trade. Suited and booted, people moseyed up the high street chatting, having a well-earned break from their work. Leaning my bike against the bakery glass, I saw that the queue of people was already spilling out onto the street. Lucinda and her staff were behind the counter, shovelling sandwiches and pasties into the hands of the hungry customers. I managed to catch Lucinda's eye. She waved me into the shop and threw open the hatch to the counter. I made my way through the crowd of hungry people.

Lucinda smiled at me. 'It's always manic at this time of the day,' she said whilst ringing up the amount of a customer's purchase and throwing his money into the cash register.

'It's over there.' Lucinda pointed to a paper bag on the counter behind her.

'What is?' I asked, perplexed.

'Your lunch order. I thought you were here to collect it?' Lucinda replied whilst serving another customer.

'I've not ordered anything.'

'Tom telephoned through about twenty minutes ago. I thought you were here to pick it up?'

Peeping inside the bag there were pasties and sandwiches and my favourite – flapjacks.

'I think Tom and Jeannie were going to grab it on the way to yours. He said something about popping in to see you as you were feeling under the weather.'

'I'll take it.' I was famished and the smell of the warm chees-and-onion pasty was making me feel even hungrier.

'Tell Tom he can take the money off the egg order in the morning.'

'Excellent, thanks Lucinda, see you soon.' I smiled and grabbed the bag and squeezed back past the rest of the customers that were still queuing up. It was such a lovely thought to bring me lunch. Throwing the carrier bag full of food in my basket, I pedalled towards the Lodge.

Cycling up the long drive, I stared at the steps of Brambleberry Cottage. I pictured Violet standing on those very steps the day after I was born, holding me in her arms. It was strange to think I had been here before. Maybe Mum and Dad had brought me back to the Lodge to show me off to the proud grandparents and aunty before they headed home.

Placing my bike against the office wall, it struck me – where was everyone? Tom and Jeannie were nowhere in sight and I wondered if Tom had told Jeannie about the photograph of Violet.

Strolling through the yard swinging the carrier bag full of food, I checked all the barns, but there was still no sign of either of them. Turning the corner, I headed down to Conker's field. Sometimes, depending on the weather, Jeannie liked to sit on the old wooden bench at the top of the field and let the sun beat down on her face.

There they both were sitting on the bench. I could see they were deep in conversation. Tom had a serious expression on his face and his arm was draped around Jeannie's shoulder. She was talking but dabbing her eyes with a tissue. She then rested her head on his shoulder and Tom kissed the top of her hair.

Tom glanced up and spotted me. He sat upright and removed his arm from Jeannie's shoulder. We exchanged looks.

His face dropped.

I felt an instant pang.

They must be talking about the baby. I didn't hang about. Holding the bag of food in the air so Tom could see it, I placed it on top of the water butt and swiftly turned and hurried back towards my bike. I pedalled home, leaving my lunch behind.

CHAPTER 24

Fifteen minutes later there was a knock at the door. Standing on the other side was Tom, smiling, holding up a cheese-and-onion pasty. He looked so handsome.

'You forgot this,' he said.

I was shocked to see him here – he must have upped and left Jeannie as soon as he saw me standing at the top of the field. He touched me lightly on the arm. 'Can I come in? I want to talk to you.'

I didn't know how much more I could take today. I was an emotional wreck. I didn't need to sit and listen to Tom whilst he explained to me he was about to become a father. I already knew. I wasn't sure I could sit there and pretend I was happy for them. I wished with all my heart that Jeannie wasn't pregnant with Tom's baby. The hardest thing for me was the way he looked at me, the way he smiled. My gut instinct told me he liked me too; it was as if he felt the connection, but it just wasn't meant to be. Well not in this lifetime anyway.

'I already know, Tom.'

He paused.

'You do?' he said, puzzled.

'Well, that was easier than I thought it was going to be. How do you know?'

'Jeannie told me.'

'That's such a relief; I did wonder if she might.'

Tom was standing in front of me, grinning like a Cheshire cat. I couldn't blame him; he must be so excited about becoming a father and starting a family. I was leaning against the door frame about to burst into tears. I couldn't even bring myself to congratulate him.

'Tom,' I managed to say, 'do you mind if you don't come in. I'm feeling a little under the weather, and I just want to curl up.'

'Of course I don't mind. Here, take this,' he said, handing me the pasty. 'Make sure you eat something; you need to keep your strength up.'

He leant forward and kissed me tenderly on the cheek. I wanted to turn my head and kiss him properly, but what good would that do? Jeannie needed the support of her friends at the moment and no matter how I felt about Tom I wasn't going to let her down.

I shut the door behind him and burst into tears.

CHAPTER 25

7 November 1960

My heart is broken. I lay deep below my bed sheets today and cried. I couldn't move. It's been twenty-four hours since I found out T has a new baby daughter. Mum thinks I'm ill. Well I am ill, but not in the way she thinks.

He told me he loved me; he melted my heart. I believed him when he said one day we would spend the rest of our lives together.

It was T who had sought me out in the first place; we'd met by a bandstand in the park one evening. Then he used to pass me in his van every morning. That's how it started. I knew it was love at first sight. He was older than me, but that's what made it more exciting. He promised he would look after me; he promised nothing would ever hurt me but look – now he himself has.

I never knew he had a wife. He told me we had to wait before we could tell anyone; we had to wait because of the age difference. It was only a matter of time. I believed him. He's a liar. All along, he's been married with a family. I never want to see him again.

8 November 1960

I woke up in the middle of the night to the sound of tapping on my window. At first I thought a bird had flown into the glass. Wearily I looked out to find the light of a torch shining below on the ground. T was staring up at me. I opened the window. He wanted to talk; I didn't.

After a little persuasion I found myself sneaking downstairs and we stood beneath the old oak tree at the bottom of the driveway. He looked pained. I was shivering; he put his arm around me and pulled me in close. He kept telling me it wasn't what I thought. How could I think any different – his wife had just given birth to a baby girl, their child. It couldn't be clearer to me: sexual relations with his wife were well and truly current.

He leant his chin on the top of my head and promised me that no matter what happened I should always remember two things: everything he ever said was true and he would always love me.

We kissed for one last time. I didn't want it to end. He felt so good; it was so good. He tasted divine. Then he was gone.

Flicking over the page, I felt like I was living every moment with Violet. Glancing down at the diary, I saw the next few entries were missing. The following one was a week later. Suddenly I was startled by the ringing of the telephone. I picked up the receiver to find Jeannie on the other end. I could hear the excitement in her voice when she spoke. 'I believe Tom has told you.'

For a moment I'd been lost in Violet's world, then all of a sudden I was crashing back into mine. I didn't know what to say. I made my excuses, telling her that I was just getting into the bath and I would ring her back later. I wanted to read more; I wanted to know what had happened to Violet, and I couldn't face talking to Jeannie at that moment.

15 November 1960

It's been a week since I last wrote to you. I'm sorry – I just didn't want to face life. Ethel has been an amazing friend.

She has spent every spare minute with me trying to cheer me up. George doesn't mind either. He said we always need our friends, and true friends are difficult to find and that Ethel should never put him before a friend in need. Ethel is lucky to have a boyfriend like him.

16 November 1960

Alice is back home with Julian. There had been a few further complications but no one has had the decency to tell me. All Mum has said is that it's between the adults. I don't honestly know what she must think of me. I'm just concerned for my sister. Alice has written me a letter; she writes to me often now she's moved out of home. I look forward to reading about her life away from home.

I turned the page and a piece of cream paper folded up into quarters fell out of the diary onto the duvet. I picked it up and carefully unfolded it. Immediately I recognised the handwriting: it was my mother's. I was shaking.

To my dearest sister, Violet,

First of all I must tell you that my friend Bea has given birth to a gorgeous little girl.

I am so pleased to tell you it was a natural birth and she is a real beauty. She has the loveliest, sweetest face and Bea is a very proud mother.

And now for my bit of news: Bea has asked me to be godmother. I was absolutely thrilled and accepted immediately. She apologised if her asking made me feel uncomfortable after losing my baby, but on the contrary I'm pleased I will be a part of her life. They're still deciding on her name.

I hope life is bearable without me at home. I know it's difficult for you at times. I think Mother forgets you're a young woman now. Please be patient with her; she does mean well and has a heart of gold.

Julian and I look forward to your visit after Christmas; the spare bedroom is already made up and I'll meet you off the train.

We will speak soon.
Love,
Alice

The emotion was running through my body and the tears began to run down my cheeks again. I needed to stop crying, but I couldn't help it. Why had my mum never mentioned Violet? It didn't make any sense to me at all. Her letter to Violet was very loving, and reading the diary it was obvious, even though there was a ten-year age gap between them, that they'd been close, so there was no logic to keeping Violet hidden.

CHAPTER 26

The following morning back at the Lodge, apart from Dotty strutting around the yard, it appeared I was on my own. I spotted a note from Tom pinned to the office door, flapping in the wind. The scribbled, rushed handwriting read that he had been called out to an emergency at a nearby farm, something to do with a calf that had been tangled up amongst barbed wire that had been disposed of illegally in the stream that ran through the farm. Even though the local vet had been called, it turned out that a fence had also been broken and all the cows needed herding back to the fields. It was all hands on deck. Jeannie was also unwell today; morning sickness had kidnapped her body and was not looking to relinquish it any time soon.

I needed to get on and check the chickens had been released from the coops in the bottom field. The air was crisp and it was a little breezy. Walking past Conker's field, I saw he'd already been released from his stable and was happily chomping away on a bale of hay that Tom must have thrown over the gate for him before he left.

Squinting, I spotted a figure in the distance. I recognised Robin in his overalls and wellington boots; he was wandering back up towards the stable. I felt a little anxious; I hadn't seen Robin in person since he declared he 'liked me' at the Easter-egg hunt, even though I had spoken to him on the phone a couple of times. I'd been preoccupied since then reading Violet's diary.

Approaching the stable, I peered around the door; Robin was emptying bags of feed into the huge buckets. Startled, he swung round and faced me.

'You made me jump,' he said, smiling.

'I'm sorry; I didn't mean to. What are you doing here?' I asked.

He glanced down at his watch. 'I've been here for at least an hour. Tom received a call from Willard's farm. They needed help: a calf was tangled in some wire and he's gone to help them rescue it. I telephoned him to tell him Jeannie wasn't feeling well just as he was leaving and I offered to come down to let the chickens out.'

'That was extremely kind of you; it saves me a journey to the bottom field.'

'I'm a very kind sort of a guy.' He laughed. 'But I did have an ulterior motive.'

'Which was?'

'To see you.'

I felt myself blush.

'Kitty Lewis, I think we need to talk.'

He took my hand, and we walked back towards the office in silence. My entire body was trembling; I had the urge to pull away, but I held his hand until we got to the bench.

As we both sat down, he folded his arms and stared at the floor. I mirrored his stance. Within a couple of seconds Robin turned towards me, his hazel eyes gazing deeply into my mine. I knew we were about to have a serious conversation. He was a catch, he was certainly handsome, and also a kind, considerate and funny guy, but I didn't get those fluttering butterflies like I did every time I was anywhere near Tom.

I felt my face heating up and began to fiddle nervously with the strap on my watch.

We exchanged looks; for a moment I thought he was going to kiss me but he didn't. Why did this relationship lark always need to be so complicated? No wonder I had shied away from it for most of my life.

I knew some of this situation was my fault; I let him get close to me in the field when he told me he liked me. I'd responded and told him I liked him too. I was confused at the time; I'd discovered the romantic setting in the stable laid out for Tom and Jeannie. Even if I couldn't have Tom, it was unfair of me to give Robin any false hope.

He stared at me anxiously.

With a slight hesitation, he spoke. 'I'm not looking for a quick fling, Kitty. I may have been once, but not now. I really like you and you're gorgeous, funny and kind, and I think we could make a go of it. We could be really good together, Kitty. What do you think?'

I was dreading this moment. I couldn't quite put my finger on why I didn't have any romantic feelings for him but I didn't.

I felt myself sigh and my shoulders sag. I reached for his hand and held it gently. This wasn't going to be easy. Our eyes locked.

'I'm so sorry, I really am.'

'I can feel a "but" coming,' Robin whispered.

'But … I don't feel the same. I wish I could explain why but I can't. You're such a special person, Robin, and I know one day you'll make someone very happy but I know that person isn't me.'

Robin looked down at the floor; he placed his head in his hands.

'It's not very often I wear my heart on my sleeve and this is one of those times I wish I hadn't.'

'Don't be daft. It's absolutely lovely you can be honest with me and don't you ever apologise for being such a lovely person.'

'Do you think you will ever change your mind?' he asked hopefully.

'I'm sorry, I don't think I will.'

He let out a defeated sigh.

My heart was clattering; it wasn't nice to let anyone down and even worse when they'd just declared their feelings for you. His friendship without a doubt was important to me but there was no spark. Robin felt more like a brother to me. He didn't set my heart on fire, not like Tom did.

I could see the disappointment in Robin's face, but he put on a brave smile.

'Friends?' he asked.

'Friends,' I agreed.

Suddenly the awkwardness had lifted and I actually felt that, even though there was no romantic connection between us, Robin was going to be in my life forever. I threw my arms around him and gave him a hug.

'You pair seem very cosy.'

Neither Robin nor I had heard Tom approaching. Startled, we both looked up to find him standing in front of us, clearly agitated. It must have been a stressful morning rescuing the calf.

'We're just clearing a few things up; I think we're done here now though.' I smiled at Robin.

'I didn't think you would still be here,' Tom said to Robin. I wasn't entirely sure whether I sensed an atmosphere. Maybe Tom was just exhausted.

'I'm just off,' he replied. As he stood up, he squeezed my knee and began walking down the long drive.

'How's the calf?' I asked Tom.

'We managed to untangle the poor thing. He was stressed in the water, but he's happily grazing alongside his mother. All's well that ends well.'

Tom sat next to me.

'You're acting a bit weird,' I said.

'Am I? I wonder why that is,' he replied curtly.

Something in his tone made me flick my eyes towards him. He was staring at me. His gaze was dark and thunderous.

'I have no idea,' I replied, nonplussed.

I waited for him to answer.

He stood up and looked me straight in the eye. 'I don't like being made a fool of.' And before I could even answer him, he strode off up the yard and disappeared around the corner, leaving me wondering what the hell all that was about.

CHAPTER 27

I didn't see Tom for the rest of the day; I assumed he must have an awful lot on his mind with Jeannie and the baby. I'd never seen that moody side to him before, but I didn't take it to heart; we were all entitled to an off day.

I cycled home as fast as I could that evening. My mind hadn't been on my work and without Jeannie at the Lodge the day seemed to drag. I was forever checking the time on my watch, willing the hours to pass quicker.

The temporary farmhands were working flat out too, and I was going to suggest to Tom that maybe it would be possible to make a couple of them permanent.

After grabbing a bite to eat and feeding Alfie, I once again retreated to my bed. I sat upright and pulled the duvet up over my knees. Once Alfie had finished eating his tea, he was as loyal as ever and snuggled down next to me on top of the bedcovers.

Opening the diary, I placed the letter that my mother had written to Violet on the bedside table and carried on reading.

17 November 1960

I'm happy that Alice is now back home with Julian. I'm looking forward to visiting them very soon.

At the moment I'm working alongside Mum and Dad at the Lodge and I am being very helpful. There is a method to my madness. The harder I work, the less I think about T. I don't think I will ever trust a man again as long as I live and considering I'm only sixteen that could be a very long time. In the mornings I've stopped waiting by the side of the road to wave at him. I don't know if he still travels along the same route to work, but I think it's best if I don't find out. What good will it do? The sooner I forget about him the better, but it's easier said than done. Every night he's the last thing that I think about before I fall asleep and he's always the first thing I think about as soon as I wake. I'm hoping in time this will change.

18 November 1960

Today has been the most dreadful day. I've spent the whole day in bed with only a plastic bucket for company. Mum called the doctor out to me at 2 p.m. Every time I attempted to sit up I felt dizzy and now I've been vomiting for nearly six hours. I've not managed to eat anything and even water isn't settling in my stomach.

19 November 1960

My body aches, the tiredness is unbelievable and I still feel sick. The doctor thinks I may have a dose of food poisoning; either that or it's just a bug. My mum must be worried because she keeps checking up on me, expecting me to be up and about, but I can't even lift my head off the pillow. All I want to do is sleep.

20 November 1960

Mum must have spoken to Alice. When I woke up this afternoon she was sitting next to my bed and had been watching me sleep. She was holding my hand and wiping my brow with a cold facecloth. Every part of my body feels clammy and I've not had a wash for a couple of days now. I've not even got the energy to stand up.

Alice, my kind sister, helped me to wash and shampooed my hair over the bathroom sink; she said I would feel better if my hair was clean, and she was right, I did a little. Ethel has tried to visit me but Mother thought it was better if she didn't see me in case I transferred any germs to their household. Mum didn't want that on her conscience. It would've been lovely to see her but she's promised to come back in a couple of days' time to check if I'm any better.

As I lay in bed with Alice mopping my brow she told me all about her new goddaughter. She sounds so adorable with her small fingers and toes and chubby cheeks. The parents still hadn't agreed on a name, but Alice told me they needed to hurry because they wanted to arrange the christening soon after Christmas.

Alice promised I could go shopping with her for an outfit as soon as I was better. Julian had been putting some money aside maybe for a holiday, but now he's given it to Alice. He wants her to treat herself to a new dress for the christening, as being asked to be godmother is such a privilege and one I know will be taken very seriously by Alice.

22 November 1960

I can't take much more of this illness. It's been a few days now and I'm still being sick. I feel so weak and tired. All I want to do is sleep. Mum has called for the doctor again.

Scanning the next few pages, I noticed that the next entry of Violet's diary was nearly a week later.

28 November 1960

This has been the worst week of my life. I've spent the past week either asleep or being sick. Looking at my reflection in the mirror, I am half the woman I was a week ago. My face is white and gaunt and my weight loss is extremely noticeable without a doubt. My nightie is hanging off me. This is the worst sickness bug I've ever had.

Finally my mum has let Ethel in to see me. She is such a good friend — every day she's called in to see how I am. She brought me a letter. I didn't know what to do with it. I didn't want to read it, but I knew I would eventually. The letter is from T. It wasn't anything I didn't already know. He had heard I was poorly.

My dearest Violet,

I want you to know that I am thinking about you and wish you a speedy recovery.

Every morning I miss your wave and now I know why you haven't been waiting by the roadside recently.

I miss you and always will.

Love always and forever,

T x

I began to sob and handed the letter to Ethel. The look on her face was one of utter disbelief when I shared with my best friend what I'd discovered that day at the hospital. Neither of us had any idea that T was married with children. Ethel was extremely clear in her instructions to me — I must forget him immediately. I had no choice. Time was a great healer.

I was trying my best, but he was still sneaking into my thoughts at every opportunity.

Reading Violet's diary, I had such mixed emotions. I felt like I was with her every step of the way. I was feeling helpless that she was so poorly yet that was a daft feeling to have because the diary must be several decades old.

Feeling a little parched, I sauntered into the kitchen to make a drink. Noticing the empty milk carton on the worktop, I could have kicked myself. I was that eager to arrive home to carry on reading the diary that I'd forgotten to pick up a pint on my way home from work.

Slipping my feet into my trainers, I grabbed my bike and purse. The evening air was very pleasant and I began cycling towards the shop. Balancing my bike against the windowpane of the shop, I pushed the shop door but it remained firmly shut. There in front of me I read the sign that was pinned to the door. 'Sorry for the inconvenience but due to a family emergency we will be closed for the rest of the day.'

'Damn,' I muttered, rolling my eyes. Now I would have to pedal further down the road to the small newsagents on the other side of the park. Looking down at my watch, I saw time was ticking. I was hoping the next shop would still be open. Pedalling fast, I put on a spurt, steering the bike around the corner and in through the open gates of the park. The entrance was a narrow path lined by ancient oak trees. Their branches intertwined, creating a canopy over the path. The late-evening sun shone through the gaps in the newly sprouted shoots, leaving a mottled effect reflecting on the ground. As a gentle breeze blew, a grey squirrel shot in front of my bike, causing me to wobble as it scampered off up the gnarled tree trunk ahead. There were children still running around, happily chatting and kicking footballs backwards and forwards to each other. The ducks were gathered at the edge of the pond quacking at an old lady who was throwing them scraps of leftover bread from a plastic bag. I dodged a couple of joggers and dog walkers, and as the path widened towards the top of the hill, I pulled my brakes and placed both feet on the ground. I stared as I spotted a familiar figure further along the path.

It was Jeannie; she was perched on a bench, her legs entwined around another person's. A man. A man who certainly wasn't

Tom. From a distance, I watched the pair of them. Jeannie threw her head back and laughed. They seemed very at ease in each other's company; he too was grinning. A few seconds or so later he pulled Jeannie towards him. He cupped his hands around her face, and they kissed. She didn't resist. Their kiss was deep and full of passion.

'Oh my,' I found myself muttering, I was rooted to the spot, watching. I recognised the man but couldn't quite put a name to the face. I racked my brains but still nothing. Where did I know him from?

From what I was witnessing I certainly wasn't overly impressed with Jeannie; in fact I was utterly disgusted. How could she treat Tom this way? For God's sake, she was pregnant with his baby. And yet here she was in broad daylight openly cavorting with another man. They both stood up. Jeannie's head was resting against his shoulder and his arm was firmly wrapped around her body as they began to stroll towards me. There was a feeling of panic burning in my chest. Maybe I'd got it wrong – I hoped I'd got it wrong – but my gut instinct told me the way that man kissed her, he was certainly not just a friend.

With my plans now thrown into disarray, I sighed. The milk would just have to wait because there was no way I could carry on cycling past them through the park. They would spot me. Turning around I mounted my bike and cycled off home in the opposite direction.

CHAPTER 28

After sipping some water, I placed the glass on the bedside cabinet and snuggled back under the duvet. My mind was whirling with every scenario possible as to why my friend was cheating on Tom. He deserved better. I rubbed my temples and closed my eyes whilst I tried to decide whether I should tell Tom or not. I had to consider how this would affect everyone's working relationship at the farm. Staring out of the window from my bed, I smiled as I remembered one of Mum's useful pieces of advice. I heard her voice in my head: 'Always remember to stick your nose in a book and not other people's business.' I think Mother might be right on this occasion; no one knew that I had seen Jeannie and eventually she would have to come clean, unless Tom discovered her secret first. At some point there was the possibility that she may even confide in me and at that time, if it happened, I would encourage her to tell Tom the truth.

There – that's what I was going to do. I would wait and see what happened, but in the meantime I was going to take Mum's advice and stick my nose back in a book – in this case Violet's diary. Mum always knew best.

29 November 1960

I've ripped T's letter into tiny pieces. Ethel is right – I need to forget him. Sometimes I get so angry when I think about him. Why did he lie to me? If he'd been honest enough to tell me the truth, then I could have made my own mind up. I'm not sure what I would have done but at least it would have been my decision and I would only have myself to blame when and if our relationship was ever discovered. Honestly, I thought he was playing it safe because of the age difference. It didn't bother me he was ten years older, but my parents' reaction was one I didn't really want to think about. But in time they would have come round; I know they would have, especially when they saw how much we loved each other and he did love me, I know he did, he must have. The way he looked at me, the things he said to me and the way he kissed me – I felt it, so why, why, why?

1 December 1960

It's been a few days since I've written. I weighed myself on the bathroom scales this morning and I've lost nearly half a stone with the sickness. I still feel weak and dizzy but my parents needed help on the farm today. Mum said it would do me good to get some fresh air and put some colour back in my cheeks.

I can't believe it's 1 December already; this year has flown by and Alice has been in touch. She's very excited. Remember I told you her friend has asked her to be godmother? Well the christening has been booked for 22 December. Alice has asked Mum if she can spare me for a few days so I can go shopping with her to find the perfect outfit. Mum has agreed and thinks the change of scenery will do me good after my illness. I am so excited. I've missed Alice since she left home and sometimes I feel really lonely.

5 December 1960

I am sitting in my bedroom at Alice's house. Well technically it's not my bedroom but Alice said it can be my room every time I come and stay. I hope I can come often. I joked that no doubt they would need it for a nursery very soon and Alice changed the subject very quickly. Maybe she isn't coping as well as we all thought with the loss of her baby.

Her house is very clean and tidy; it's the first time I've been over since they got married. Their married life started at Julian's parents' house; they have a huge house and it was nearer to work for Julian, so he didn't need to travel very far.

Alice is very proud of her house; she is very clever and has made her own beautiful cushions with a second-hand sewing machine that Julian's mother gave to her. Alice has promised she will teach me how to use it. She told me it's a very valuable skill to have and she makes some of her own clothes too.

Tomorrow we're catching the bus into town to search for a suitable dress for the christening. Alice isn't religious as such but is thrilled at being asked to be godmother.

6 December 1960

Alice woke me up early this morning; she was eager to hit the shops. Julian left for work at approximately 8 a.m., but once he had retrieved his bike from the outer house he popped his head around the back door to warn us to wrap up warm, as the air was nippy outside this morning. He was right – there was definitely a winter chill as we set off to catch the bus. I was so glad I'd wrapped up tightly in my warm duffle coat, scarf, hat and gloves.

Alice was like an excited child. She loves Christmas as much as me and as the bus pulled into the stop at the main high street we both gasped. The Christmas tree in the square stood tall and proud, wrapped in all its glory with twinkling, sparkling lights that shone out amongst the busy street. The place was already swarming with shoppers laden with bags. The bus was packed and Alice and I remained seated whilst we watched the droves of people filtering off the bus onto the street below. Harassed mothers weaved in and out of the chestnut stalls with their small children, who were being dragged along by their hands. People were pushing and shoving and we watched whilst they mumbled under their breath. Once Alice and I hopped off the bus we giggled as she took my hand and we skipped along the high street looking for her first bargain of the day.

Our first stop was the cafe on the corner; the aroma was divine and Alice warned me they whipped up the most delicious hot chocolates ever, and she wasn't wrong. This was just what we needed to warm us up after the bitterly cold journey.

The day was fantastic and even though my feet ache and I feel extremely tired our mission was accomplished. Alice purchased the most fabulous dress, shoes and hat to wear for the baby's christening.

7 December 1960

I'm so happy staying at Alice and Julian's house. They treat me like I'm a proper person and not a child. Everything is so relaxed and I'm allowed to sit downstairs with them at nighttime. When I'm at home, Mum always shoos me upstairs to my room. She tells me that that time is for her and my father to relax quietly after a hard day's work at the farm.

I haven't thought about T until now, which means I must be coping. I'm starting to think about him less and less, and maybe I should see if the friend of my mother's son, 'Winston Smithells', is still available to take me out to the Christmas party at Handover Place. It can't hurt and maybe I will like him after all.

Alice's friend is definitely visiting tomorrow and bringing the baby over late afternoon. I've never ever held a small baby before. I've delivered a few lambs during the lambing season but I think that may be a little different. I'm looking forward to meeting Alice's friend and her new baby.

Staring at my bedside clock, I saw it was approaching 10 p.m. My eyes were beginning to feel tired now. I'd been reading for a while. As usual Alfie was snuggled beside me. I stroked his fur, and he purred softly. My mind drifted towards Tom. It didn't take a lot for my mind to drift towards him; he was always there, in my thoughts. I felt kind of safe every time I thought of him.

Wandering over to the window, I stood there for a moment and watched the cars weaving up the road around the parked vehicles. Hearing a horn beep, I swung my head around and saw Tom's face smiling back at me from behind the wheel of his van as he drove past. I had no idea where he'd been this evening but he seemed in a better mood than earlier today. I watched him until he disappeared around the corner and finally, when I could see him no more, I tore my eyes away from the window and closed the curtains.

Climbing back onto the bed, I wrapped my arms around my knees. I had a nagging feeling inside me and began to think more and more about Violet. As far as I was concerned there was only me left in this family; I had no other family, but someone somewhere must know more about Violet.

Exhausted, I picked the diary back up; just one more entry wouldn't hurt.

I turned the page over.

The entry was short.

8 December 1960

This has been the worst day of my life.

CHAPTER 29

Waking up startled, I sat upright in bed. The sound of the letter box continuously clanging was echoing noisily through the hallway.

'Are you in there?' came a muffled shout.

Jumping out of bed still half asleep, I grabbed the keys from the small table in the hall and stumbled towards the front door. Flinging it open, I found Tom standing on the other side, staring at me, looking concerned.

'Are you OK? I've been ringing the house for the past few hours but there's been no answer.'

He stood waiting for a reply.

'What are you doing banging my letter box at this time in the morning? You'll wake the neighbours. Where's the fire?' I snapped, staring back at him and trying to focus my eyes.

'I very much doubt I'll wake anyone at 11 a.m. Your neighbours should have left for work hours ago, unlike you,' he replied, tapping his watch.

We exchanged looks.

'11 a.m.? There's no way it's that time,' I responded, beginning to panic.

'I think you'll find it is!'

'Oh no, I am so sorry! I must have overslept.'

'Well, are you going to invite me in? And, more to the point, are you thinking of coming into work anytime today? Nice PJs by the way.' Tom grinned.

As I looked down at my love-heart pyjamas, I suddenly felt embarrassed.

'Now let me in and you go and get ready for work. Unfortunately Jeannie's still under the weather and hasn't made it in again today.'

I stared at Tom, suddenly remembering what I had witnessed yesterday between Jeannie and the guy in the park.

'What's the matter now? Go and grab a shower and wake yourself up and I'll switch the kettle on, if that's OK with you?'

'Go ahead,' I replied, leaving him standing in the hallway while I headed back into the bedroom to get ready.

Once I'd showered and dressed I walked back into the kitchen. Tom was leaning against the worktop reading the newspaper. I hesitated in the doorway for a moment, watching him.

Sensing I was there, he swung round and smiled. 'Tea,' he said, pouring boiling water from the kettle into two mugs and placing them down on the table.

'Forgive me for saying, but you look like you haven't slept?'

I paused. 'I must have slept because I'm late for work, but honestly I'm OK,' I said hesitantly.

'Honestly?' he said, raising his eyebrows. 'I don't think you are. I'm no Sherlock Holmes but the amount of used soggy tissues thrown on your worktop suggests to me you've been crying,' he continued, sliding a mug of tea over the table in my direction. I sighed. Maybe this was the time to confide in him about the diary, Violet and Jeannie, oh and not forgetting my feelings. However, once Tom was in possession of all the facts, things could change; his friendship was important to me and it was possible I could lose that. What's more, I couldn't bear to hear his response when he rejected me. There were no ifs, buts or maybes about it.

Tom sat down next to me and slid his arm along the back of my chair. I glanced nervously into his eyes and took a deep breath. My heart was clattering and I could barely breathe. He moved his face towards mine; I moved closer to his.

My head was fighting my heart. I'd never felt this feeling before. My mind whirled; his touch, his smell, the spark was explosive. Surely he felt it too? My pulse was racing and my skin was tingling. This is it, Kitty Lewis, the voice inside my head was saying; I'd made up my mind to hold back but all my best intentions had suddenly gone out of the window. I thought I might just kiss him. I was so glad I was sitting down because my legs would've collapsed underneath me by now.

He brushed the tip of his finger against my lips and tilted my chin; I could feel his breath on my face. He moved closer.

The moment was interrupted by the phone in the hall ringing.

'You'd best answer that, it might be important,' Tom said and smiled.

I felt a surge of disappointment run through my blood. Reluctantly, I got up and walked over to the phone. 'Hello?'

'Hi, Kitty, it's Robin, Tom wouldn't be with you by any chance, would he?'

'Yes, he is, I'll just get him.'

Placing the receiver on the table, I shouted Tom.

'It's for you – it's Robin.'

I watched as Tom made his way towards me. He placed the telephone to his ear.

'Hi, Robin. What's up, mate?'

I was just making my way back to the kitchen when I heard the tone of Tom's voice change.

'Yes, of course, I'll be there straightaway. No problem. Bye.'

I could only hear one side of the conversation yet instantly I knew something was wrong.

'Is everything OK?' I asked.

He didn't answer me.

'What is it, Tom?'

'It's Jeannie; she's been taken to hospital.'

I shivered.

'I have to go.' He paused. 'Shall we catch up later?'

I took a deep breath.

'Yes, of course.'

Tom kissed my cheek.

Suddenly the guilt swept through my body. What had I done? I'd let Jeannie down, I'd let myself down – whatever was I thinking? She needed Tom and when she needed him most, he was with me and she was all alone in the hospital.

CHAPTER 30

I spent the rest of the day in a blind panic, feeling guilty about my selfish actions. There was nothing else for it except to throw myself into work, and I had never worked so hard in my life. Every muscle in my body ached, including my heart, and that wasn't so much from the work but the emotional strain of the day.

Both Jeannie and Tom were on my mind all day. I prayed that she and the baby were safe and well. All I could do was wait to hear from someone. No news was good news.

Throughout the day I sporadically broke down in tears. Luckily for me the only witnesses were Conker the Shetland pony and hundreds of chickens, who were more interested in foraging on the ground searching out worms, so I think my secret was safe.

I scrubbed all the coops clean until there was not one ounce of dirt left on them; they were spotless, all laid out with fresh bedding. Egg orders were boxed and completed and the invoices were all up to date.

Once all the chickens were locked up and Conker was safely back in his stable, I grabbed my bike and began to cycle home. I'd had my share of bad days in the past, but this had to be the worst one in a while.

Halfway up the road I recognised Lucinda's van parked up, and there she was, standing on the pavement, talking to a woman I didn't recognise. Lucinda turned round and spotted me cycling towards her; she waved in my direction then patted the woman's arm and I heard her say, 'That's not a problem, if you pop into the shop tomorrow I'll take the order for the wedding cake.' The woman smiled and walked off in the opposite direction.

'Good evening, Kitty, you OK? Business is booming! I've just been stopped on the street and asked to make a wedding cake. You can't get better than that, can you?' She laughed.

Pulling my brakes on, I placed both feet on the ground and halted straight in front of her.

I forced a smile. 'Well you are the best cake maker I know.'

'How's the Lodge today? You look exhausted, have you been working hard?'

I nodded. 'Yes, I've been on my own all day.'

'Why, where is everyone?'

Panic hit me as I realised that Lucinda might not even know Jeannie was expecting a baby, never mind the fact that she was currently in hospital.

Lucinda placed her hand on my arm. 'You look like you have the weight of the world on your shoulders.'

'I'm just having a bad day.'

'Do you want to talk about it?'

Lucinda always made time for everyone, even though she was one of the busiest people I knew. I could see from her face she was genuinely concerned and not just prying.

'I'll be OK, honestly, but thanks. I just need to go home and run myself a warm bath and climb into my PJs.'

'If you're sure?'

'Yes, I'm sure, but we definitely need a girly catch-up soon.'

'I promise.'

And with that I put my feet back on the pedals and rode home as fast as I could.

I was more than flustered arriving at the steps to the flat. Fiddling inside my pocket for the front-door key, I finally let myself in and heaved a huge sigh of relief.

What a day.

If I hadn't ridden off at that particular moment I would have spilled all my problems to Lucinda in the street. What would she think of me? What would Jeannie think of me? The only decent thing I could do now was to step back and let them become a family.

After a long hot soak in the bath and a huge bowl of pasta, I was beginning to feel a little better. Wrapped up in my dressing gown on the settee with Alfie curled up next to me, I reached for Violet's diary and opened it up. I was about to read why she'd had the worst day of her life.

12 December 1960

I've been too distressed to write for a few days. Why me? Why does everything have to happen to me? I was enjoying myself spending time with Alice and now it's gone awfully wrong. Alice is so mad at me. I thought she would be on my side. It was only a mistake, I didn't do it on purpose, but I have been sent home disgraced. She has promised not to tell Mum, which is a relief and a blessing, and hopefully in time Alice will forgive me.

It was all going well until Alice's friend came to visit with the baby and her young son. The baby was gorgeous, gurgling away, lying in her pram, kicking her feet in the air. Alice was smitten. Bea had named her Jeannie. I thought it was an unusual yet pretty name. It's only a little over a week to the christening and both Alice and her friend Bea were excited, chattering about the gathering and the outfits they were going to wear. Alice had prepared afternoon tea; that too was delicious.

She'd cut the sandwiches into small triangles and had baked scones, which we all enjoyed with butter and strawberry jam.

Jeannie had drifted off to sleep. Once she awoke and was fed she was even more adorable. Alice went into the kitchen to make a pot of tea and Bea was cuddling Jeannie. I asked if I could have a hold of the baby. We joked that if Alice was godmother that would make me a godaunty and we were all giggling. Bea handed me the baby, but she made sure I was sitting propped up against the arm of the settee before she placed Jeannie in my arms. She was so cute. I thought she smiled at me, but both Alice and Bea laughed and said it was only wind. Her fingers and toes were so tiny; I'd never seen anyone so small. I couldn't take my eyes off her.

Then there was a knock at the door and Bea said that would be her husband; he was coming to collect them all. As the door to the living room opened, I froze when I recognised the voice, and then I found T standing in my sister's living room staring straight at me. His face was one of utter shock. I began to shake with fear, and I didn't mean to but I dropped the baby. She hit the floor and let out a horrific cry and everyone rushed towards her. T started to shout at me, calling me a stupid little girl and yelling that if his daughter was hurt he wouldn't be held responsible for his actions. I was crying. I was just surprised to find him standing in my sister's living room, not to mention that I'd spent the afternoon with his wife and family. I didn't even know he had a son. It was all so heartbreaking.

He cradled his daughter in his arms and his son was hanging off his leg. Bea was shaking, and once they knew the baby was OK, they all promptly left, but not before T muttered in my direction, 'I hope I never lay eyes on you again.'

I fell to my knees, the tears rolling down my cheeks. He meant those words; they were uttered with such venom.

All I could hear was Alice continuously apologising to them – she was so sorry and hoped Jeannie would be OK. Then the front door shut and all was quiet. I knew I would never see or hear from T ever again.

When Alice returned to the living room she ordered me to gather my belongings and I was on the next train home.

Staring at the words on the page, I couldn't believe what I was reading; my mind was in a whirl and the cogs were beginning to turn. I was racking my brains trying to remember a conversation that had taken place between Tom and I a while back. I couldn't even remember when and where we'd had the conversation, but I was sure he'd told me that Jeannie's mother was called Bea. Surely this wasn't a coincidence? Was it?

My mind was in overdrive; my hands were sweating. Fumbling, I began to quickly flick back through the previous diary entries. I knew what I was looking for, but I just couldn't remember the date. Scanning the pages, my eyes rapidly flitted up and down, and there it was, the entry for 6 November, the day Violet had visited Alice in hospital after her miscarriage.

My pulse was racing and my heart was thumping as I reread the entry.

As Violet had made her way across the maternity wing towards the exit, she had identified T's voice and found herself standing within a few metres of him, his wife and his newborn baby girl.

My mouth fell open as the penny dropped; this surely was no coincidence? I knew immediately if Jeannie's birthday was 6 November then my young Aunt Violet was more than likely having an affair with Jeannie's father, Ted. In fact there was no question about it, my aunt Violet had had an affair with Jeannie and Robin's father.

Right then there was a knock on the front door. Maybe it was Tom, I thought. Ever since he'd left this morning there had been no further communication whatsoever, even though he'd promised we would catch up later.

Opening the door, I found Robin standing on the other side. 'Can I come in?'

He looked pale and tired.

'Of course you can,' I answered, opening the door wider so he could squeeze past me. I wasn't expecting to find him on the other side of the door and my heart was racing. I had no idea why he was here. He must have brought news of Jeannie. How was she? What had happened? Then the guilt hit me again. Robin wouldn't be thrilled to find out I had nearly kissed Tom, and even less thrilled to find out it had happened when his sister had been admitted to hospital. Maybe he already knew; maybe that was why he was here.

I followed Robin down the hallway and he sank down onto the settee.

'It's been a very long day. I hope you don't mind me dropping in on you like this?' He looked weary.

'Of course not,' I replied

'Can I trouble you for a glass of water?' he asked.

I nodded and quickly hurried to the kitchen to fill up a glass of cold water from the tap.

On my return he was still sat on the settee with his head in his hands. Looking up, he said, 'Sorry, I've forgotten to take my boots off.'

'Don't be daft – it's OK. How is everything? How's Jeannie?'

'I've never been so scared in all my life. I found her collapsed on the bedroom floor, her pulse was weak, her eyes were shut and there was vomit next to her. I rang for an ambulance immediately. I didn't leave her side until they arrived. My dad was down in the bottom field attending to the cows. He only knew something was wrong when he heard the ambulance speeding up the drive with the sirens blaring.'

Robin paused again and looked at me. 'I was so scared, Kitty. I thought we'd lost her. I've never felt so helpless in all of my life.'

Robin buried his head in his hands and began to sob. Tears pricked my eyes and I blinked them away. I sat down next to him and put my arm around his shoulder. He turned and faced me and we hugged. I could feel his whole body shaking.

'Thanks, Kitty – I needed that hug. I didn't know where else to go.'

I smiled at him. I was touched he'd come to me; it was a relief to know after everything he still considered me a friend – a good friend.

'How is Jeannie now?'

'She's dehydrated. It's the constant sickness, they said; it's caused the rapid loss of fluids and electrolytes from her body. She's currently hooked up to a drip and has to stay in hospital for a few more days to be monitored.'

'So she's going to be all right? What about the baby?' I added.

'They're both going to be just fine.' The look of relief on Robin's face said it all.

CHAPTER 31

I stared at Jeannie in her hospital bed; she looked so pale and weak. I sat with her for about half an hour and just watched her sleep – I didn't want to wake her. She was hooked up to all sorts of machines; the wires dangled and the monitors were bleeping away consistently.

A nurse walked in pushing a trolley. She examined the numbers of the display on the machine that was bleeping. All seemed to be in order. After refilling Jeannie's water jug and checking the chart that was hanging from the bottom of her bed, she took a pen out of her pocket and placed a tick on the paper. She smiled in my direction then left the room.

'Hey, how long have you been sitting there?' Jeannie opened her eyes.

'Hello, you, how are you feeling?' I said softly. 'You've given us all a bit of a scare.'

'I feel like a pincushion.' Jeannie smiled, holding out her arm for me to see. She was covered in plasters and bruises, and there was a cannula in her arm.

'But you're smiling – that's a good start. Do you want a drink of water? The nurse has refilled your jug.'

'I want a damn good wash and need to clean my teeth. The last time I felt this manky I'd spent four days at a festival.'

'Are you able to sit up? I could pour some of the water into the cup and you can dip your toothbrush in it.'

'I'll try in a moment but my blood pressure is so low that even the slightest movement makes me feel dizzy and faint. If I stay in this position it's not too bad, but I keep drifting in and out of sleep.'

I patted her arm soothingly. 'You don't need to move, just stay where you are.'

'It's awful. You hear about women who don't even know they're pregnant until they're in labour, but not me; I've never felt so ill.'

'You poor thing, it must be awful.'

'I feel so damn useless and stupid being in here. I'm so sorry I'm not at work.'

'Sorry? Did you really just say you were sorry? Don't be daft. Don't worry about work; Tom and I have it all under control.'

I didn't actually know whether Tom had anything under control. I hadn't seen or heard from him since we'd nearly kissed in the kitchen. I wanted to telephone him last night after Robin had left my flat, but I didn't know what to say. I was half expecting him to be sitting next to Jeannie's bed when I arrived, but he wasn't there.

Pouring some water into the cup, I placed it on the cabinet next to Jeannie's bed.

'Now, where's your toothbrush? Let's try and get you feeling at least semi-human again.'

'I haven't got one.'

'What do you mean you haven't got one?'

'Yesterday when they brought me in the ambulance I was barely conscious. I didn't have time to grab anything: no clean nightwear, no washing essentials and certainly no toothbrush.'

'Well we can't have that.'

'Robin is just as useless. He travelled with me in the ambulance whilst Dad followed in his car. Neither of them would even think to put some toiletries and clothes in a bag.'

'That's men for you.' I laughed. 'Shall I nip to the hospital shop for you?'

'I was hoping you could do me a massive favour?'

'Of course.'

'Would you be kind enough to go up to the house for me and put me a bag of essentials together? You'd have more of a clue what I need than Robin or my dad and I think I'm going to be in for a few more days yet.'

'Of course I can. Do you want me to go now?'

'Would you? I know Dad and Robin are out today; they both have an important meeting with a supplier that they couldn't rearrange but they promised to pop in and see me on their way home. Dad always leaves a spare key under the cartwheel to the side of the front door of the farmhouse. My bedroom is the second door on the right at the top of the stairs.'

'Consider it done. I'll telephone the Lodge from the payphone in the hospital corridor and let Tom know it'll be a couple of hours before I'll be back up there. Any message for him?'

'For Tom? No, I don't think so.'

'Is he popping in to see you today?' I was fishing for information.

'I wouldn't have thought so,' Jeannie replied, closing her weary eyes.

I touched her hand and gave it a quick squeeze. 'I'll be a quick as I can.'

Jeannie didn't answer; she was already fast asleep.

Standing up, I placed my arms inside my coat and zipped it up, then I hesitated. Hovering over the table, I was fighting with my conscience. Should I or shouldn't I? Eyeballing the door to make sure I wouldn't be spotted, I quickly grabbed the chart that was hanging from the end of Jeannie's bed. My palms were sweating. Glancing down at her medical information, there it was staring me in the face in black and white: Jeannie's date of birth. She was indeed born on 6 November. It seemed that both Aunt Violet and I were guilty of similar indiscretions.

CHAPTER 32

I glanced up the drive towards Jeannie's family home. In many ways it seemed no different to the Lodge. From what I could see, the farm was sprawled across approximately twenty acres of open land. The view went on for miles and miles. Everywhere I looked there were animals grazing – cows, sheep and ponies and even a couple of goats butting heads over in one of the far fields. The edges of the farm were flanked by enormous trees that must have stood there for centuries. Oak, I thought. Their branches were enormous, swaying in the breeze. The quaint farmhouse was standing between two barns. Entwined around the doorway, I recognised the climbing wisteria that hugged the beams of the wooden archway. No doubt in the summer months the blast of colour from the plant would be truly spectacular.

Spotting the wooden cartwheel propped up on the ground to the side of the front door, I bent down and reached behind it. I rummaged along the ground until I found the key. Placing the key in the lock, I pushed open the door. The layout was similar to Tom's cottage, with a living room situated to the right of the hallway and the kitchen straight in front. The kitchen door was open, and I spotted numerous pots and pans hanging from the old wooden beams that ran across the ceiling. Picking up the pile of post that had landed on the mat behind the door, I placed the brown envelopes on top of the antique-looking sideboard in the hall.

Climbing up the creaky stairs, I remembered that Jeannie's room was the second door on the right. The landing area was adorned with shelves and shelves of books. I paused for a moment, running my fingers along the spines – they were mostly classics. Someone was an avid reader. The heavy tapestry curtains that hung either side of the window were embroidered with foxes and ponies and very suitable for a farmhouse; they certainly gave the cottage a homely feel. Opening the door to Jeannie's bedroom the first thing I noticed was the red antique Persian rug sprawled across the wooden floor. Bending down, I picked up Jeannie's slippers from the floor and placed them on the bed – she would need those. Grabbing her toothbrush, paste and flannel from the bathroom, I searched through the cupboard under the sink for a washbag. Moving over to the chest of drawers, I retrieved clean nightwear, underwear and not forgetting the hairbrush and deodorant that were sitting on top of her dressing table. Noticing a small rucksack hanging from the arm of a chair, I shoved all her belongings in the bag. She would also be in need of clean clothes for her journey home, once she was released from hospital. There, I thought; I'd remembered everything. Staring out of Jeannie's window, I saw the view was impressive. I loved my flat and loved the fact it was situated on the busy high street. Sometimes I would sit there for hours people-watching; I'd wonder about their lives and who they were and what they did for a living, but waking up to the sight of this each day would be something else. Turning around with the rucksack in my grasp, I noticed a wooden desk in the corner of the room. There were numerous photo frames of all shapes and sizes. There were the usual types of photos: Jeannie standing next to an old couple, most probably her grandparents, and one of her standing next to Robin under a huge oak tree in a park. There was one in particular that stood out: it was positioned right in the middle of the desk. Picking the frame up, I glanced at the photo. It wasn't a recent one. The picture was of a woman holding a baby with a small boy reaching up and grasping onto the baby's blanket. Turning the frame over, there was an inscription scrawled on the back: *Bea, Robin and Jeannie*. I could only assume this was a photo taken just after Jeannie was born.

Bea was stunning – now I knew where Jeannie and Robin had got their looks. Remembering what Tom had said, I realised it wouldn't have been long after this photo was taken that Bea would have passed away. I was hit by a twinge of sadness. How devastating for Jeannie and Robin, never knowing their mother. It felt strange to see the face of a woman that my mother also knew. There was no doubt in my mind that both our families were connected. This was her friend, the friend that had asked her to be godmother to her child – Jeannie. If all the writings in Aunt Violet's diary were true then my mother, Alice, was indeed Jeannie's godmother. It was very odd that my mother had never mentioned these people; maybe it was simple as the two families just drifting apart once Bea had passed away.

Gently placing the photograph back on the desk, I knew I needed to be careful about the information I shared from Violet's diary, because it appeared my aunty had had an affair with Ted, Jeannie's dad.

CHAPTER 33

After dropping Jeannie's bag back at the hospital, I'd cycled to the Lodge. I hadn't seen or heard anything from Tom in the last forty-eight hours. I'd telephoned the Lodge from the hospital, but there had been no answer and there was no sign of him at all. Brambleberry Cottage was plunged in darkness.

I'd begun to have that feeling in the pit of my stomach, the feeling you get when you know someone is more than likely avoiding you. My gut instinct was screaming that Tom knew he'd made a mistake, a huge mistake, in getting close to me, and who could blame him? With Jeannie in hospital I bet he was riddled with guilt. I knew I was.

Maybe he couldn't face me, but whatever was going to happen we both needed to act like adults. We still had the Lodge to run, and no matter what my feelings were towards him, we were going to bump into each other on a daily basis.

I worked for the rest of the day up at the Lodge and then headed home. After a quick shower and a bite to eat, I lay down on top of my bed. Since the discovery of Violet's diary I'd begun to shut myself away more and more. Each night I carried out the same routine: food, shower and more reading of her diary.

Opening up the diary, I turned to her next entry.

13 December 1960

At the moment I am not enjoying life. There's still no word from Alice; she really must still be cross with me. I need to wait until she calms down, which I'm sure she will do soon. Surely she can't stay mad at me; it will soon be Christmas, the season of goodwill and all that. I have confided in Ethel about what happened at Alice's. She's assured me the baby is absolutely fine; she knows this for a fact because she spotted T in the park with his son and he was pushing a pram. Even though it cuts me deep that he's pushing his daughter in a pram in the park, I am relieved that Jeannie is OK. It was purely an accident; I wouldn't drop a baby on purpose, and soon, hopefully very soon, Alice will realise this.

Ethel thinks it's a good idea to keep busy and I've spoken to her about the Christmas party at Handover Place. She thinks courting another man is just what I need to take my mind off T and she said I might actually like Winston Smithells. Why am I not convinced? He probably already has a date for the party; after all it is only next week.

14 December 1960

I have made my mother the happiest mum alive, but can I just make it clear I am not attending the party to marry Winston Smithells. I'm attending the party to take my mind off the love of my life. I'd only briefly mentioned last night over dinner that I might have been a little hasty in rejecting his offer to be wined and dined for the evening. My dad swiftly reminded me that I would in no way be wined because I was only sixteen. I didn't mean literally – it was just a figure of speech. Sometimes my dad can be so stuffy about things. I'd never seen my mum finish her dinner so fast. Within ten minutes of the conversation ending she had grabbed her coat and was sprinting towards Green Park. She wanted to talk to Winston in person.

Twenty minutes later, she'd bounded back through the front door and announced it was a date. Winston Smithells would pick me up at 7 p.m. sharp on Christmas Eve eve. I can't wait (note the sarcasm).

15 December 1960

What have I done agreeing to go to a party with Winston Smithells? I've now become my mum's new best friend. All she talks about is the Smithells. I don't think she gives two hoots what I think, but she's practically married us off, and I've not even spent more than ten minutes in his company. I'm not sure I want to spend any time in his company; they all seem very la-di-da and pompous. He's sent me an official invite through the post. It's been requested I wear a dress; well that's what the invite states. My mum has abandoned my dad at the farm today and has been busy on her sewing machine making me a dress.

16 December 1960

It's official – I look like an idiot. Ethel was biting down on her bottom lip trying not to laugh when my mum insisted that I strut around the living room to show her the dress. Ethel, being the best friend that she is, had come to the rescue; I love Ethel. She popped back round with a dress that her older sister had worn for a posh do. It fitted perfectly. Mum was a little put out at first that I didn't want to wear the dress that she'd made, but when I threatened not to go at all she soon started to fuss around me again. I think she thought I was dating royalty.

I sat in bed laughing at the last few entries. It reminded me of my own mother, years and years ago, when I was without a costume for the school play. It was soon after my father had died and we didn't have much money. She ripped up some of his old overalls and made me a Christmas pudding outfit. I wore it just for her. She was the proudest mother in the audience when I stood up on that stage, yet I looked undeniably ridiculous. Violet was obviously stronger willed than I had been.

23 December 1960

I'm sorry I've not written for a few days again but the sickness bug has been back in full force. I heard whispers from the landing before the doctor entered the room. My mum's voice was cross. All I could hear were the words, 'Don't be ridiculous, it is most certainly not a possibility.' This time the doctor prescribed some antibiotics and has put it down to the time of year – there are lots of viruses and colds going around. Mum went into complete meltdown. She was panicking that I was going to let Winston down. I'm sure he would've understood if I was too ill to attend; it wasn't as though he had a date in the first place if he could fit me in at such short notice. But it's tonight and I am ready and waiting to be picked up by Winston. Ethel has curled and pinned my hair. I feel like a movie star, and it looks truly amazing. My mum has let me wear the necklace that she wore on her wedding day, which is stunning and very exquisite. Even if it turns out I don't like Winston Smithells, I still feel like a million dollars.

Turning over the page, I discovered it was blank. I flicked over the next few pages; they were also blank. There were no entries over Christmas or over New Year, absolutely nothing at all.

Hearing the doorbell ring, I jumped out of my skin; I wasn't expecting anyone. Placing the diary on the bedside table, I walked up the hallway and fished about in my handbag, trying to locate the front-door keys and finally I managed to open the door.

'Grab your coat – we are on a mission to cheer up a poorly mum-to-be,' Lucinda ordered from the doorstep. 'Come on, get a shifty on.'

'OK! Give me a minute.'

'Robin phoned me earlier. He's filled me in on the situation. Poor Jeannie! Robin and Ted nipped in to see Jeannie after their visit to the suppliers and she's all on her lonesome tonight, so I've stocked up on the latest trashy magazines, chocolate and I'm hoping to catch a glimpse of any dishy doctors that may be on duty. There's nothing like a bit of eye candy to cheer up an evening.' She laughed.

I grinned back at Lucinda. 'You are so funny.'

After promptly stuffing my feet into my shoes, I grabbed my bag and keys and followed Lucinda to her van.

'I live in hope, and to be honest I'm actually getting a little lonely in the evenings; I need some company – any company. It's that bad I was even thinking of getting a dog.'

'Ha ha, well let's see if we can find a dishy doctor, and if we do, maybe you could swap places with Jeannie and see if he can take your pulse.' I winked.

'Now there's an idea! I like your way of thinking.'

We both laughed.

'Anyway, Miss Kitty, what have you been up to lately, anything on the romantic front happening for you?'

My thoughts immediately turned to Tom. Flicking my hair over my shoulder, I concentrated on the road in front. 'Absolutely nothing is happening for me,' I answered.

'Before I forget, are you free to try out the new local bistro tomorrow night? I fancy giving it a whirl.'

'Most definitely; I'll look forward to it,' I replied.

Arriving at the hospital, we saw the car park was almost full. Lucinda manoeuvred into a space at the far end before anyone else spotted it. Clutching the magazines and swinging the carrier bag of chocolate, we walked through the rows of parked cars, heading towards the hospital entrance.

'I'm not sharing my chocolate,' Lucinda said, laughing, and nodded towards another vehicle in the car park.

'What do you mean?' I queried.

'Over there.'

Turning my head, I noticed Tom's van parked up.

I felt my stomach lurch. I wasn't sure why I felt this way. Tom had every right to be visiting the mother of his baby, but I had to do everything in my power to put on a brave face.

'Me neither,' I managed to say.

Feeling anxious, I followed Lucinda to the ward and entered the room behind her. Jeannie was propped up in bed and what a difference a few hours had made. She looked human again; there was colour back in her cheeks and she was smiling. Tom was seated at the side of her bed, his hands clasped around one of hers. I felt a pang in my heart.

'The cavalry has arrived,' Jeannie announced. 'You are now relieved of your duties, Tom.' She laughed. 'I hope that's chocolate in that bag,' she said, nodding across at Lucinda.

'Of course!'

Letting go of her hand, Tom shot us a smile of relief and stood up. 'Thank the lord for small mercies – there was only so much talk I could take about soap operas and baby names.' He laughed and bent over, kissing Jeannie on her cheek.

Lucinda sat down in the chair and tipped the carrier bag full of chocolate out onto the bed. 'Take your pick,' she laughed.

'This is so why you are my friend, Lucinda.' Jeannie and Lucinda both giggled.

'I'll be off then and leave you all to it.' Tom smiled and walked towards the door. He looked absolutely exhausted.

'Hi,' Tom said hesitantly as he approached me.

'Hi,' I managed, hoping my voice didn't sound as shaky as I felt.

He nodded towards the door. 'Have you got a minute?'

'Is it work?'

He raised his eyebrows then nodded.

I knew full well it wasn't anything to do with work, but I didn't want Jeannie to worry about me slipping out of the room with Tom.

'I'll be two minutes, girls. Do not eat all that chocolate without me.' Both Jeannie and Lucinda began flicking through the magazines and were chatting away whilst I slipped out of the room behind Tom.

'Shall we find somewhere quiet to talk?' he suggested.

I nodded and followed him down the maze of corridors. Pushing open the double doors to the exit, we made our way to a wooden bench positioned not far from the hospital entrance. We sat down; things felt tense.

Tom broke the ice. 'Are you OK?'

Staring into his eyes, I gave him a nervous smile.

'You're shaking,' he noticed.

'It's the chill in the air; it's a little nippy now.'

'Here, take this,' he said, slipping his jacket around my shoulders, his arm lingering for a few seconds.

'Thanks.'

His eyes seem sad. The poor man was most likely confused, because I knew I was. He was probably looking for a nice straight-forward relationship and in a short space of time his girlfriend was pregnant and he'd nearly ended up kissing me.

'I should have known someone like you wouldn't be single for long.' He looked down at the floor, avoiding all eye contact.

What the heck was he going on about?

He lifted his head up, but his eyes were closed and he shook his head. 'I just wish you'd been honest with me.'

Me be honest with him? I was lost for words; what the hell had I managed to do wrong?

He opened his eyes and looked straight at me; my eyes met his with disbelief. I shook my head and laughed self-consciously. 'I'm sorry, I don't follow.'

'There's no use pretending, Kitty. I saw you; I saw you both.'

I was completely flummoxed. I had no idea what he was talking about.

'I wanted to call you but I couldn't. I thought about it for hours, but I don't want to stand in your way.'

'My way?' I questioned. 'What about your way?' I was beginning to feel a little agitated now.

'My way?' he repeated. 'I've been honest with you right from the very start.'

'I wouldn't go that far,' I retaliated.

'I'll come straight to the point then,' he blurted. His voice seemed distant and cold.

'Please do.'

Just then the double doors to the entrance of the hospital were flung open. 'There you are, Kitty. Come on, we're here for a girly chat and at this rate all the chocolate will be eaten!' Lucinda shouted across to me.

'Unfortunate timing,' mumbled Tom.

Turning towards him, I said, 'I best go and I'll look forward to hearing all about the baby names you and Jeannie have come up with.'

'What on earth are you on about?' he demanded.

Standing up, I didn't answer him. I was fuming. How could he sit there and accuse me of not being honest? I handed him his jacket back and walked off in the opposite direction. I didn't look back.

CHAPTER 34

The following evening I met Lucinda on the corner of the high street and we walked to the bistro. Sitting down at a table, we ordered a bottle of crisp white wine to share. It was a quaint little place; the lighting was dimmed, with tea lights flickering on every table. The whole place had an olde-worlde feel about it. The menu was simple but offered a delicious range of food. We both ordered penne along with a fresh green tomato salad accompanied by garlic bread. I was looking forward to a decent meal. I didn't have any inspiration when it came to cooking for me; it was always easier to bung a meal for one in the microwave. So this was certainly a welcome change.

Taking a sip of the wine, I began to relax. I was glad my working day was over. Things were strained at the farm; Tom had barely spoken to me and I'd barely spoken to him either. For most of the day he'd stayed out of my way, mending the fences down at the bottom field. The only words I can remember him saying were, 'You've done a grand job of cleaning those coops; you could eat your dinner off the floor in those.' I'd nodded and he'd disappeared again. I didn't see him after that.

'That was a huge sigh. Have you had a difficult day?' Lucinda asked, pouring more wine into my glass.

'I have to say this wine is going down way too quickly,' I answered, 'and I'm certainly glad today is over.'

'Me too. I'm ready for some me time. The bakery has been so busy in recent weeks, I feel like I've lost all contact with the outside world. So what's been going on today? Tell me all about it.'

I contemplated spilling the life of Kitty Lewis to Lucinda, including my feelings for Tom, but before I could think about it anymore the waitress was wandering over to our table, balancing two bowls of pasta, salads and garlic bread in her hands. Placing the plates of food down in front of us, she asked whether there was anything else we needed before disappearing off to fetch the bill for the table next to us.

'Wow, this looks delicious. You go first. The bakery being busy must be a good thing, right?' I asked, changing the subject quickly.

'It most definitely is. I've had a couple of extravagant wedding cakes to bake this week and in-between the usual orders I've been interviewing for new staff. I'm expanding.'

'That all sounds very exciting – tell me more,' I enthused.

'I've been doing a little research into opening another shop and I think it may just happen. I've been interviewing for a manager, someone I could trust to take over the daily running of the bakery and manage the staff, which will take the pressure off me whilst I set up the second shop.'

'Lucinda, that's fabulous! Have you found some new premises?'

Lucinda nodded. 'I've seen a few places and I've settled on one in a brilliant location in the next town, so fingers crossed. It's in the early stages and I'm still in the negotiation phase, but I've got a feeling the small shop will be mine very soon. I'm also toying with the idea of opening up a small teashop attached to it,' she said, grinning.

'You could easily do that with your talent. And owning your own little teashop? Wow, that's every little girl's dream. Vintage teacups, slices of home-baked cakes, I'm there already!'

'Keep it under your hat until all the Is are dotted and the Ts are crossed; I don't want to tempt fate.'

'Your secret is safe with me.'

'The only downfall is that I'll have less time to find a man,' she said, laughing.

'They'll be flocking to you once you've made your first million; you'll have the pick of the bunch.'

'Let's hope so because I'm not sure I can spend many more evenings as a lonely woman. I'd just love a cuddle from time to time.'

Visions of Tom seeped into my mind again. For the past few evenings I'd woken up sweating – I'd begun to dream about him. The dreams were so vivid, so real, and my mood had most definitely dipped when I awoke, knowing that the fantasy was just that – a fantasy. I knew exactly how Lucinda felt, but luckily for me I had Alfie to keep me company.

A few seconds later the waitress ambled back over and asked us whether everything was OK with our meals. We both nodded and she smiled and flitted to the next table. It was the most delicious meal I'd eaten in a long while. Being reckless we decided to order another bottle of wine.

'What about you, Kitty, what's happening with you?' Lucinda was looking straight at me. 'You seemed a little preoccupied last night at the hospital, and I don't think I'm speaking out of turn when I say Jeannie is worried about you too.'

Placing my knife and fork down on the table, I met Lucinda's gaze. 'Jeannie? Why's Jeannie worried about me?'

'She's not daft, Kitty; she could see you were upset last night when you came back in the room after speaking with Tom. We both could.'

She reached across the table and squeezed my hand. 'She's worried about you and Tom.'

My stomach lurched and I felt physically sick.

Lucinda was still staring at me.

'I'm so sorry,' I managed, blinking away the tears.

'You don't need to be sorry, but the only advice I can offer you is that you need to sort the situation sooner rather than later.'

I brushed away a lone tear that had escaped and was now running down my cheek.

'How long have you known?' I asked.

'Jeannie told me all last night when you'd disappeared after Tom; she's been really upset about it.'

'I can't apologise enough. I didn't mean to upset her – with everything she's going through too. I've been such a rubbish friend. I tried to fight it, I really did but …' Placing my head in my hands, I couldn't bear this conversation; it shouldn't be happening. I felt so low, but it was probably nothing compared to what Jeannie was going through knowing that I had feelings for Tom.

'Hey, there's no need for these tears; I'm sure we can sort this out.' She smiled kindly, rummaging in her handbag, then handed me a tissue over the table.

'Thank you, but I don't deserve your kindness. I would understand if neither of you wanted to speak to me again. You must both be disappointed in me,' I said wearily.

'Don't be overdramatic. Why wouldn't we want to speak to you again?' She laughed. Why was she being so kind to me?

I looked up and our eyes met. She pulled a sympathetic face. 'You and Tom just need your heads banging together.'

'What do you mean we need our heads banging together?' I was confused now.

'Can I ask you a question first?'

I had a feeling if I'd have said no, Lucinda would have asked anyway, and I wasn't going anywhere fast. If both she and Jeannie knew of my feelings towards Tom, I may as well get it out in the open.

'Go on …' I waited.

'Out of curiosity, do you have any feelings towards Robin?'

Well, that wasn't a question I was expecting. 'Robin? What's Robin got to do with anything?'

'Just answer me; it's not a trick question,' she said, smiling.

Taking a huge gulp of wine from the glass, I swiftly filled it up again.

'Such a cliché I know, but Robin and I are friends. I have no romantic feelings for him at all. Truth be told, I feel very comfortable in his company, but I think of him more as the big brother I never had.'

'So nothing whatsoever has happened with him?'

'Er no, of course not. Why do you ask? Where is this going?' I was even more confused now.

'Because before we arrived at the hospital last night, Tom had told Jeannie that you were dating Robin.'

'He needs to get his facts straight! Where the hell would he come up with that from? I've been straight with Robin, and he knows the situation between us.'

'Tom saw you.'

'Tom saw me doing what?'

'He told Jeannie he saw you through the window.'

'What window?'

'Your living-room window.'

'Lucinda, you're talking in riddles. Please just tell me what you know,' I begged.

'Tom spent an hour by Jeannie's bed; he was beside himself. Eventually Jeannie extracted the information out of him. He told her about his feelings for you, he revealed the moment in the kitchen when he was sure you would kiss. He came back that night, Kitty, and he spotted Robin's car outside. He waited for an hour or so and it was still there. The curtains to the living room were open, the light was on and he was about to knock on the door, but when he looked in the window he spotted you both with your arms around each other on the sofa. He left and went home.'

My mind was in a whirl – what must Jeannie think of me? I couldn't believe Tom had revealed we nearly kissed. She had every right to be cross with me. Not only was she lying in hospital with low blood pressure, hooked up to a drip, she had to lie there and listen to the father of her baby stating we'd nearly kissed. Whatever was he thinking? Why would he tell her without thinking of the consequences and why didn't he discuss it with me first?

'I'm so sorry, I really am.'

'Stop saying sorry; he was honest about his feelings for you and thought you were making progress until Jeannie was rushed into hospital.'

'I need to go and see Jeannie and apologise. I hope she'll forgive me; I didn't mean for her to be upset.'

'She has nothing to forgive you for. No, Kitty, it's you talking in riddles now.'

I paused.

'Why do you want Jeannie's forgiveness?' Lucinda's eyes were locked on mine. She took a sip of wine and waited for me to answer.

'Because I'm in love with Tom, and he's the baby's father,' I blurted.

Lucinda burst out laughing.

'You silly fool, whatever gave you that idea?' she asked. 'Tom's not the father. Jeannie was upset because you pair seem to be going round in circles, and not realising that you're totally perfect for each other. Quite simply, Tom has fallen in love with you, Kitty, and thinks you don't want him.'

'Well if Tom isn't the father, then who the heck is?' I asked.

'I'll leave Jeannie to tell you that one.'

'I can't tell you the relief I feel! So there's nothing stopping me being with Tom after all?'

'Absolutely nothing at all,' Lucinda confirmed.

CHAPTER 35

Stepping off the bus, I gazed up at the hospital building in front of me. The trees were rustling in the light breeze and despite the people bustling around me and the constant drone of the traffic in the street, I felt a sense of calm. Last night I'd slept right through; in fact a full eight hours. I couldn't remember the last time I'd had a decent night's sleep, and I certainly felt better for it.

Right now I needed to see Jeannie; I couldn't believe I'd got the situation so wrong. I knew once I'd seen her I would go and find Tom; he'd be up at the Lodge and I would try to put this situation right. He was probably wondering why I hadn't turned up for work as yet, but I'd be there soon enough. Walking up the light and airy corridors of the hospital towards Jeannie's room, I smiled to myself. I had a feeling today was going to be a good day.

Opening the door to her room, Jeannie was sitting up in bed, flicking through a magazine.

'Good morning,' I said cheerfully.

'Good morning, yourself. I'd get out of bed and give you a hug but unfortunately I'm still hooked up to these wires,' she said, smiling, and nodded towards the bleeping contraption beside her. 'I think they'll let me out tomorrow now my ketones are back where they should be. They just want to make sure they're stable for twenty-four hours.'

'Ketones?'

'Something to do with dehydration; some women suffer for the whole of the pregnancy, but it varies.'

I settled on the chair next to her bed.

'Well, you're definitely looking more alive.'

'Ha ha, do you reckon? Because I think I look a mess, and I without a doubt I feel yucky.' Jeannie grinned.

'Don't be daft; you don't look a mess. But to be honest you could be arrested by the fashion police for wearing that hospital gown; it doesn't do anything for you!' I teased.

'I wish I could get out of here now; my patience is wearing thin and I'm bored silly staring at these four walls. I know it's only been a few days, but there are only so many celebrity magazines I can read before my eyes start to glaze over. I'm sick to death of reading about their latest fad whilst they flaunt their perfect bodies.' Jeannie tossed the magazine down on the bed.

I laughed. Picking up the magazine, I perused the photo on the front cover advertising yet another celebrity exercise video, with the before and after picture of a woman parading around in a bikini and sparkly silver high heels. I didn't have a clue who she was.

'Have you eaten this morning?'

'Now you sound like my father,' she replied. 'Hospital food isn't the best, but my appetite has returned thanks to the secret stash of goodies Lucinda's been sneaking in.' She nodded towards the drawer of the bedside table. 'If it wasn't for her I'd have been starving, never mind dehydrated, and I never want to see another creamed potato as long as I live.'

'I've been feeling like the worst friend in the world recently,' I admitted.

'Why, what have you been up to? I've only left you alone for a few days; surely you couldn't have got yourself into that much trouble?'

'Do you want a bet? Being single, an idiot and not getting the correct end of the stick is no easy run,' I joked.

'And here was me thinking I was the only idiot around here.' She winked.

'It was way back at the Easter-egg hunt at the Lodge, I stumbled across the romantic setting in the stable and I assumed that it was for you and Tom.'

Jeannie's mouth fell open and her eyes widened. 'Me and Tom, whatever gave you that idea?'

'The double-date fiasco. The night at the pub – the one we shared with Robin and Tom.'

'Fiasco? I had a fun time. Well maybe just a little too much fun in my case.' She smiled, rubbing her stomach.

'We were sitting in my kitchen and you told me you were dating Tom and my date for the night was Robin. At that point I already had feelings for Tom. I was in two minds whether to go but I talked myself into it only because I'd convinced myself it was unethical to have any type of relationship with Tom except a working one, me being his boss and all that, and I thought you two were together.'

Jeannie rolled her eyes. 'Tom isn't my type. I prefer the rough-and-ready type of guy; Tom is more the dependable, loving sort.'

'But you set me up with Robin.'

'Yes, initially, only because Robin spotted you at the market, and yes it was his idea for us all to spend the evening together. But anyone with an ounce of intelligence could see the sparks were flying between you and Tom that night; the pair of you barely took your eyes off each other.'

'I thought I'd hidden it well.' I smiled broadly.

'That would be a big fat no! You could see Tom was on pins all night, thinking you were going to go out with Robin.'

'I feel awful now.'

'There's no need to feel bad, Tom jumped at the chance to come along, and the only reason for that is you, Kitty. He's attracted to you, not me. Unfortunately Robin was caught up in it all, but I'll let you in on a little secret.'

'Ooo, go on.'

'I'm trying to fix him up on a date with Lucinda. I'm sure they would be the perfect couple, and I'm not sure why no one has thought of it before. Sometimes Robin needs taming and, unquestionably, I think she's the woman to do it. Let's hope she thinks so too.'

'Yes, they'd make a lovely couple,' I agreed.

'And let's face it, with Robin's appetite for all things sugary, those pair would be a match made in heaven.'

Pouring us both a glass of water from the jug on Jeannie's bedside table, I asked the question that had been burning inside me for the last twenty minutes.

'But he followed you into the toilet – I saw him.'

'Who did?'

'Tom.'

Jeannie dropped her head in her hands. 'I wasn't with Tom, honestly.'

She paused. 'Is that why you disappeared home that night, Kitty?'

'Yes, if I'm truly honest, I ran out because I thought you were together in the toilets. I heard your voice – you were with someone – and I'd seen Tom disappear in after you. The hurt was too much to bear.'

'Why didn't you mention this sooner?'

'Because you're pregnant and I thought Tom was the father.'

'You put two and two together and made five more like.'

'What was I meant to think? I'm sorry.'

'There was a perfectly reasonable explanation: I didn't sneak off to the toilet to be with Tom.'

'Who then?'

'Remember I was so keen to get the drinks from the bar?'

I nodded.

'Well that was more to do with a drop-dead-gorgeous barman that I'd had my eye on for a while.'

'The barman! What was his name?'

'Danny!'

'Oh yes! Danny! The cheeky chappie.'

'The one and only.'

'Wow! I'd never have guessed.'

'Well clearly not!'

We both laughed.

'So had you known him for a while?'

Jeannie hesitated. 'Long enough. He'd been having a casual fling with one of the barmaids for a while. It was one of those arrangements where if neither of them had anything else better to do they'd end up together in the sack.'

'Friends with benefits.'

'Yes, that's the one.'

'There was something about him. We hit it off straightaway; the chemistry between the pair of us was unbelievable, but I would never let anything happen. We came close on numerous occasions, believe me, but I always had this nagging feeling in the back of my mind about him and her. I thought he was a player. I didn't want to admit my feelings, and I certainly wasn't going to put myself in the firing line to be hurt, knowing he would more than likely be sleeping with the both of us. Then that night in the pub, he leant across the bar and told me he'd made it clear to her that their current arrangement had to stop because he had his eye on someone else, someone special – me.'

'Was this all at the beginning of the night?'

'Yes, once he served the drinks, I put my hand out to pay him the money, and he grabbed my wrists, hauled me over the bar and kissed me full on the lips. I was taken aback at first; I wasn't expecting it, and then he made me promise to meet him on his break. I didn't need much persuading.'

My mind began to run over the events of the evening. 'I remember Danny coming over to the table and then I remember him disappearing through the front doors.'

'Yes, he did – that was more for his boss's benefit. The girl he'd been dating on and off, Stacy, was the boss's daughter and he didn't want to cause any conflict at work. He wandered out of the front door and straight back into the pub through the side entrance that leads down the long corridor to the toilets.'

'So there's another entrance?'

'Yes – the tradesmen's entrance. There was a method to his madness. He didn't want to get spotted and he was waiting for me inside the cubicle.'

'So who was the romantic set-up for in the stable?'

'The night of the Easter-egg hunt?'

'Yes.'

'It was for Danny. I'd been up bright and early setting the scene. I didn't think anyone would venture that far down after I'd let Conker out of his stable. On the day of the egg hunt there was no access to the general public in that area and I thought you guys would be too busy to notice.'

'I think I may have led Robin on a little that day.'

'Why, what makes you say that?'

'After I saw how much trouble you'd gone to, I was devastated because I thought it was for Tom. Wandering down to the field, I started to cry. When I looked up, Robin was standing behind me. He put his arms around me, hugged me and told me he liked me. I told him I liked him too, but I was confused. Then

I noticed Tom; he was standing at the top of the field leaning against the fence. He was watching us, and then he strolled off in the direction of the stable. I thought he was meeting you.'

'Well this is all a bit of a mess!' Jeannie exclaimed.

'I have no feelings for Robin. He's lovely, don't get me wrong; I feel comfortable in his company, but it's like I've known you both for years. It's just platonic, but with Tom it's different. The first time we met I just knew he was special. My heart melted the minute I saw him. I was wheeling my bike up the drive towards Bluebell Lodge and unfortunately somehow got caught up in the pedals and ran over Dotty. The next thing I knew I'd landed on the ground with a bump. When those strong tanned arms hoisted me back to my feet and I looked into his eyes, I knew there was something about him. I literally fell for him,' I said, laughing.

'Danny didn't turn up that night, the night of the Easter-egg hunt. Stacy had decided she'd fallen for him and wanted a proper relationship with him. He explained to her straight that he was with me now, and there would never be anything romantic between them. She wasn't happy to say the least and went running back to daddy, no doubt telling him how Danny had been using her. That wasn't the case. They were both consenting adults; it was just an arrangement they had. The very next day her father sacked Danny.'

'She was a woman scorned,' I chipped in.

'Most definitely. Danny felt he had to keep the pregnancy quiet for a while. He knew about it the day after the hunt, but we'd already decided to be together before then. We'd been meeting up most nights in the park until things had settled. His parents were upset he'd been sacked from his job, so we both thought it was best to keep quiet about the baby for the time being. However, all's well that ends well. We told his parents when I was admitted to hospital this week. He couldn't hide it for much longer. While you lot were visiting in the evening, he was been nipping in in the afternoons.

'Argh, bless him, is he happy about the pregnancy? And what's he going to do about work?'

'Yes, he was a little taken aback; the result of our rendezvous the night in the pub obviously got out of hand.' She smirked. 'But Lucinda's come to our rescue regarding his work. I confided in her a couple of days ago when you slipped outside with Tom, and she's kindly given him a job on the vans. The timing couldn't have been better; she was just about to advertise for a driver when I mentioned Danny's predicament. She offered him the job immediately and he starts on Monday.'

'That is fantastic news; I'm really pleased for both of you.'

'Not as pleased as my father. It was difficult enough explaining to him I was pregnant, which came as a massive shock, as he wasn't even aware I had a boyfriend. I was dreading telling him Danny was unemployed as well, but thanks to Lucinda we were spared that conversation. I have a good feeling about Danny. I think we'll go the distance and my father's agreed that he can move into the farmhouse with us; there's plenty of room and he may be able to give Danny some shifts on the farm too.'

Feeling like a huge weight had been lifted off my shoulders, I said, 'What am I going to do about Tom? I feel like a complete idiot.'

Jeannie smiled across at me. 'You pair are already friends and the attraction is there – anyone can see that.'

'Can you?'

'Yes! And Tom spent an hour pouring his heart out to me just before you and Lucinda arrived to visit me. He was devastated. He claimed he'd witnessed you and Robin through the living room window and he felt you weren't being honest with him.'

'And I felt he wasn't being honest with me because even though I was sure I was receiving the signals that he was attracted to me, he never once mentioned the baby.'

'Well he wouldn't, would he? He's not the father!'

'Robin was at my flat that evening. He turned up out of the blue; he was upset because he was the one who found you lying on the floor, and he felt helpless. I hugged him because he needed a hug – that was all there was to it.'

'Trust Tom to pick that moment to peer through the window.'

'Why didn't he knock on the front door? Robin would have been pleased to see him.'

'That's men for you – always jumping to conclusions.' Jeannie smiled.

'I thought when he received the phone call saying you'd gone into hospital that he'd shot straight here to be with you.'

'Nah, the only place Tom shot was up to our farm because my father was here with me and hadn't finished the milking.'

'I've got this so wrong, haven't I? I don't know what to do now,' I said, shrugging.

'You go and find him now and that's an order!'

'Do you think so?'

'I know so. He cares about you and that's a good thing. I'm sure he's battling the same dilemma. Now go and find him – why are you still here? Go, go, go,' she said, shooing her arms in my direction. 'And don't come back until you're a couple and living happily ever after.'

'One last thing before I go, Jeannie. Can I pinch a piece of Lucinda's flapjack off you?' I grinned.

'If you must, but you can only have one piece – the rest is all mine!'

CHAPTER 36

After my visit to Jeannie, I travelled straight to the Lodge. I wanted to talk to Tom and sort this mess out but he was nowhere to be found. The office was locked up and his boots were missing from outside his cottage. I asked a couple of the farm workers but they hadn't seen him either. I assumed he must be up at Jeannie's farm helping her father. He was working so hard, but that's the kind of man Tom was – he wouldn't let anyone struggle. No wonder he'd looked exhausted and tired the last time I saw him.

I scribbled him a note and posted it through the door of the cottage. I'd taken the liberty of booking us a table in a fancy restaurant in town. I was hoping that would set the tone; we'd be away from familiar ground and hopefully that would give us a chance to open up to each other. Thinking about it now, I realised it was probably the last thing Tom needed after a hard day's work at the farm. He would possibly prefer to put his feet up and enjoy a takeaway accompanied by a beer instead of getting washed, dressed and making his way to a restaurant he'd probably never heard of.

Me and my bright ideas.

Apart from being nervous, I had no clue what to wear and back at the flat I'd thrown myself into a blind panic. I was beginning to get agitated with myself for not thinking this plan through well enough. In the end I plumped for black leggings, a white tunic and a pair of baby-pink ballet pumps. I was constantly listening out for the phone to ring but it stayed silent.

A couple of hours later I was standing at the impressive entrance to the restaurant. I felt shaky and couldn't make up my mind whether it was down to the cool air of the evening or the nerves. I thought maybe a little of both.

Entering the restaurant, my eyes quickly flitted around the room – Tom was nowhere to be seen. Feeling apprehensive, I was approached by the waiter. After confirming the booking, I followed him to our table.

'Your dinner guest hasn't arrived as yet but would you like me to bring you a drink in the meantime?' the waiter asked, pulling out my chair so I could sit down.

'I'll just have a glass of water for now, thank you,' I replied, deciding to play it safe. If Tom didn't turn up I could drink the glass of water and go. I'd not managed a morsel of food since lunchtime and the last thing I needed on Tom's arrival, if he did appear, was to be tipsy on one glass of wine. Sipping on my water, I began fiddling with the strap on my watch. Tom was already ten minutes late. I took my book out of my bag and began to read. Sitting there on my own, I felt as if the whole restaurant must be looking at me, but they weren't. And as my eyes darted around the room, I saw the majority of couples were staring off in different directions, not even speaking to each other. I couldn't make up my mind whether this was sad because they no longer had anything left to say to each other or whether it was a comfort knowing that they were so relaxed with each other that they didn't need conversation all of the time.

Just then the restaurant door opened and I heard the waiter's voice.

'Yes sir, your dinner guest is already seated; I'll show you to your table.'

Firstly, I was relieved Tom had turned up and secondly, I was speechless. He caught my attention the second he walked through the restaurant door. He was most definitely worth the wait.

'Hello,' I said, smiling shyly as he sat down.

'What can I offer you to drink, sir?' the waiter asked now, passing both of us a menu.

Tom turned to me. 'Do you like red wine?'

'Yes,' I nodded.

'Then a bottle of your finest would be grand, thank you,' Tom replied confidently.

The waiter acknowledged Tom's request with a nod and walked away towards the bar area to retrieve the wine.

'Finest? Is it a special occasion?'

'I hope so. I was happy to receive your invitation.' He smiled and sat down at the table opposite me but not before kissing me lightly on the cheek. For a moment we sat in silence perusing the menu.

'Have you chosen yet?' Tom asked. 'What do you fancy?'

I smiled.

Tom smiled back then laughed. 'I mean food wise.'

'Damn.' I raised my eyes playfully.

He grinned at me knowingly and I began to relax.

'You look lovely.' My heart soared.

'Thank you – you do too.'

'I'm sorry I didn't manage to phone you. I got back late and when I read your note I rushed to get ready to make sure I was here on time.'

'You're forgiven.' I smiled.

The waiter came and took our orders and once we were left alone again I decided to be brave and reveal to Tom what an absolute idiot I'd been, getting the wrong end of the stick about Jeannie's baby.

Once I'd finished talking, Tom didn't speak for a while. 'Are you going to say something?' I asked gently.

'Words fail me, and actually I don't know what to say. Did you honestly think that was my style? Really?' He looked saddened, disappointed in me.

I couldn't answer; when he put it like that, I was actually disappointed in myself. All I could manage was a shake of my head.

He paused for a moment while the waiter placed our food in front of us. Once the waiter was satisfied we were happy with our meals he disappeared over to the next table. Tom leant over and squeezed my hand. 'Kitty, I can't ever be hurt again.'

'Again?'

'Yes, it was a long time ago and I never want to be in that position again – ever.'

'Do you want to talk about it?'

'I think I do,' he answered, taking another sip of his wine. I began to eat slowly while I listened. He cleared his throat and began to talk. 'I've not been in a relationship since Rose. I didn't know if I could ever handle being in a relationship again.'

The hurt on his face was clearly visible. He took a bite of his food then he carried on. I remained silent and listened.

'We met at school. She was vibrant, full of fun, and we soon became inseparable. She was like no one I'd ever met before; I'd had the odd flirtatious moments before with girls, but when I met her it all stopped. I wasn't interested in anyone else, and I wasn't expecting to fall in love – it just happened.

'Rose was ambitious; she wanted to become a doctor. She was certainly intelligent enough and her grades were always top-notch, whereas I don't have a qualification to my name. I knew I was destined to work in farming – that's what I'm about, the great outdoors. It didn't bother me at all that one day she would earn more money than me. As long as we were both happy, I was all for that.

'Her studies began to take over her life; it was expected with the amount of work she needed to do. It was her suggestion that we get married. There was no grand gesture on my part, no going down on one knee, but I was happy to go along with it if it made her feel secure. However, things began to change and she began to mix with different circles, distancing herself from our friends. At times it felt like we were an inconvenience; all she ever talked about was her new circle of friends. Hanging out with the medical students and the staff from the hospital started to become a regular occurrence. From what I could gather the majority of them were young, trendy types who were engaged or planning their weddings. I think she wanted to be part of the crowd. She wanted the wedding so she had something to share with the group.'

'Did you ever socialise with them?'

'At first she did invite me out for a drink with them on numerous occasions but I felt like a fish out of water – they weren't my kind of people. I felt inferior, often intimidated and I most definitely didn't understand their medical speak. She would constantly put me down in front of them, calling me the farm boy, and sometimes I felt I was only there for their entertainment, so they'd have someone to ridicule. In the end I stopped going along and Rose went by herself. I think she preferred it that way.'

Listening to Tom, I heard the sadness in his voice. How could anyone ridicule him or make him feel like that? It was unacceptable in my book.

'What happened to Rose?'

'Apart from her medical career, she wanted to travel the world. I didn't mind that she wanted to experience different places but I was quite happy with the simple pleasures in life, like working on the farm. I had no desire to travel. I thought she was my soulmate and I worked my fingers to the bone saving up for the wedding she wanted, and then it all went horribly wrong.' His tone was sad.

'What happened?'

'It was six weeks before the wedding day, everything was booked and paid for and it was a Tuesday – I can remember it vividly, like it was yesterday. I was feeling unwell at work; my body ached and I was shivering. I thought I might be coming down with the flu. I'd gone home; we rented a house, as there was no way we could afford a mortgage. I was going to start to save for the deposit for a house after the wedding. I made myself a hot drink and climbed the stairs. I thought a few hours' sleep before Rose finished work would recharge my batteries. Opening the bedroom door, I was shocked to find Rose was already home from work. She was lying in our bed with one of her medical colleagues. Her wedding dress was hanging in the room next door.'

Staring open-mouthed at Tom, I didn't know what to say.

'It was grim to say the least,' Tom continued.

'I'm so sorry, Tom; that must have been awful,' I said gently, squeezing his hand.

'I was crushed and never saw her again. Within ten minutes of finding them together I removed every single item that belonged to her from the house and you'd never have known she'd lived there. I can only assume he took her in. Soon after, I moved back in with my parents until Agnes offered me the farmhouse. I wasn't entitled to any refunds due to the fact the wedding had been cancelled so near to the day and all the outstanding balances had been paid. I lost nearly £7000. The last I heard of her she'd graduated as a doctor and was working abroad.'

'And now I feel even worse for jumping to such silly conclusions,' I said.

Tom looked at me and reached out across the table. 'Let's put all this behind us.'

I swallowed a lump back in my throat and couldn't believe I was getting a second chance. I exhaled sharply. 'Thank god for that! I'm all for forgetting about the last few weeks.'

We smiled at each other.

We finished our meals and the rest of the evening passed in a lovely blur. The waiter returned and began to clear away the plates. 'Would you like to see the dessert menu or order any more drinks?' he asked politely.

'I'm OK, I'm not sure I could manage to eat another mouthful,' I replied. 'What about you, Tom?'

'I think I'm all done too. Can we have the bill please?'

The waiter nodded.

'On the whole it's been a great night. I'm so glad you booked the table.' Tom's eyes met mine and sparkled.

I smiled at him. 'I'm so glad I did too.'

'Let's hail a cab and get you home,' Tom suggested.

Standing on the edge of the pavement waiting for a taxi, Tom stood close to me. I shivered in the cool night air. 'Come here,' he said, pulling me in close, wrapping his arms around me and resting his chin on top of my head. He smelt divine. Tucking my hands deep into the pockets of my coat and leaning into him, I felt so happy and was hoping this bubble wasn't about to burst anytime soon.

The cab pulled up in front of us, Tom opened the door and I climbed in. Sitting in the back of the cab, he never let go of my hand as he gave the driver my address. Watching the lights of the town pass us by, we stayed silent. Our eyes locked and the shadows of the night passed across the contours of his face. He smiled at me and there was one thing I knew for sure: being wrapped up in Tom's arms couldn't come soon enough. I'd waited so long for this moment.

CHAPTER 37

Tom was standing behind me while I rummaged in my bag looking for the front-door keys. I was all fingers and thumbs. My heart was thumping and I forced myself to breathe calmly. Feeling Tom's presence so close to me, my whole body was trembling. Pausing, I tried to compose myself as I placed the key in the lock. I stumbled through the door and Tom caught my arm; fire ripped through my veins from his touch. My heart was beating so fast I thought I was going to explode; I hadn't felt desire like this in a long time.

A yellow glow shone onto the hallway from the table lamp I'd left on so I didn't come home to complete darkness. Tom shut the door behind him and Alfie appeared in the doorway. Purring, he wound himself around Tom's legs; Tom promptly picked him up and stroked his fur.

Leaning against the hall wall, I smiled at Tom and he placed Alfie gently back on the floor.

I lifted my hand up to Tom's face and stroked his stubble. Our eyes stayed locked; neither of us faltered. He moved my hand towards his mouth and kissed it. I got goosebumps. He pressed his body against mine and I groaned with desire. 'Kiss me,' he murmured. He lowered his head towards mine. I couldn't wait any longer. I grasped at his hair and my lips met his. I kissed him hard. The electricity was flying. Tom pushed me against the wall. I pressed myself against him; I wanted to be closer. Still kissing,

I guided him backwards towards the bedroom; the tingle in my body was immense and I didn't want it to stop.

Animal instinct took over and we started to rip at each other's clothes. I couldn't believe Tom's body: his toned torso, his strong arms. I was scared to look. It had been a while since I'd seen a man's naked body, let alone touched one. Tom's face was in my hair, kissing my neck, his hands tugging at my clothes.

He unbuttoned my jeans. We both fell onto the bed, his hands exploring all over my body. Every nerve tingled as he lifted my blouse over my head and unhooked my bra. He rose above me, his strong arms either side of my body.

'Kitty, are you sure?'

'I've never been so sure about anything in my life.' I kissed him passionately.

'I'll go slowly and if you want me to stop, I shall.'

I was breathless and dizzy.

He entered me. I gasped, and his eyes locked with mine. I didn't ever want him to stop.

Lying in bed entwined in Tom's arms, an overwhelming feeling of happiness surged through my body. I tilted my head up and kissed him lightly on his lips. Tom's face was flushed as he smiled at me and kissed the top of my head.

'Thank you,' I murmured.

'You don't have anything to thank me for,' he replied softly.

But I did: it was perfect, he was perfect and I couldn't help but smile – this was a night I would never forget.

CHAPTER 38

Waking up with Tom's arms tightly wrapped around me, I glanced at the clock. It was only 3.30 a.m. yet I felt like I'd been sleeping for hours. Tom was fast asleep, and I smiled to myself while I watched him for a further few moments.

I closed my eyes but I knew there was no chance of me returning to my slumber anytime soon. Lying next to Tom I felt so content, so safe – the happiest girl on the planet.

Ten minutes later I was still wide awake. Gently removing Tom's arm from around my body, I slipped silently out of bed. I pulled on my jeans and top and quietly padded into the kitchen. Maybe a hot drink would help me to sleep. I closed the kitchen door while the kettle was boiling so the sound wouldn't wake Tom. Settling down on the settee with my mug of tea, I picked up Violet's diary, which was lying on the table.

'Hey, what are you doing?'

I swung round to find Tom leaning against the doorway.

'I woke up and you were gone. What time is it?' he asked softly.

'It's 3.30 a.m.'

'Kitty, that's way too early – even for me.'

I smiled at him. 'I couldn't sleep, so I thought I'd grab a drink and read for a little while to see if that helped.'

'You're dressed – are you running out on me?'

I laughed. 'Don't be daft! This is my house – where would I run to?'

'What are you reading?'

I hesitated and looked up at his face. The moment felt right to share my secret with Tom. 'It's not just any old book, it's a diary.'

'Whose? Yours?'

'No, not mine. Aunt Violet's.'

Tom look confused. He came and settled on the settee next to me.

'Where did you get that from?'

'The safe.'

'Come again?'

I paused. He waited patiently for my reply.

There was no point lying to Tom; I didn't need to hide the fact that I'd cracked the code of the safe in the office. OK, maybe I should have mentioned it sooner, but I wanted time to read and discover its contents by myself.

'The safe from the office at the Lodge.'

'You cracked the code? How did you do that? Please tell me you aren't secretly a bank robber?' He laughed.

'Of course I'm not; to be honest it was quite simple.'

'Cracking a code to a safe is simple? Tell me more.' Tom pulled me in tightly and I rested my head against his chest.

'The numbers on the front of the safe—' I looked up and met his gaze.

Tom nodded, willing me to carry on.

'I stared at them for a while. I had a few random attempts but I knew, I just knew, when some of the numbers were more worn out than others: the combination had to be those four numbers.'

'Which were?'

'Zero, one, five, seven.'

'It was as simple as that?'

'Well nearly – they needed rearranging first to one, five, zero and seven.'

Tom hesitated and stared at me, puzzled. 'Those are the same numbers as the combination code to the lock on the gate, the one at the bottom of the drive leading up to the Lodge.'

I nodded. 'Yes, I know.'

'It wouldn't even have crossed my mind to try that sequence only because the safe has been there for years and the combination to the lock didn't exist until just before Agnes passed away. It had always been a padlock with a key but unfortunately I lost the key and we used bolt cutters to free the chain. It was only then Agnes changed it to a lock with a combination. What a coincidence!'

'There's another coincidence – 1507. That's the fifteenth day of the seventh month, i.e. 15 July, which is my birthday,' I butted in.

'Wow.'

'There's more.'

'What do you mean?' Tom asked, intrigued.

I hesitated. Once I'd told Tom what I'd discovered about Aunt Violet and Jeannie and Robin's father there was no going back, but it was time to tell him everything.

'According to the diary, it's more than likely that my sixteen-year-old aunt had an affair.'

Tom looked at me; his eyes were wide.

'An affair? Who with?'

'This is the part where you have to promise not to say a word. I'm trusting you, Tom.'

'Go on.'

'With Ted.'

'No. I can't believe that. Ted's been traumatised for years over the death of Bea; surely you've got that wrong.'

I shook my head.

'Here, have a look through while I make you a drink,' I said, handing him the diary and stealing a quick kiss on the lips. 'It makes for interesting reading.'

Walking into the kitchen, I discovered Alfie too was now wide awake and sitting patiently by his bowl. I bent down and scooped him up in my arms. 'It's not breakfast time yet,' I whispered softly. Alfie purred and I couldn't resist pouring a few cat biscuits into his bowl. 'Maybe having something to eat will help you sleep too.'

'Shall we take the drinks back to bed?' I asked, drifting back into the living room.

Tom was still sitting on the settee flicking frantically from one page to another of the diary.

He glanced up and I could see the panic in his eyes.

Instantly I knew something was wrong.

'Tom, what is it?'

'Kitty, you need to see this,' he said, thrusting the diary in to my hand

'See what? You're frightening me now, Tom. What is it?'

'The entries for July 1961.'

'What about them?'

'I think you need to read for yourself, Kitty.' He kissed me lightly on my lips and cupped both his hands around my face. He stared me straight in the eyes. 'I think we'll need something stronger to drink.' Tom passed me the diary and I settled on the settee next to him.

Since finding the diary I'd been reading it in chronological order. I'd only got to December. My hands were shaking as I opened the diary and scanned the pages in search of July.

CHAPTER 39

1 July 1961

I couldn't have made it through the past six months without Ethel; she's been my rock. If our calculations are correct, it could happen anytime now – it's just a waiting game. I'm scared witless. I have no idea what to expect and soon the whole world will know. There's nothing we can do except wait.

2 July 1961

After work today Ethel and I visited the library. The librarian was watching us like a hawk. We weren't members and there was no way we were going to join today. The librarian knew my mother from the reading group she attends on a Monday and if we borrowed the types of books we needed, my mum would surely find out and then there would be questions, too many questions. I distracted the librarian while Ethel smuggled a couple of the more factual books under her jumper. We weren't necessarily stealing the books; we were going to return them once we'd found out what we needed to.

3 July 1961

Ethel came round after tea. Mum tutted when she opened the door and made a sarcastic comment: 'We may as well get her a key cut the amount of times she's here'. Ethel has come round every night for the past six months, since we found out. She's no longer stepping out with George. That is entirely my fault. I feel dreadful but Ethel has assured me it's OK and that I have enough to worry about. George was unhappy about the amount of time Ethel was spending with me – who can blame him? – but as far as she's concerned no man will ever come before her best friend – especially when she's the only one who knows my secret.

Tonight we locked ourselves in my bedroom; we wedged a chair under the door handle so no one could enter the room. Once we were certain no one was going to barge in Ethel removed the books from her bag. We sat next to each other on the bed, staring at the pages in disbelief – the images were so graphic. I began to sob and I told Ethel I didn't think I could do it; I didn't want to do it. But I didn't have a choice; it was all too late.

Ethel squeezed my hand and told me she would never leave me.

4 July 1961

I've had the worst sleep ever; I tossed and turned all night. I couldn't get comfy. I managed to get out of work today; Mum and Dad think I'm looking peaky and ordered me to stay in bed. That suited me down to the ground. I slept for most of the day and only woke up when Ethel appeared at my bedside. Ethel thinks we need to come up with a plan. I'm not sure how a plan is going to help us at such a late stage. My only plan is hoping I get out of this alive. Ethel suggested we confide in Alice. I don't think that's a good idea because she will certainly share the information with Julian and no doubt with Mum. Things have been so strained with Alice since the incident before Christmas.

5 July 1961

I am exhausted. I've managed to take another day off work. Mum and Dad have advertised for farm help. I'm relieved about that but I can't tell them why.

6 July 1961

Ethel appeared tonight with a holdall. It is her father's; she said he wouldn't notice that it had disappeared because it's been stored in the back of the wardrobe for as long as she can remember. Ethel said we need to store the bag in a safe place and make sure it's packed with the relevant items. I didn't have a clue what she meant by 'the relevant items' but she'd made me a checklist that she'd copied from one of the library books we'd borrowed. Ethel thinks of everything. We looked down the list together. Some of the items we could muster up: a nightie, washbag and towel. Other items would prove a little more difficult but Ethel said she'd seen a couple of items in the local charity shop's window so she would purchase them tomorrow after work.

7 July 1961

Ethel is a diamond – she's managed to collect every item on the list. We stuffed it all in the holdall and hid the bag back under the bed. We waited and waited some more. Nothing was happening tonight but it most definitely had to happen very soon.

8 July 1961

Dad made a remark this evening around the dinner table that made my mum look up and stare. She was placing our food down on the table when Dad suggested that she give me a smaller portion. She asked him why she would want to do that. He replied that I was getting a bit tubby and the pounds were creeping on. Mum eyed me up and down and made a comment that no wonder I look like I've put weight on because the baggy clothes that I was wearing don't do me any favours. Actually I've put about two and a half stone on and I think I've done a fantastic job keeping it under wraps.

I gasped and looked up at Tom, who was reading the diary over my shoulder.

'Are you thinking what I'm thinking?' I asked him.

'Yes, I think Violet is pregnant.'

'And nobody knew except for Ethel?'

'It certainly appears that way.'

'The poor girl,' was the only response I could muster.

Tom put his arm around my shoulder and squeezed me gently. I snuggled into his chest. We carried on reading.

9 July 1961

We are waiting.

10 July 1961

And still we wait.

11 July 1961

Maybe we've got this all wrong.

12 July 1961

Nothing as yet.

13 July 1961

Can't put my finger on it but I feel kind of strange today.

14 July 1961

I'm writing this to keep my mind off it. As usual Ethel came round after work. She teased me, laughing at the state of my bedroom – it was spotless. She'd never seen it so clean and tidy. I don't know what had come over me; I like living in clutter but not today. Ethel claimed it was a nesting instinct. Standing up to go and get Ethel and I a drink, I heard a pop and felt a weird sensation from within followed by an immediate gush of very warm fluid, which soaked through my pants. The fluid began to trickle down my legs. I started to have lower-back pain and a dull ache. Ethel and I stared at each other. I sat back down on the bed, holding onto my bump. The dull ache became worse, followed by a tightening across my stomach; it became so tight I couldn't breathe. Ethel reached under the bed for the holdall. I have no idea what she thought we needed from there but the books said we needed it. This was it, Ethel was by my side and the baby was coming. The pain became too much to bear and I began to scream. We heard a barrage of footsteps running up the stairs. I was scared.

As I read the diary entry, the tears were free falling down my cheeks. Tom leant over to grab me a tissue from the box on the table. I didn't have a good feeling about this; in fact the gut-wrenching emotion that was gripping my body told me that what I would read next was going to change my life. Tom held me tight.

'Are you OK?' he asked gently.

Our eyes met briefly before I wiped the tears away. I shook my head and swallowed. I couldn't speak.

'This isn't going to change who you are. You're beautiful inside and out, and I love you.' He kissed my tears.

Hearing Tom say those words should have been one of the happiest moments of my life but now I was petrified to read on. In my heart of hearts I knew I was about to discover Aunt Violet was no longer my aunt but my mother.

CHAPTER 40

Tom had moved away from the settee and I could hear him rummaging around in the kitchen cupboards. Sitting back down next to me, he passed me a glass full of brown liquid.

'Here, drink this.'

'What is it?' I asked, placing the glass under my nose and taking a whiff of the repulsive substance. I winced.

'It's whisky. Just take a sip; it'll take the edge off.' He passed the glass to me and I took a gulp. It burnt my throat and almost instantly I felt a warm rush through my body.

'Where did you find that?'

'In the very back of one of the kitchen cupboards. I think it's been there a while. Are you ready to read on?'

I could see the concern in Tom's eyes.

'I think so. I can't put it off any longer; I need to know the truth,' I replied, blinking away the tears.

Turning the page, I saw there was no entry for 15 July. My heart was pounding.

16 July 1961

Yesterday I gave birth to a beautiful baby girl. She weighed in at exactly seven pounds. The pain was immense; pain like I'd never felt before. Mum and Dad had burst into the bedroom after hearing my screams. They didn't know what was wrong with me until I told them I was having a baby. They didn't believe it and shouted at me. I can still hear their words ringing all around: 'Don't be ridiculous.' Ethel confirmed it was true. My secret was out.

My mum's face said it all: a look of disgust. All I could hear in-between my screams was her muttering away about what the neighbours would think followed by how I'd brought shame on the family. I didn't care what the neighbours would think; I only cared about receiving some pain relief. My dad couldn't even look me in the eye. I just remember him saying, 'I'll fetch the truck – we need to get Violet to hospital.'

Travelling in the truck was the worst experience of my life. Ethel was with me every step of the way. She squeezed my hand and ordered me to take deep breaths – she'd read that in one of the books we'd smuggled from the library. The pain was getting worse; the tightening across my stomach took my breath away. By the time we reached the hospital I could feel the head. I wanted to push. I did push and my baby was born safely a few minutes later on the maternity ward.

Of course, the hospital and midwives had no notes about me; I hadn't shared my secret with anyone until now. My mum kept shaking her head. 'How could you do this to us?' she repeated over and over again. Ethel produced the holdall and pulled out the smallest white Babygro I had ever seen, one she'd managed to purchase from the charity shop. I stared down at my baby; she looked so tiny. Her fingers and toes were so small and there was no doubting she looked like T. A wave of sadness flooded through me. This was not how I pictured myself having a family. I wanted the dream, I wanted T and I wished with all my heart he was here. I knew the question was coming and I was surprised it hadn't been asked already but right on cue the words spilled out of my mum's mouth with venom. 'Well, come on then – who's the father?' she demanded.

'Where is he now?' Ethel was staring at me; she didn't dare speak and waited for me to answer. All eyes were on me but there was no way I could divulge that information. T didn't know about the baby and that was the way it had to stay. He had his own family now and I had my baby. T was always going to be in my life because of my beautiful baby girl. I would have a piece of him with me every day for the rest of my life, but no one else except Ethel would ever know.

'This can't be true,' I gasped. I shook my head. 'Tom, please tell me this isn't true.'

'We don't know what the baby's called yet – it may just be a coincidence.' I could hear the hesitation in his voice.

'It's way too much of a coincidence that I'd have a cousin somewhere out there in the huge wide world who has exactly the same birthday as me.'

'I suppose, when you put it like that.'

I took another swig of whisky and turned the page.

'Look, whatever we find out here, we can deal with it together; I'm here for you, always.'

Even though Tom's arms were wrapped around me, I felt sad and lonely. I wasn't sure I was ready to face the fact that my mother and father were in fact no longer my mother and father.

CHAPTER 41

17 July 1961

My heart is breaking. They have decided for me. I hate my mum and dad. I didn't think I would ever use that word about them but it's true, I do. They haven't given me any alternative. As far as they're concerned, I'm a disgrace. They've guessed the father is a married man and they will 'out' him some way or another unless I do as they demand. I can't let them discover that T is the father. It'll spark even more hatred and his family will be torn apart. They have also made it crystal clear they will disown me. They will not provide for me or my baby. Ethel too is disgusted by their decision. She calls it blackmail. I'll have nowhere to live, no support and no money. I can't provide for a baby. We've racked our brains but we can't come up with an alternative and they are refusing to listen to us.

The hospital says I can be released today; I can take my baby home. I don't want to go home; I want to stay here forever. Once I go home they'll take my baby from me. They've arranged for Alice and Julian to arrive at the house just after dinnertime. They will raise the baby. I hope they never arrive; I hope they see sense and let me keep my baby. She is my baby. This will be the worst day of my life.

18 July 1961

The last few hours with my baby at home were spent rowing with my mum and dad. What gives them the right to decide that I cannot bring up my own child? Except my mum said she had every right to make that decision. She is head of this family and what she says goes. There was no way on this earth I was bringing shame on them. My voice is hoarse; I can barely speak from the screaming. I have begged and begged, but she is adamant. Mum AGAIN has made it clear that I won't have a home or a job, and she said did I want to end up living on the streets with a baby? I've told her I'll run away. She looked at me like I was dirt on her shoe and said, 'Oh how very mature, putting your baby's life in danger, which just shows the sort of mother you are already.'

I'm too scared. I wouldn't know where to run to. I haven't got any money or a place to stay.

She said that if I tell them who the father is then maybe he could help. I could marry him. That way I wouldn't bring shame on the family.

My heart is breaking. I can't disclose who the father is. T would never forgive me. It would tear his family apart and he has chosen them. All the children would end up coming from a broken home. I couldn't do it. If I thought there was a slight chance he would marry me, I would say who he was, but I can't. He's married – it's impossible.

There are no words that can describe how I felt, hearing Alice and Julian arrive, having the baby I love torn out of my arms. I held onto her for as long as I could. I screamed, I kicked and I fought for her, tears rolling down my cheeks. Mum restrained me and Alice paused for a moment. I could see she was torn. She whispered, 'I will love her with all my heart; she'll want for nothing, I promise.' She took the baby from my arms. My baby was now with her new doting parents – parents that could never have children of their own after Alice's complicated ectopic pregnancy.

Not only was this the last day I would ever set eyes on my baby, it would also be the last day I ever set eyes on Alice and Julian. My family are sending me away before word gets out. I am to speak about this with no one. I have no choice; if I don't go then I'll have nowhere to live. I could try and get a job and a flat, but I have no money at all. I'm to be shipped off to my father's sister who lives in Canada. They thought it was safer that way. My aunty has agreed to provide a home for me. I have agreed to go because this is my only safe option. I don't want to spend another minute in my mother's company. At least it will give me time to think. Time to make a plan. My mother has told me I am never to return and I am never to contact my sister again. They are bringing the baby up as their own.

I screamed after them and begged for them to let me hold her one last time. My mum said no, but Alice agreed and they took a photograph of me standing on the steps of the Lodge holding my baby. She was gorgeous, wrapped tightly in her white blanket. I will treasure that photograph forever. It will go with me wherever I go. They may have taken my baby away from me but she will be in my heart every day.

I watched them as they climbed into the car, Julian looking like a proud father. Just as Alice was about to shut the car door, I began running towards them. Mum grabbed me but I shouted like I had never shouted before for my baby. They drove away and didn't look back; I'll never know if they heard me. But one day I will see my beautiful baby Kitty again.

19 July 1961

My bags are packed and I leave for the airport in fifteen minutes. I want to get out of this house now. Ethel doesn't know that I'm leaving. For Alice and Julian to have any chance of bringing the baby up as their own, I have been ordered not to share this news with Ethel. My mum will tell Ethel that I've moved away with the baby to start a fresh life, away from the stigma I have caused. No matter what they say, I cannot leave without saying goodbye to my best friend. I've managed to write her a letter; I stuffed it into the hand of the farm boy, who promptly got on his bike in search of Ethel. I told her they were sending me away to Canada. I told her Kitty was now Alice and Julian's child. They could love her and provide for her; they had a proper family set-up, unlike me. The only comfort I have is that no matter what I think of my family, I do know that Alice and Julian will dote on my child; I know she will want for nothing, but what she will never know is how much I love her. I love her so much it hurts.

Looking back at the Lodge for one last time, I watched the farmhouse became smaller as my father drove me away down the long driveway. My mum was standing on the steps watching the car drive off. We never spoke; I didn't have anything left to say to her. As far as she was concerned I was damaged goods; she'd told me so during our last row. She said I would thank her one day; a girl of sixteen could never bring up a baby on her own. There is one thing I do know for sure: I will never thank her.

As my father indicated left at the bottom of the track I could hear shouting. Looking out of the window through my tears, I saw Ethel. She was running so fast, waving my letter in her hand. I placed my hand against the glass window and watched the sadness in her eyes as my father drove off. Ethel slumped to the ground sobbing. I knew that would be the last time I'd ever see my best friend.

CHAPTER 42

My whole world came crashing down all around me. Everything I had ever known was a lie. Tom sat in silence, his arms placed firmly around my shoulders. There was nothing he could say or do. My heart ached with sadness for Violet. We had been torn apart. I had been ripped from my mother's arms. I despised Agnes with a passion – what gave her the right to take the decision into her own hands? All to save the reputation of her good name. She'd been right about one thing though – I was loved by Alice and Julian, and throughout my whole life I hadn't wanted for anything. It was strange that they'd suddenly become Alice and Julian instead of Mum and Dad, and now I understood why there was never any mention of Aunt Violet. I buried my head in Tom's chest and let the tears flow.

'Kitty, look at me.' Tom tilted my head up and our eyes met. 'Without a shadow of a doubt your mum and dad loved you. They brought you up as their own, and you had a good upbringing, Kitty. Don't ever forget that. OK, so you're in shock from discovering a family secret that everyone tried to hide, but your past is your past, and you've spent it in a loving household. The bond you had with Alice and Julian was a real bond, a bond that was formed from proper love.'

'Tom, there are still so many questions.'

'I know,' he replied, kissing the top of my head.

'How could they take me from her arms – she wanted to keep me.'

'Times were different back then. Things have changed over the years but being pregnant at sixteen by a married man would have been frowned upon. Families would hide their secrets in order to save their reputation.'

'I'm sorry,' I said.

What are you sorry for?'

'I bet you didn't think our first night together would end up like this or that getting involved with me would be so complicated.'

'Don't be daft. I'm here for you,' he replied gently.

I felt a lump rise in my throat. 'I think I'm going to be sick.'

Quickly standing up and rushing to the bathroom, I threw up. It must have been the shock, and I could feel my whole body shaking. I looked in the mirror; my pale tear-stained face stared back at me.

Tom was still sitting on the settee waiting for me when I came back. I sat down next to him.

'Kitty, this is a huge shock. I know it's going to be difficult, but how about we try and get a couple of hours' sleep?'

Suddenly I felt exhausted, not to mention battered and bruised. 'Will you stay?'

'I'm going nowhere. Come on – let me hold you. Please try and manage a few hours' sleep.'

Climbing under the duvet with Tom's arms wrapped around me, I felt safe; I was relieved he wasn't going anywhere. I needed him now more than ever. There were lots of questions I needed answers to and I knew the very person who might have those answers, but first I needed to sleep. I knew what I would have to do in the morning. The next few days were going to be some of the most difficult I would ever face.

CHAPTER 43

The sunshine streamed through the gap in the curtains when I finally awoke. I stretched my arms above my head and gazed over at Tom. He looked so handsome lying next to me.

'Are you awake?' I whispered.

'I think so. What time is it?'

'It must be about 9 a.m.'

I turned to face Tom. He smiled at me and slipping his arms around my waist pulling me in close. I grasped hold of his arms tightly and tilted my head upwards. He dipped his head towards mine and we kissed.

'I'm so glad you're here,' I murmured.

'I'm so glad to be here.'

I closed my eyes and began to explore his body with my hands, every inch of him, savouring every touch, every moment.

Alfie jumped onto the bed and startled us both. 'He nearly gave me a heart attack.'

'Me too.' I smiled.

'Did you finally sleep?' Tom asked.

'Yes, I must have eventually, but, Tom, what am I going to do?'

He pulled back. Looking me straight in the eyes, he moved my hair away from my face and tucked it gently behind my ear.

'Whatever you do, it's going to set the cat amongst the pigeons, there's no doubt about that.'

'I know, but I need answers, and you know who I need to speak to, but I'm scared; I'm scared of his reaction.'

'I'm assuming you mean Ted?'

'Yes. Do you think he knows I exist?'

'Well, to be honest, Kitty, there's only one way to find out. Whether he does or whether he doesn't, you need to decide what you're hoping to gain from this situation. Yes, I know you want answers but the truth will also rock their world too. It isn't going to be easy.'

'What do you mean?'

'Whether or not Ted knows you exist, Jeannie and Robin are also going to discover they have a sibling, and that their father conducted an affair with a sixteen-year-old girl behind their mother's back. They have a good relationship with Ted, and who knows what damage it may cause. All I'm saying, Kitty, is don't do anything hasty. Just think about it carefully, and of course whatever you decide to do, I'll be by your side.'

Letting out a huge sigh, I slumped back onto my pillow. Tom patted my arm. 'I'll go and feed Alfie and make us a drink.' Throwing back the covers, he strode out of the bedroom with Alfie close at his heels. Looking up at the ceiling, my head was whirling, a question burning fiercely inside me: where was Violet? I wanted to find her.

Tom wandered back into the room holding two steaming-hot mugs of tea. I felt myself smiling while I watched him. It was strange having company but also very comforting knowing I wasn't on my own.

Tom perched on the edge of the bed and passed me a drink. 'What's the plan of action then? Have you decided on anything?'

I stared up at him and held my breath.

Tom sat in silence, waiting for me to answer.

'I think … I'm going to visit Ted today. I'm going to find out whether my father knows I exist.'

'Do you want me to come too, Kitty?'

'What about the Lodge? Don't you need to sort out the animals first?'

'Yes, I can nip there now to check on things, but no doubt the farmhands will have it all running like clockwork. I'll pick you up after I've finished. I know Robin is collecting Jeannie from the hospital at 2 p.m., so the coast will be clear and we can gauge from Ted's reaction what to do next.'

I nodded.

'Are you sure this is what you want, Kitty? Because once you've revealed who you are there'll be no going back.'

Of course I was nervous, though that was an understatement. However, there was a burning desire inside me; I needed to know what had happened to Violet and I wasn't going to surrender that need anytime soon.

'Yes, I'm sure.' I let out a long sigh. I met Tom's gaze and managed a nervous smile.

Tom took the last gulp of his tea and touched my arm. 'I'll be back within the hour.' He kissed me lightly on the lips.

'I'll be ready. Well, as ready as I'll ever be.'

CHAPTER 44

Tom was waiting for me outside in the van. I grabbed my bag and my keys from the table and I was just about to follow him when the phone rang.

It was Jeannie.

Hearing her voice, I felt strange. It was confusing knowing that my relationship with Jeannie had changed overnight yet she had no clue she was now ringing her sister and not just a friend.

'Hi, Kitty, it's only me. Robin is collecting me in an hour or so but do you fancy coming over to the house tonight? I could do with some company and, to be honest, if you're there it saves me from the constant fussing of Dad.'

I hesitated for a moment. I wasn't expecting the invitation.

'Are you still there, Kitty?'

'Sorry, Jeannie, there's someone knocking on the door. Can I ring you back when you're home? Will that be OK?' I asked, not knowing how to answer.

'Yes, of course, speak to you later. But first tell me, have you spoken to Tom?'

'I have indeed.'

'Is everything OK between you two? Are you finally an item?'

I laughed. 'Yes and yes.'

I could hear Jeannie let out a huge cheer before she clicked the phone off.

As Tom drove me to Ted's farm, we travelled in silence. I was feeling apprehensive.

He pulled the van up in front of the farmhouse. We both sat and stared at the quaint old building for a moment. Tom placed his hand on my knee. 'Do you want me to come in with you?'

'This is something I need to do myself, Tom, but will you wait here for me?'

'I will, I promise.'

I paused and took a deep breath.

Walking towards the front door, not only could I feel Tom's eyes watching my every step, but my heart was thumping so loud I was convinced he must have been able to hear it. For the last hour or so I had imagined the conversation between Ted and I, but now I was here I hadn't a clue what I was going to say when he opened the door. I felt terrified.

Rapping the lion door knocker with my sweaty hand, I waited. I heard the patter of a dog's paws running along the wooden floor, followed by the sound of sniffing. 'Come here, boy, in the kitchen.' The paws clattered back up the hallway, and a door slammed. Then I heard footsteps approaching the front door.

I felt my heartbeat quicken and a feeling of nausea surged through my body.

Glancing back at Tom, he gave me a reassuring smile. Turning back round, I saw Ted standing in front of me in the open doorway. Our eyes met for the first time. Looking up at the man standing in front of me I saw the resemblance between us was striking. We stared at each other and my heart was pounding. His face didn't falter. I waited for him to speak; I waited for him to ask who I was and what I wanted but he didn't. I couldn't speak. I bit down on my lip; I could feel it beginning to tremble and I could feel my eyes filling with tears.

I thrust my hand towards his; I didn't know what else to do. He shook it but still he didn't speak – he just watched me.

'Pleased to meet you.' My voice was shaking. 'I think you may have known my mother.'

'Violet?' he questioned yet didn't look surprised.

I gasped.

'Come on in.' He opened the front door wide. I followed Ted towards the living room, where he gestured for me to take a seat. Nervously, I sat down. The view from the living-room window was spectacular. It looked out towards the back of the farm with fields that went on for acres and acres. Cobbled walls criss-crossed the fields, disappearing into the distance.

'Can I get you anything?' Ted asked politely. He wasn't what I was expecting. Even though there appeared to be a strange tension in the air, he had still welcomed me into his house. From reading Violet's diary I thought he might be a little standoffish, however, even though he was watching me carefully, the relief on his face that I was there seemed apparent.

'No thanks, I'm fine,' I replied.

I reached into my bag and pulled out Violet's diary and placed it on the wooden table that separated the pair of us.

'What's this?' Ted asked, picking up the diary and thumbing through the pages.

'Violet Porter's diary – she wrote it when she was sixteen,' I answered firmly.

The colour instantly drained from Ted's face and he buried his face into his hands. He took a minute to look up and asked, 'Your mother's diary?'

I nodded.

'Do you know who I am, Ted?' There – I'd said it now.

He nodded. 'Yes, I do.'

I hesitated. 'Now that I'm here, I have no idea what to say to you.'

Ted paused and glanced out of the window. His face seemed to soften as he began talking.

'Shall I go first?' he asked softly.

I could only manage a nod.

'I heard you were here. As soon as Jeannie mentioned the new Lodge manager named Kitty, I knew it had to be you. It was the Easter-egg hunt. I sneaked into Tom's cottage and watched you from behind the curtains; there was no mistaking you were Violet's daughter.'

'So that was you sneaking around in the cottage?'

He nodded.

'It wasn't long after that I went to visit Tom at the cottage. It was one lunchtime and I noticed you sitting on the bench outside the office with Jeannie.'

'Why did you visit Tom?'

'Because you were on my mind all the time. I was trying to discover whether you knew or not. Tom must have thought I was acting strangely, popping in with no real reason. I asked him a few questions, but it was obvious he didn't know anything. You knocked on the door and I watched you walk back up the path and cycle down the drive towards the gate. I didn't say anything to Tom and left shortly after.'

'How did you meet Violet?'

'I first met Violet one summer's evening at the local bandstand. She was leaning against an old oak tree wearing a beautiful dress and she was the most stunning girl I'd ever set eyes on. I'd never seen her before, but all through the evening my eyes kept flicking over in her direction. She was enjoying the evening with her friend. Her eyes sparkled, she was young and vibrant, and her laugh was infectious. I was mesmerised. I couldn't take my eyes off her. I wanted to find out more about her; I wanted to know her name, and as the evening went on I found myself staring at her more and more. I was married and had a child, and more to the point it wasn't right, but I was drawn to Violet. Eventually she noticed me and smiled back. As soon as the band had finished playing, the crowds began to filter away. I lost sight of her for a brief moment but once the hordes had dispersed, she was standing there, smiling back at me. I plucked up the courage to walk over and we began chatting. Not only was she beautiful, but we also clicked straightaway. It wasn't my usual style, chatting up women in the park, but there was something different about her. She told me she'd seen me about; she told me she saw me every morning as I drove past her in my van. Violet looked up at me with her beautiful eyes and made me promise I would look out for her on Monday morning, and of course I did. I couldn't believe my luck that morning – she was standing on the edge of the pavement smiling at me. I pulled my van over, she climbed in and we chatted some more. I felt so at ease with Violet. It became a frequent occurrence. Every morning I would pull the van over for a chat unless I had one of the farm boys with me. Violet made me feel alive; she made me feel young again, although obviously I was quite a bit older.'

'You also had a wife,' I blurted out.

Ted and I stared at each other; there was a strange tension in the air. Looking me straight in the eye, he continued, 'I'm not proud of what I did, far from it. There are also no excuses. Violet ignited a flame in me. I felt like I was myself whenever I was around her; there were no demands. She made me feel like me. Does that sound weak, Kitty?'

Our eyes locked. Ted continued, '*Yes*, I know who you are, but honestly I didn't know what had happened to you until your mother died. That's when I found out you'd inherited the Lodge.'

My heart felt like it had been ripped from my chest. 'Violet's dead?' I gasped.

'No, Kitty, I mean your mother – Alice.'

Ted stood up and walked around the table and sat next to me. 'This is going to be difficult for all of us.'

'All?'

'Yes – Robin and Jeannie. I knew one day the truth would come out. It always does.'

'Did you ever want to look for me?'

'I did, Kitty, I promise I did. Let me make us a pot of tea and I can explain. You do like tea, don't you?'

'Yes,' I answered.

'I'll be back in a minute.'

I watched him walk out of the living room. I was a bag of nerves; looking down at my hands I could see them shaking.

Five minutes later Ted returned with a pot of tea on a tray with a couple of mugs. Placing the tray on the table, he poured the tea and handed me a drink.

'I don't know about you, but I've thought about this moment on many occasions – what I would say to you. I've played the conversation over and over in my head.'

I shook my head. 'I only found out yesterday that the people who I thought were my parents were actually my aunt and uncle. I'm still in complete shock.'

I could see the tears welling up in Ted's eyes. 'How did you find out?' he asked.

I raised my eyebrows and nodded towards the diary on the table.

'Where did you find it?'

'It was locked in the safe up at the Lodge. I had no idea who Violet Porter was or that she even existed. No one in my family had ever spoken of her.'

It took a few seconds for either of us to speak, and then Ted continued.

'I didn't realise Violet was so young when we first met. The way she held herself, her knowledge of the world, led me to believe she was older. You know I was married at the time. I'd been married to Bea for five years; we were childhood sweethearts, swept away with the romantic notion we were soulmates and would spend the rest of our days together. Bea's parents gave us this house, this farm,' he said, looking all around him. 'And what a magnificent wedding present it was. We had friends who couldn't even afford their first house. We had well and truly landed on out feet.'

I took another sip of my tea and let him continue.

'Once Bea had given birth to Robin, family life became more strained. I imagine everyone goes through their rough patches; new home, new child, but Robin never slept. Bea was up most of the night every night and, as for me, I was that tired with the work on the farm that nothing or no one would disturb my sleep. Bea began to struggle; looking back she was more than likely suffering from post-natal depression, but things like that were taboo back in the day. My escape route from it all was Violet. I was dishonest with Violet and it's something I've never forgiven myself for.'

'What do you mean? Why were you dishonest?'

'I promised her the world, Kitty, yet I lied to her. I never told her I was married. I made Violet believe the reason we couldn't be together was due to the age gap between us. I made her think if she waited until she was eighteen it wouldn't be a shock for her parents, but of course I couldn't ever be with Violet because I was married.'

'Why couldn't you just have been honest with her?'

'I had my reasons, but the simple answer to that, Kitty, is that I didn't want to lose her. I knew the minute she found out she would be off and I could never imagine life without her.'

'But you thought it was OK to have another baby with Bea. How was that fair on Violet?' I was now struggling to get my feelings under control. 'It sounds like you were in love with Violet but couldn't give up Bea?'

Ted gave a knowing nod. 'I think you may be right. I loved Bea, of course I did, but it was a different love; it was comfortable. However, I was in love with Violet. When I was at home, Violet was the one on my mind constantly; she was the last person I would think about at night and the first thing I would think about when I opened my eyes. She was the woman I loved. It was the timing – the timing was all wrong. I couldn't leave my wife and baby. I knew what the right thing to do was, but I couldn't do it. I loved Violet. In a way, a part of me will always love Violet.'

'You broke her heart the day she saw you in the hospital with your wife, holding your new baby daughter in your arms. How could you do that to anyone?'

'I didn't have a clue Violet was at the hospital that day. I remember looking up and she was standing in the doorway of the maternity ward. She didn't utter a word. I think that was the moment it hit me.'

'She was at the hospital because my mother, Alice, had just come out of surgery. She'd suffered an ectopic pregnancy. The result of the surgery meant she could never have children.'

'I am so sorry to hear that. I honestly didn't know. I made the heartbreaking decision to put my family first – we had the children and I threw myself into life at the farm. I broke down on many occasions; the pain of not seeing Violet ever again was unbearable, but I had no choice. Then I heard through the grapevine she was ill. I was distraught; I remember I risked everything to get a note to her. I told her she must remember I would always love her. I did mean it.'

'Violet was already pregnant then.'

Ted shook his head; his eyes were blurred with tears. 'I never knew she was pregnant.'

'I don't understand. You said you knew I existed.'

'Bea was close friends with Alice. My wife had asked her if she would do us the honour of being Jeannie's godmother. At the time, I wasn't aware that Alice was Violet's sister. It all came as a bit of a shock when I walked into her living room before Jeannie's christening to find Violet holding my daughter in her arms. She looked just as shocked as me and dropped Jeannie. I went berserk. I panicked and thought she was going to tell everyone I'd been having an affair with her. I wasn't ready for my marriage to crumble all around me. I wasn't prepared. I'm ashamed of my actions and how I treated Violet that day. I shouted at her.' Quickly he added, 'I didn't mean it; I still loved her.'

The knots in my stomach took my breath away. This was like a tragic love story: two people that seemed besotted with each other but could never be together.

Ted looked exhausted from reliving the past, but he still hadn't answered my question: how did he know I existed.

'Ted, I need to know everything,' I urged.

I knew there was more.

'Soon after Jeannie, Bea got pregnant again.' Suddenly Ted's voice became shaky and I watched a tear roll down his face. He wiped it away with the back of his hand. 'There were complications and I lost them both – my wife and our baby. Words cannot describe the pain and guilt of that night.'

'Guilt?'

'Yes – Bea was a good person and a loving mother. I lied to her and cheated on her, and some would say I got what I deserved. The guilt began to eat away at me. Bea threw her whole life into our relationship and how did I repay her? She deserved better than me.'

'But you'd already decided to save your marriage,' I offered.

'At the time yes, but I always knew one day I would go looking for Violet. I could never get her out of my system. She was always there, in here,' he said, bringing his fist up to his chest and thumping his heart.

'I was left to bring up Robin and Jeannie by myself. In all the years gone by, I've never had another relationship. I couldn't face it.

'Shortly after Bea died, Alice sent the most beautiful bouquet of flowers. Once the funeral arrangements had been decided I travelled over to the house to thank her personally and let them know the time of the service. I was surprised when Alice opened the door – she was holding a baby. At first, I thought she must have a visitor and I apologised for disturbing her. She told me not to be daft and invited me in. The house was cluttered with baby paraphernalia. I didn't even know Alice had been pregnant. Bea had never mentioned it. She made me a drink and asked me to hold the baby. I asked what the baby's name was and Alice replied Kitty.'

Ted hesitated for a moment. 'I can remember looking at you and thinking how much you looked like my other two children. You smiled up at me and lay in my arms, gurgling away. The resemblance was so strong that there was something inside me urging me to ask questions. Alice looked so tired and tearful. I thought it was due to the devastation of Bea's death – I'm sure that took its toll on her – but Alice broke down and cried. She kept apologising for crying. I made a comment that most mothers felt this way after giving birth, and it was normal to feel emotional, and it was at that moment she confided in me. She told me the baby belonged to her sister Violet.'

'You held me?'

Ted nodded. 'I did and immediately I knew there was something about you.'

'What happened next?' I urged.

'I asked her where her sister was. I wanted to know for my own selfish reasons and it was then Alice told me that Violet had now moved to Canada. Not only had I lost my wife, but Violet was also gone.'

'Did you say anything to my mum?'

'About Violet and me?'

'Yes.'

'Not at that moment. I knew you were mine; I could see it in your eyes. Even though Alice was emotional I could see how much she loved you. It didn't matter that you weren't biologically hers. I didn't mean to pry but I asked her why the baby hadn't travelled to Canada with Violet. Alice said it was a family decision, however I kind of got the impression it wasn't Violet's decision at all.'

'It wasn't,' I snarled. 'Violet was distraught when I was taken from her. How could they do that to her?'

'I'm so sorry, Kitty; I can't imagine what you must be going through.'

'Why didn't you tell them the truth? Why didn't you tell them that you were my father? Why didn't you want me?'

'Oh, Kitty,' he said, touching my knee. 'You have to believe me – it wasn't as simple as that. I'd become a widower overnight; the grief of losing my wife and bringing up two small children was the most difficult thing. I had no one to help, a farm to run and I struggled. I didn't have a clue about running or managing a house – that had been Bea's strength. The only comfort I had was I knew you were in the best hands. Alice and Julian loved you like their very own; you were their own, and I couldn't take you away from them. They gave their life to you, which makes them very special people in my heart, and they would have been devastated to lose you. There wasn't a day went by that I didn't think about you. If I'm honest, I existed on a day-to-day basis and learnt to carry on; I learnt to cry without making a sound.' Ted looked down at the carpet, no longer able to maintain eye contact with me.

The two of us sat in silence, for a moment lost in our own thoughts.

Both of us had lost special people: Violet, Alice, Julian and Bea. I understood that the circumstances had spiralled out of control but sadly my heart twisted for Violet – she had lost everyone.

'Alice and Julian knew you were mine and that's when all communication broke down between us,' Ted continued.

'How did they find out?'

'They asked me to be your godfather. Alice was Jeannie's godmother and they thought it was a kind gesture after Bea's passing. It was then I told them; it was the hardest thing I ever had to do. Alice crumbled before my eyes – she thought I was there to take you away. I promised them both I would do no such thing; I had no intention of causing anyone any trouble or pain, I just wanted to know how you were from time to time.' Ted stood up and walked over to the old oak dresser in the corner of the room. Bending down, he retrieved an old tin box from the cupboard and sat back down next to me.

'Open it,' he said softly.

'I don't understand.'

'Just open it, Kitty.'

Lifting the lid off the old tin box, I peered inside. Thumbing through the pastel-coloured envelopes in the tin, they all had one thing in common: they were addressed to me.

'I don't understand.'

'These are yours, Kitty – letters, cards I'd sent to you every Christmas and birthday. They were returned to me unopened. I didn't want to take you away from Alice and Julian, but I did want you to know I was always thinking about you. I've struggled for years knowing you were out there, and when your mother died—'

I interrupted Ted 'How did you know Alice had died?'

'Ethel contacted me.'

I was stunned. 'Ethel? You know where she is?'

'Yes. Ethel is the most loyal friend anyone could ever wish for and she's looked out for Violet for all these years.'

I gasped – my head was whirling trying to take in all this information.

'Where's Ethel now? And, more to the point, where is Violet?'

'Ethel lives in the village, and Violet, as far as I know, made a life for herself in Canada. She never came back.'

'Are you sure?' I queried.

'She never returned, not to my knowledge anyway.'

'And when Alice died?'

'I went to visit the grave where she was buried next to Julian. Your father's death was such a tragic accident and after her passing I laid some flowers on the grave with a small note thanking them for taking such wonderful care of you for all these years. They were amazing people.'

'That note was from you?' I let out a long breath, remembering the note left on the graveside.

'Yes, I knew Agnes had left the Lodge to you and I knew it was only a matter of time before you came looking for answers and I knew, Kitty, that I would be here, waiting. I know I'm far from perfect but hopefully you'll give me a chance to get to know you?'

I nodded, happy and relieved I hadn't been rejected. I knew the relationship would take time to build but time was on our side.

Standing up, I said, 'I best go now; Tom is waiting for me outside.'

Ted nodded thoughtfully and stood up beside me. He stretched his arms out to me. 'I'm so sorry for everything. We can't change the past, but we can still look forward to the future.' I fell into his arms and he hugged me tight. I sobbed. I'd hugged my father for the very first time. Now I had found my father I had a burning desire to track down Violet too.

'Does someone want to tell me what the hell is going on here?'

I spun around to find Jeannie, Robin, Danny and Tom standing in the doorway.

Tom was staring at me, his eyes wide.

I glanced at Jeannie; her face was thunderous.

'I'm sorry, Kit, I didn't know what to do,' Tom said.

She stared straight at me with such hatred. 'You and my father?'

I shook my head immediately. 'No, it's not what you think!'

However, Jeannie didn't want to listen and before anyone else could speak she pushed past everyone and ran out of the room. All we could hear were her footsteps running up the stairs followed by a slam of the bedroom door.

'Jeannie?' Ted's voice petered out as he followed her up the stairs.

CHAPTER 45

Robin was the last person we expected to see today. Tom and I had left the farmhouse rapidly on Ted's request. Jeannie had locked him out of her room and he'd come back downstairs. He'd touched my arm lightly and reassured me that everything was going to be all right. I had no choice but to trust him. They were his children and he wanted the chance to be honest with them now. I understood completely. Although it didn't stop me feeling apprehensive, I didn't want to hurt Jeannie or Robin, but I knew when Ted explained the past there was going to be anger and hurt flying about.

Opening the front door to the flat, I found Robin standing on the doorstep with Lucinda. He raked his hand nervously through his hair and there was an awkward silence. 'Can we come in?' Lucinda asked.

'Yes, of course, go through. Tom's in the living room,' I said, opening the door wide so they could filter past me. So many things had changed in my life in such a short space of time. No matter what had happened in the past I had hope – hope that Jeannie and Robin would accept me into their family and hope that they would forgive Ted for his actions as a young man. For me, Ted had suffered enough; I understood perfectly his reasons for leaving me with Alice and Julian.

Robin was quiet and settled on the sofa, Lucinda firmly grasping his hand. He looked pale and battered and stared down at the carpet. Tom stood up and patted his shoulder. 'I'll put some tea in the pot,' he offered, leaving the room.

'Robin, I don't know what to say,' I said softly.

I noticed Lucinda squeeze his hand and she gave me a reassuring smile.

'That makes two of us,' he said.

He looked sad, and I felt my heart sink.

He looked up, and our eyes met. 'How long have you known, Kitty?'

'Around twenty-four hours.'

'So my father wasn't lying about that then?'

'No, he wasn't. It's a huge shock for all of us. I know it's not easy for you and there are bridges that may need to be rebuilt, but Ted's carried this burden around for a long time and he's always put you and Jeannie first. He loves you both dearly. I know this doesn't make it any less painful. You still have your father; I've just found out my parents were never my parents and I can never have a conversation with them about any of this. I don't love them any less. In fact I may love them more; they opened up their heart and their home to me, and I never had an inkling about any of this. And as for Ted, Jeannie and you, I hope you feel the same as me.'

'Which is?' Robin asked

'That I've gained a new family.' I smiled warmly at him.

Robin nodded. 'I hope so too. I knew there was something about you. Remember when you first arrived and we were competing against each other in the chicken show? I can remember you saying something and you laughed. I was amazed how much you looked like Jeannie.'

I smiled.

'I always felt a connection between us, there was no denying that – it felt like you were the big brother I never had.'

'I *am* the big brother you never had.' Robin sighed then followed it up with a half smile. 'And thank god ...' said Robin, feeling awkward.

'Stop there,' I said quickly. I couldn't believe how close Robin and I had come to going on a date!

Tom placed a pot of tea on the table along with some biscuits and handed Robin a bottle of beer.

Robin nodded his appreciation towards Tom and took a swig.

'New start?' I asked hopefully.

'Is it all that simple, Kitty?'

'I think it is. We can't change the past; what's done is done. Your dad dedicated his life to you and Jeannie, and Alice and Julian did the same for me. If anything, me arriving at the Lodge has given me a new lease of life. I have a job, a home and this gorgeous man.' I smiled at Tom. 'And hopefully a new family that in time will accept me.'

'I agree with everything that Kitty's said,' Lucinda added.

Robin and Lucinda smiled at each other. Lucinda touched his knee affectionately.

Tom smiled and raised his eyebrows at me.

'Are you two together by any chance?' he asked.

'We're getting there.' Lucinda beamed. 'Even though I was hoping for a quiet start to our relationship,' she added, laughing.

'Didn't we all,' Tom said and grinned.

'I'm so glad for you both.'

Robin smiled at us. 'I'm glad too, and it looks like I've not only got myself a girlfriend but I've also gained another little sister.' He stood up and stretched out his arms towards me. 'Can I have a hug?'

'You certainly can,' I answered, feeling relieved.

'Can I ask a question, Kitty?'

'Yes, of course.'

'What are you going to do about Violet?'

'I'm going to find her, Robin. I'm going to find her.'

CHAPTER 46

The next morning I lay awake in bed next to Tom. I found my-self staring up at the ceiling. It had only been twenty-four hours since I'd discovered the contents of Violet's diary and everyone's lives had been catapulted into disarray. There were no more en-tries in the diary after the last one we read. It felt like once her father had driven Violet out of the village, she'd disappeared. Her voice was no longer heard. It couldn't be that difficult to find Violet – if Ethel was still in contact with her, surely it would be very simple? Without a shadow of a doubt I knew I wanted to find her. However, the thoughts inside my head were niggling away at me. What if Ted wouldn't provide me with Ethel's ad-dress? What if Ted didn't want me to find Violet? And what if Violet didn't want anything to do with me? These were all ques-tions that I would discover the answers to very soon.

'Are you awake?' I heard Tom's sleepy voice.

'Yes, wide awake.'

'What's the plan of action?'

I let out a sigh. 'I don't know what to do for the best.'

'What do you mean?' he asked, stroking my hair.

'I want to go and see Ted again. I want him to give me Ethel's address so I can start searching for Violet, but I have no idea how the land lies with Jeannie. What do you think I should do?'

'Now there's a question.'

I turned my head towards Tom and he kissed me lightly on the lips.

'Why don't you give it a day or two? Let the dust settle and wait until you know what Jeannie's feelings are. She may need a little time, and let's not forget she's pregnant and has just been in hospital – her emotions will be all over the place.'

'I think you're right, Tom, but it's that feeling I want sorted and I want it sorted now.'

'Yes, I felt like that too.'

'What, with your ex?'

'No, silly, with you!' he joked, tickling me.

'But on a serious note, Kitty, wherever Violet is, a couple of days isn't going to make a difference. She has no idea you've discovered the diary or that Ted's children finally know the truth. Let's just hang on until we hear how Jeannie is coping with all this.'

'OK, but in the meantime we best get up to the Lodge. I'll jump in the shower and you can make breakfast.'

Tom pulled a sulky face. 'You mean you don't want company in the shower? You're fed up with me already.'

'You, my dear, can wait until later. Now go and make breakfast,' I insisted, pushing him out of bed.

'OK, OK, I know when I'm not wanted!' he claimed, strolling out of the bedroom with a pretend hurt expression on his face.

'Men,' I shouted after him before jumping in the shower.

Up at the Lodge, we'd fallen behind with the workload in the last couple of days. Conker needed mucking out, the coops needed cleaning and the invoices were piled high.

'No slacking today,' Tom shouted after me as I headed towards the bottom field to feed the chickens and unleash them into the fields. I shook my head and smiled to myself. Even though this week had been traumatic, Tom made me happy; I was so glad he was there for me.

Walking up the yard, I realised this place felt like home. Six months ago I'd never heard of it, yet now I'd truly started to have a sense of belonging. I thought back to the conversation this morning with Tom regarding Jeannie. He was right about seeing how the land lay in a couple of days' time. Robin had taken it all in his stride. Of course he was hurt by his father's actions, but they couldn't be undone, and it seemed he was prepared to find a way to move forward. I was hoping Jeannie would be OK; for her it had all come at the wrong time, with the baby and her being unwell. I spotted Conker already grazing on the lush grass and then I saw a figure sitting on top of the hay bale outside the stable door. I squinted – it was Jeannie and she was staring across the fields. Even from this distance I could tell she was lost in thought and had been crying. I walked over in her direction. She looked up, startled.

'Hi,' I said.

'Hi back,' Jeannie replied, still staring across into space.

'You OK?'

'I've been better,' she replied sadly.

'Can I join you?' I asked.

'Of course.'

'Are you OK?'

'Honestly?'

I nodded.

She dropped her gaze to the ground. 'I feel cheated in a way.'

'Cheated? How?'

She brushed the tears away from her cheek with the back of her hand.

'I suppose I had this vision that everything was perfect. My father has been my rock – someone I admired, looked up to. I placed him right on the top of a pedestal and guess what? He's just come crashing down to the floor. I believed everything he'd ever told me: how Mum was so wonderful and how he'd never wanted another relationship due to the grief and how no one would ever grab his heart again. It wasn't about that, though, was it?'

'Your mother was wonderful,' I said, touching her knee. 'That certainly hasn't changed.'

'What makes it worse is that I can't remember her. I try and try; I squeeze my eyes shut and there's nothing, absolute nothing. I can't remember her and it hurts so much.'

'You were too young. What you have to focus on, Jeannie, is that at the time Ted was technically two people: your father and a husband. Whatever mistakes he made as a husband, he didn't make any mistakes as a father – he loves you and Robin.'

'Do you think Mum knew about Violet?'

I shook my head. 'I don't think she did. According to Violet's diary as soon as she saw your dad in the hospital, holding you as a baby, it all stopped. In the end, Jeannie, your dad did the right thing and put his family first. We don't know what other people think and feel, but I do believe he loved your mum. He just got lost for a while.'

'And what about you?' Her eyes met mine.

'What about me?'

'I can't begin to imagine the turmoil you're going through.'

'It's been a strange six months, believe me. Finding out my parents aren't really my parents in the biological sense ... but in my heart they'll always be my parents. I could never think of them any differently. I never knew my grandparents; they were never spoken of. But what I have to assume from the diary is that maybe they were acting with the best intentions. Violet was only a young girl, with her whole life in front of her. The world was her oyster, and my mum could no longer have children after her ectopic pregnancy. The stigma attached to an unmarried mother at that time, the father a married man – it would seem the obvious solution to them. They saved the reputation of one daughter and gave happiness to another, while keeping the baby in the family. What they failed to take into account was Violet's feelings in it all.'

'How did the diary end up in the safe?' Jeannie asked.

'You know what, I have no idea, but as it was my grandmother's safe it must have something to do with her.

'Do you forgive Ted?' I asked gently.

Jeannie sighed. 'I know everything is screwed up, but he is my father. We're all human, born to make mistakes, and even though he made a huge mistake back then that's affected so many lives, there is one thing I can thank him for.'

'What's that then?'

'You,' she said, smiling at me. 'I have a sister. And I wonder if I can get away with being a bit stroppy now I'll have middle-child syndrome.'

'More stroppy?' I laughed.

'Shut up and give me a hug,' Jeannie ordered.

'With pleasure.'

I rested my head on her shoulder and looked out across the fields – everything had become so calm.

'Do you think you will ever call him Dad?'

'I think we should all take one step at a time.'

'Never say never, hey.'

'How do you feel about me looking for Violet?'

Jeannie pulled away and shrugged. 'I'm not sure.'

'Well let's face it, Violet may not even want to be found.'

'Can I be honest with you, Kitty? I know you have a right to search for your biological mother but I'll have to prepare myself to come face to face with the woman my dad had an affair with.'

I nodded; I understood that completely, but Violet was the last piece of this unfinished jigsaw and the desire inside me burned so brightly. I needed to find her; I needed to see her.

'Maybe it's the maternal instinct in me but you do what you need to do, Kitty, and don't let me stand in your way.'

I flashed Jeannie a grateful smile.

CHAPTER 47

By 6.30 p.m. Tom and I were absolutely shattered. The Lodge was in tip-top condition and all jobs were completed. Jeannie worked for most of the day but by late afternoon she began to feel tired again and went home to sleep. She was certainly suffering with the pregnancy. We chatted all morning about anything and everything. As planned, Danny was moving into the farmhouse this weekend and would be living with her, Ted and Robin. His job with Lucinda was going from strength to strength and he was now her right-hand man. I was so glad it was working out for them all.

'Are you all done?' Tom shouted up the yard while I was locking the office door.

'I think so.'

'Did you need to get straight back for Alfie or do you fancy a drink at mine?'

'A quick drink sounds great.'

'Great,' he replied, grabbing my hand, and we walked over towards the cottage. I couldn't help but smile to myself: even though my life was in turmoil I felt so happy when I was around Tom.

'What are you smiling at?' he said, grinning.

'You, taking my hand. I feel like a proper couple.' I laughed.

Tom stopped and turned towards me.

'We are a proper couple.' He gently wove his fingers through my hair and brushed it away from my face. 'I love you,' he whispered softly and kissed me. I closed my eyes and kissed him back.

I, Kitty Lewis, was kissing the most handsome man on the planet.

'So this is what it's like to fall in love?' I murmured.

'Do you like it?' he teased.

'Like it? I love it!'

'Let's go and put that kettle on – I'm parched. What do you fancy for tea tonight?'

I slipped my arm through his as we walked towards the cottage gate.

'We are most definitely a proper couple if we're eating together as well!'

'I fancy you for tea, but if that isn't on the menu until later on, how about a takeaway back at yours?'

'That sounds like a perfect plan.'

'I'll need to grab a quick shower first,' Tom said, opening the door to the cottage. 'You know where the kettle is,' he added, playfully pushing me towards the kitchen door.

'Charming! So you invite me back for a drink then I have to make my own?' I replied, taking a swipe at him.

'There was a method to my madness.' He kissed the tip of my nose and bounded up the stairs like a big kid.

I made my way into the kitchen and filled the kettle up with water. It was strange to think that I was actually standing in the same house my mother had lived as a child – well, both my mothers in fact. Sitting down at the table, I tried to visualise them all sitting here eating their tea – my grandparents, Alice and Violet. The only photograph I had seen of Violet was the one of her holding me when she was sixteen years old. I began to wonder if she resembled me at all. Hearing the water running in the shower up above, I walked into the living room. I imagined my granddad sat in the old armchair in the corner, smoking a pipe while the open fire roared. I had no idea whether he smoked a pipe, but that's what I imagined old men did. The old dresser took pride of place at the back of the room; I could imagine it being jam-packed with books, photographs and a dinner service that only ventured out at Christmas time.

Wandering back into the kitchen, I took a couple of mugs off the draining board and placed a teabag in each of them. Hearing a knock at the door, I stood still for a moment to see if there was any movement from Tom upstairs. There was nothing – he must still be getting ready. There was another rap on the door. Making my way up the hall, I glanced up the stairs but still Tom hadn't appeared. Opening the door, I found a woman standing on the step, staring back at me. I'd never seen her before. She wasn't a customer at the Lodge – well not to my knowledge anyway.

'Hi, can I help you?' I asked politely.

'Kitty?' she answered, staring at me.

I felt myself stiffen then I began to tremble all over. I managed a nod.

She hesitated.

'V-Violet?' I stuttered, fighting the lump in my throat.

'No, no, I'm not Violet, I'm Ethel,' she said, swiftly thrusting her hand forward.

I shook her hand. For a split second I battled the crush of disappointment. It wasn't Violet standing in front of me. However, Ethel was the next best thing.

'Please forgive me for dropping in on you so unexpectedly,' she said.

'No, no, not at all. Please forgive my manners. Come on in. This isn't my house, it's Tom's. I'm just making a drink. Do you want one? The kitchen is just through here,' I babbled.

Ethel smiled. 'Yes, I know. I've been in this house a fair few times, but not in recent years.'

'Oh yes, of course you have.'

Ethel followed me into the kitchen. 'Would you like tea or coffee?'

'I'd love a cup of tea, one sugar please.'

I could hear Tom's footsteps echoing down the stairs. He appeared in the doorway all showered and shaved and looked a little taken aback that we had a visitor. 'Who's this?' he asked, wandering towards me and kissing me lightly on the cheek. He grabbed a mug of tea off the side.

'Hi, Tom, I'm Ethel,' she said politely.

Tom's gaze met mine then turned back towards Ethel. 'Ethel as in Ethel from the book – the diary?'

'Yes, Tom, Ethel as in Violet's best friend.'

'Wow, I have to admit I wasn't expecting that,' he replied, pulling out a chair and settling himself down at the table.

Tom and I sat and stared at Ethel, waiting for any information about Violet.

'I'm actually lost for words,' I managed to say.

'I didn't know whether to come, but Ted told me that the secret is finally out, after all these years. So I thought I'd come and find you, as I'm sure it was only a matter of time before you came looking for me. I just guessed you might be at the Lodge.'

Both Tom and I nodded.

'It's Tom that lives here; I'm in the flat on the high street.'

'How are you coping, Kitty?' she asked with genuine concern.

Tom leant forward and took hold of my hand and gave it a gentle squeeze.

'It's all very surreal I have to admit. I feel like I'm riding on a roller coaster; every time I think I've come to the end of the ride there seems to be another twist or turn. What I once believed to be the truth has shattered all around me in tiny pieces.'

Ethel nodded. 'I can completely understand where you're coming from and I'm sure you have a million and one questions, but first can I ask you – where did you get the diary?'

'Actually I only have one question, but I found the diary locked in the safe in the office, here at the Lodge.'

Ethel raised her eyebrows. 'Locked in the safe?'

'Yes, why do you ask?'

'The day that Violet was driven out of the village was one of the worst days of my life. She was my best friend and no one will ever come close to the bond that I have with your mother.'

'Violet?'

'Yes, Violet. I will always call her your mother because I was there at your birth. I harboured the secret of the pregnancy from the moment we both realised that she was carrying you.'

Both Tom and I sat in silence and listened to Ethel.

'I can remember the day she left like it was yesterday. John, the farm boy, hammered on my door; he was clutching a letter in his hand and was shouting at me to be quick otherwise I would miss her. I didn't have a clue what he was talking about. I ran while reading the letter; my heart was thumping and my legs pounded the pavements, I ran so fast. She wrote that her family were shipping her off to Canada without the baby. She didn't want to go. I reached the Lodge just in time to see the car travelling down the road. It stopped on the corner just before it turned and I screamed Violet's name at the top of my voice. She turned around and the tears were flowing down her face. She placed her hand on the window; I did the same. She mouthed bye and that I would always be her best friend. I shrieked I loved her. I too was crying. Then the car pulled away. My legs buckled underneath me and I slumped to my knees. Picking myself up, I ran after the car and watched while they got smaller and smaller. Then something caught my eye. There was an object being tossed out of the car window. I ran and ran, and when I got there I couldn't believe it – it was the diary, Violet's diary; she'd thrown the diary to me.'

'That would make sense,' I said, looking at Tom. 'There were no more entries after the day she left.'

'That's right,' agreed Ethel, 'because I had the diary. I cried all the way home; my heart was ripped out and I knew it was unlikely that I would ever see Violet again. That afternoon I went home and I read the diary from cover to cover then the letter she'd written me. My heart was breaking. Violet had had the most distressing time and even after everything, all she wanted was you – all she wanted was to keep her baby.'

The tears were flowing down my face; Tom passed me the box of tissues from the table and placed his arm around my shoulder.

'It was your grandma's decision. I may be speaking out of turn here, but Violet told me on numerous occasions that she felt like the black sheep of the family, an outcast. The age difference between her and Alice was huge and our only guess was that Violet wasn't a planned pregnancy. At the time it always felt that Agnes was hard on her, always short-tempered. Don't get me wrong, she never beat her or anything; it was more that Violet felt she was an inconvenience.'

'That's the impression I got too from reading the diary,' I said, nodded in agreement.

'Agnes and Arthur were devastated when it was confirmed Alice could no longer have children. Violet and I used to listen in to their conversations from the top of the stairs. The night she left, or should I say was driven away, I was so angry I remember marching up to this front door. Agnes opened the door and she began screaming at me, calling me all the names under the sun. I screamed back. I didn't care that I was screaming – they'd taken Violet away and I had nothing to lose. Agnes threatened me and said if I ever told anyone that Violet had given birth or Alice wasn't your real mother then she wouldn't be responsible for her actions. I was scared of her; I was only sixteen too. I threw the diary at her and it fell to the ground. She bent down and picked it up, asking me what it was. When I revealed it was Violet's diary, her face turned white. Thumbing through the pages quickly, she was shouting that the diary needed to be burnt and there was no way anyone could find out the truth. She slammed the door in my face and I could hear her shouting for Arthur. I thought she'd burnt the diary years ago; I'm surprised to know it still exists.'

'My heart goes out to Violet. From what I could gather from reading the diary she was besotted with Ted. It seems she lost him and then her baby.'

'Ted was her first love and her only true love, but as you've now discovered, he was married. Ted was caught up in the moment, flattered no doubt by the attention. I'm not saying he didn't love Violet – I'm convinced he did – but there was no way he was ever going to leave Bea. Ted wasn't aware that you existed until after Bea died.'

'Yes, I know – he told me.'

'Unfortunately humans make mistakes and we may never forget, but hopefully in time everyone can forgive.'

I had a sinking feeling in my heart and a lump in my throat. 'Ethel, I only have one thing left to ask you.'

'Yes, what is it?'

I took a deep breath.

'Do you know where Violet is? Do you know where my mother is?'

CHAPTER 48

Travelling on the train towards my old hometown, I felt full of mixed emotions. This would be the first time I had visited their grave knowing that the two people who had raised me as their own weren't actually my parents. I wondered how I would feel looking at their gravestone, reading the special words engraved on the tomb. I'd needed a little Dutch courage. It wasn't my usual style, but I'd swigged whisky from a hip flask that was now safely stored back in my pocket. It gave me a woozy feeling but a feeling that I needed. The woman sitting opposite me on the train tutted at me. I turned my head and leant it against the window. Who was she to judge me? She wasn't walking in my shoes; she knew nothing about me.

Earlier this morning I'd left Tom sleeping, his arm wrapped around Alfie. I felt like a burglar sneaking around my own flat in the early hours of the morning and disappearing out of the door before he awoke. I left him a note by the kettle. I told him I'd be back soon and that I'd gone to visit my parents' grave. I didn't want him to worry, but this was something I needed to do by myself. Today was a day I'd been dreading for a while. A day I wanted to be over before it had begun. Tom would be disappointed to wake up and discover that I wasn't there. He no doubt had the day planned full of lovely surprises for my birthday, but I needed to be on my own – well just for a few hours anyway.

I turned back to face another person, a man sitting in the same compartment. He was mumbling to himself while he fumbled about in a battered old rucksack that was balanced between his knees. The joy on his face said it all as he pulled out a can of Strongbow and snapped the pull. The woman who had tutted at me stood up abruptly, raised her eyebrows and muttered that he should be ashamed of himself before moving to the next compartment. I didn't judge him; who knew what he had to face once the train pulled into the station. He smiled at me, shaking his head after the woman then he hugged his can like it was the last drink he was ever going to have. No one else entered the compartment for the rest of the journey and we sat there opposite each other in a comfortable silence.

Watching the landscape whirl past, my mind flew back to the good old days. The days when life was easy; the days I didn't have a care in the world. Remembering my father sitting in the front room, I smiled to myself. Every Sunday afternoon in winter we spent it together; the fire roared while we played board games and Mum would spend her time in the kitchen cooking up a roast. It seemed like only yesterday. My thoughts then turned to my mother, Alice. How had she coped shielding me from the truth for my entire life? She must have lived on a knife-edge wondering if Violet would ever turn up to claim me. I wondered what she thought when she looked at me, knowing deep down I wasn't hers. I know she loved me – I never felt I was missing anything from my mother and father, and they never gave me any reason to doubt them.

I didn't have the words to describe how I was feeling today, but sitting on the train watching the world pass me by, tears stung in my eyes. I didn't feel angry, but if I could go back in time, if that was at all possible, I wished I could speak with my grandmother, Agnes. I would never understand how she could make such a decision back then or the damage she had done to Violet's heart, but she must believed she'd had good reasons.

We rolled into the station and once the train halted, the man opposite stood up, still clutching his can. He threw his rucksack over his shoulder and turned towards me. He smiled at me and I nodded – an appreciation of whatever either of us was facing today being our business and no one else's.

It was a beautiful day, I thought, as I wandered through the streets. The sky was clear and blue, and there was hardly a cloud in the sky. I walked along the streets and made my way up the crest of the hill, the weathered wrought-iron gates still standing tall, an impressive entrance to the graveyard. I noticed the ornamental statue that had been broken on my previous visit was now completely restored.

The churchyard was awash with colour. Freshly cut blooms adorned the grey stones. The lawns had been recently cut and the hedgerows trimmed. It was all looking very well maintained, a far cry from my last visit.

My eyes darted around the graveyard; it was deserted except for a woman walking towards me. A pretty lady, her brunette curls bounced on top of her shoulders as she walked by. Her tear-stained face said it all – the emotion was raw. I nodded politely as I passed her. The woman nodded back, barely giving me a second glance. Her expression suggested she was lost in thought.

As I approached the gravestone I stared at the same words that I'd read on my last visit.

In Loving Memory of Julian Lewis and his beloved Wife
Alice Lewis
Reunited
Treasured parents of Kitty Lewis

They were my treasured parents – nothing would ever change that. Blinking away the tears, I didn't feel disappointment, only love and gratitude. I couldn't have hoped for a better upbringing: they both did me proud. Bending down, I placed my flowers on the ground. I brought my hand to my lips and then traced my fingers around their names. I wondered what they would think knowing that I had finally unearthed the truth. I hoped they would know I didn't feel any anger towards them.

I noticed the pot sitting in front of their gravestone was filled with fresh flowers. In fact, they were my mother's favourite flowers – pink irises. She used to say the flower represented faith, hope, wisdom, courage and admiration. I smiled to myself; Ted must have remembered what day it was – my birthday – and came to thank them again for all that they'd done for me. I couldn't imagine how he was feeling today. It must be strange for him, his daughter's birthday – the daughter he'd never known until now. Picking up the small white envelope attached to the flowers, I opened it to see what he'd written this time.

The writing was small and neat. My eyes focussed, and I realised it wasn't the same writing as before. I recognised the writing; it was the same writing from the diary and there was no mistaking it – the writing belonged to Violet.

My chest pounded as I read the message. 'To Alice, no matter what, I have always loved you, V.'

I gasped.

She'd been here; my mother had been here. Quickly standing up, I spun round. There was no one to be seen, and the churchyard was deserted. Think, Kitty, think, where is she? I hadn't seen anyone here today except the woman, the woman with the tear-stained face that had barely nodded to me as I passed her. Clutching the card, I turned and ran. I ran like I'd never run before along the path towards the wrought-iron gates. Swinging the gates open, my eyes were searching everywhere, flitting to and fro, looking for the woman. Which way had she gone? There she was at the bottom of the hill!

'No, wait, please wait,' I shouted. I began to run again, but she didn't look round. I powered my legs, pushing them hard and then I stumbled.

Falling to the ground, I lay there for a moment grasping the card and I shouted again. I shouted 'Violet' at the top of my voice but nothing. Looking up, I watched the woman climb on a bus, which drove away. Sitting up, I hugged my knees, buried my head in my lap and sobbed.

Two hours later I put the key in the door and entered my flat. Tom was no longer there, so I assumed he must be up at the Lodge. I'd been numb the whole journey home. My thoughts were all over the place and I needed to see Tom.

I felt a sharp pain on my knee as I perched on the kitchen chair. Looking down, I could see blood seeping through my trousers. I hadn't noticed the pain on the train, but now it was coming in sharp bursts. Slowly rolling my trousers up, I saw a trickle of blood had run down my leg. I had obviously cut myself when I had fallen.

'Hey, whatever is the matter?' I heard a familiar voice. Looking up, I saw Tom was kneeling down in front of me, his eyes wide with concern.

'I didn't hear you come in.'

'The farmhands are working to full capacity and the Lodge is in order, so I thought I'd nip back to see if you were home yet.'

'I've just got back.'

'You're bleeding. Let me help,' he said softly, running some warm water from the tap and filling up a bowl. Taking some cotton wool from the drawer, he cleaned the wound and pressed it against the cut.

He kissed the top of my head. 'Is that better?'

'A little,' I managed.

'Your note said you went to visit your parents' grave. Are you OK?' Tom pulled out the chair and sat next to me.

'I'm not sure if I am, Tom.'

'Talk to me. What's going on?' he urged softly.

'I think Violet has been to the grave.'

Tom stared at me.

'Why? What makes you think that?'

I took the card from my pocket and laid it on the table in front of Tom.

'There was a woman in the graveyard, Tom; I walked past her when I arrived. She'd been crying. I nodded, she nodded back and then she disappeared through the gates. I think it was her. I ran after her but I stumbled – that's how I cut my knee – and now she's gone, she climbed on the bus, and I have no idea where the bus was going.'

Tom was reading the card.

'It's the same writing as the diary.'

'It does look very similar,' Tom agreed. 'But the woman you saw, it might not be her. She could have been anyone,' he said, trying to make me see sense. 'Were there flowers on the grave?'

'Yes, my mum's favourite. It was her, Tom, I know it in here,' I said, thumping my heart. 'I can feel it in here.'

'Ethel said they lost touch about five years ago. Surely if Violet was back she would know.'

'Maybe, maybe not.'

'There's nothing we can do about it right now,' he said, wrapping his hands around mine and squeezing them tight.

'I know. Maybe we could give Ethel another visit and see if she's heard from Violet?'

'Yes, we could, but we need to wait until later.'

'Why?'

'Because we need to get you cleaned up. This afternoon we have a very special family dinner to attend,' he smiled.

'A family dinner?'

'Yes, I wasn't sure at first, but Jeannie suggested it. She's organised for us all to go up to the farmhouse. She and Ted are cooking up a roast with all the trimmings.'

'For me?'

'Yes, for you; it is your birthday after all! Everyone will be there: Danny, Robin and Lucinda.'

'I don't know what to say.'

'You don't need to say anything, but I do. You sneaked out this morning without giving me the chance to wish you happy birthday.' He tilted my chin upwards. 'So happy birthday.' Tom kissed me lightly on the lips.

'Goodness, you know how to make everything feel better,' I murmured.

CHAPTER 49

'Happy birthday, Kitty,' everyone shouted as Tom ushered me through the farmhouse door.

Wow, I couldn't quite believe my eyes. Even though we were in the middle of summer it felt like Christmas. The room was decorated with colourful balloons and 'happy birthday' bunting was draped across the fireplace.

Jeannie, Danny, Robin and Lucinda were all standing in the middle of the living room with beaming smiles on their faces. Holding up their glasses, they all shouted cheers in unison. Jeannie passed Tom and me a glass and he put his arm around my waist and kissed me on the cheek.

'I am so overwhelmed. Look at all the trouble you've gone to.' I smiled at everyone. I glanced through to the dining room; it looked magnificent. The long oak table was already set with plates and cutlery and bottles of red and white wine had been placed at either end.

'How have you spent your morning?' Danny asked, thrusting his hand towards me. 'I'm not sure we've properly met,' he said. 'I'm Danny.'

'Hi, Danny, congratulations on the baby!' I replied, determined to change the subject.

'Yes, I can't wait. We're both very excited,' he said, rubbing Jeannie's tummy and kissing her affectionately on the cheek. Looking up at Jeannie, she was smiling and her face was glowing.

'How are you feeling, Jeannie? You look blooming today.'

'About time,' she joked. 'I feel absolutely great finally. I'm ravenous, so hopefully I'm over the worst of the sickness. Maybe this pregnancy lark suits me after all.'

'You look gorgeous,' said Tom, leaning forward and kissing her on the cheek.

'Come here and give me a hug! Happy birthday, Kitty,' Lucinda said, grinning. 'Guess who's baked you a cake?'

Everyone laughed.

'Happy birthday, sis!' joked Robin, giving me a wink.

'Ha ha, it's strange to hear you say that!' I laughed. 'Where's Ted?' I enquired, looking around the room and noticing he was missing.

'I'm here,' came a shout from the kitchen. We all looked up to see Ted rushing through the door wearing a striped apron, wiping his hands on a towel.

'Nice pinny,' Robin joked as Ted looked down and quickly whipped it off. Standing in front of me, he placed both his hands on my arms. 'Happy birthday, Kitty. I've waited so long to say that to you.'

'Thank you, Ted, I really appreciate the effort everyone's gone to.'

Ted turned around to the rest of the gang. 'Go and sit at your places – dinner will be served in five minutes.'

Everyone started to walk towards the dining room. Ted touched my arm. 'Kitty, I have a little something for you, wait there.'

Ted headed over towards the dresser and pulled out the top drawer. Clutching a small wrapped parcel, he turned back towards me. Tom was standing by my side but everyone else was now seated at the dining-room table.

'What is it?' I asked.

'Open it; it's something I've had for a long time.'

Ripping at the wrapping, I revealed a small red box. I flicked open the lid to reveal the most beautiful necklace I had ever seen.

I gasped.

Taking it out of the box, I looked at it carefully. 'It's beautiful. It looks so old! Thank you so much, Ted.'

Ted nodded. 'It is old. It was Agnes's necklace; she wore it on her wedding day.'

I looked up at Ted; his eyes looked sad.

'You have my grandma's necklace? How did you get this?'

'Violet gave it to me to look after.'

'How, and when?' I asked.

'The last time I saw her.'

Quickly casting my mind back to Violet's diary, I remembered she wore the necklace to the Christmas party, the party with Winston Smithells.

'You were at the party?'

'How do you know that?'

'The diary.'

He nodded. 'Of course. Yes, I was there. I bumped into Violet coming out of the ladies' room. She'd been crying. She didn't want to be there with Winston, she found him too overbearing, but it wasn't just that. In a vain attempt to lure her away into a separate room, away from the guests, he'd gotten quite heavy with her. She'd struggled, and in the struggle he'd ripped the necklace from her neck. She was devastated. She asked me to look after it for safe keeping and I arranged for one of my friends to chauffeur her home. Sadly that was the last time I saw her and I kept the necklace for all these years. It was selfish of me; I should have given it back to Agnes, but I couldn't. I'd lost Violet and this was the last little piece I had of you both.'

I could understand his reasons.

'The chain needs fixing, but now it's back in the hands of its rightful owner.'

I nodded. 'Thanks, Ted.'

He touched my arm. 'Anyway we can talk more later. Come on, let's join the others; dinner's ready and I'm so glad you're here and a part of the family. You've made me very happy, and this one,' he said, turning towards Tom, 'is a good one. I'm so glad you're together; you make a lovely couple.'

Tom smiled. 'Thanks, Ted, we really appreciate your kind words,' he said, shaking Ted's hand before we walked through the doorway towards the dining-room table.

The next hour flew by. Ted and Jeannie had worked so hard cooking up the delicious roast dinner. The wine flowed freely and there was non-stop chatter around the table. Tom sat next to me and when he wasn't eating, his hand stayed firmly on my knee. Looking around the table at all the happy faces, I watched while they chatted and laughed together. I never imagined in a million years that I would belong to a family again. It was so surreal.

'You OK?' Tom whispered in my ear.

I turned towards him and smiled. 'Better than ever – I actually feel like I belong.'

'You do, in here,' he said, grabbing my hand and putting it on his heart.

'Now, now, you two, none of that romantic nonsense at the table,' Ted said, smiling, and clinked his glass with a spoon.

Everyone laughed and turned towards Ted.

He stood up at the head of the table.

'Please tell us you aren't about to do a speech,' joked Robin.

'This could go on for hours,' Jeannie said, winking at Danny.

'Jesting aside, I promise I won't ramble on too much.'

'That'll be a first,' interrupted Robin.

'Shhh,' said Jeannie, bringing her finger up to her lips.

'I know it's been a difficult time for all of us.' Ted glanced around the table making eye contact with each and every one of us. 'However, I've waited a long time for this moment. I'm delighted to welcome Kitty and Tom into our family and I'm sure we all feel the same. We can't change the past but I think we can all look forward to a fantastic future together, as a family. Here's to Kitty. Let's raise our glasses and join together in wishing her a very happy birthday.'

'Happy birthday, Kitty!'

We all took a sip out of our glasses.

'Can I just say a few words?' I asked.

'Of course,' Ted replied.

Tom squeezed my knee.

I took a deep breath; all of a sudden I was feeling very emotional. 'This year has certainly been an emotional roller coaster. It was difficult losing my dad at an early age,' I noticed Ted nod, 'and then my mum. In my heart that's just what Alice and Julian are – my mum and dad. I miss them dreadfully and there isn't a day that goes by that they aren't in my thoughts.' My eyes began to fill up; everyone was watching me and I noticed both Jeannie and Lucinda wipe away a tear.

I paused.

Everyone was silent.

'Coming to the Lodge has changed my life very unexpectedly. Meeting Tom has made my life complete.' I smiled at him and he smiled back, showing his appreciation for my words. 'But not only that – I've uncovered a whole new family and some fantastic friends and they're all sat around this table today. Thank you so much for accepting me and welcoming me the way you all have. You have no idea what this means to me. For the first time in a long time I feel like I belong somewhere and I hope it means as much to you as it does to me, and now I'll shut up before I cry.'

Everyone applauded and Jeannie got up from the table and walked round and hugged me hard, then turned towards the boys.

'Tom, Robin and Danny, you are on washing-up duties while us girls put our feet up and drink wine,' Jeannie said, laughing. 'Well, water in my case.' She sighed wistfully.

We settled down on the couch after topping up our glasses and quite surprisingly the boys and Ted disappeared into the kitchen without any hesitation to take care of the pots. Not only was the food fantastic but so was the company. I felt so at ease and happy.

'Come on, Lucinda, spill the beans – how is it going with Robin?' I asked with a wink.

The grin on her face said it all.

'It's going very well,' she replied coyly.

'She's blushing,' teased Jeannie.

'I am not!'

'You most definitely are!' I joined in.

'Stop it, you pair. Let's just say it's early days. However, I've got a feeling we may just go the distance.'

Jeannie and I squealed with delight.

'And what about you, Jeannie? What's it like living with Danny?'

'Is it my turn to blush now? I feel like I'm about to burst, literally,' she said, patting her stomach 'I've got everything – a man, a baby on the way and I think we'll go the distance too.'

More squeals of delight were interrupted by the ringing of the doorbell.

'Who are we expecting now?' Jeannie asked, looking around the room.

'I'll get it; you ladies sit there,' Ted shouted as he walked up the hall to open the door.

'How are you girls doing?' Tom enquired as he passed through the living room.

'Are you skiving from the dishes already?' Jeannie joked.

'What, me? No!' Tom answered, bringing his hand up to his chest in mock outrage. 'I'm just off to the little boys' room.'

'Any excuse,' I teased.

Once Tom had left the room we all laughed.

'What about baby names, any ideas yet?' Lucinda asked.

Jeannie shook her head.

'I have no clue. Every time I think I like a name I change my mind a week later. We are so indecisive. I think we'll wait until the baby's born and see what comes to us at the time. We've got a while yet.'

'It'll be here before you know it, but at least you have all of us fussing around you waiting for cuddles from the new arrival. I can't wait!'

'You aren't getting broody, are you, Kitty?'

'She is – look at that face!'

'Stop teasing. There's plenty of time for all that,' I said, laughing.

Just then Tom opened the living-room door. He stood there in silence, staring at me. 'Don't worry, Tom, I'm not broody! It's only this lot pulling my leg.'

His face didn't falter; he turned pale and looked in shock.

There was silence.

'Tom, what is it?'

We all stared at him, willing him to speak.

'There was a woman at the door. I overheard her talking to Ted. She said she saw you this morning at the graveyard.'

'Where is she now?' I stammered.

'She's in the front room with Ted.'

CHAPTER 50

Bursting through the front-room door, the adrenaline was pumping through my body. Both Ted and the woman looked up, startled, and stared at me. I recognised her immediately: she was the woman who'd disappeared on the bus, the woman I'd seen crying at the graveyard. Scattered over the coffee table were numerous papers and letters. Ted looked solemn.

Tom was standing directly behind me, peering over my shoulder, followed by Jeannie and Lucinda.

'Come on in, Kitty and Tom. Jeannie, Lucinda, would you kindly leave us alone for a while.' Ted gave them a stern look. His voice was shaky. They both glanced at each other and left the room quickly, shutting the door behind them and leaving Tom and I standing there.

My eyes met Ted's. I was searching for answers but none were forthcoming.

'Come and sit, Kitty.' Ted patted the chair next to him. My legs felt like they were about to buckle underneath me as I immediately sat down. Tom perched next to me on the arm of the chair and held my hand. The woman smiled at me.

'Hello, Kitty.' Her voice was soft. My tears were threatening to break through at any moment.

'Are you – are you Violet?' I stuttered.

I was blinking back the tears. I squeezed my eyes tightly shut, waiting for the answer.

There was a startled silence.

'Tell her,' I heard Ted say, giving the woman his approval to answer.

I held my breath.

'No, Kitty, I'm not Violet,' the woman answered warmly in a Canadian accent.

I gasped, then opened my eyes. I slumped back in the chair, not knowing whether I was relieved or not.

I shrugged helplessly.

'Then who are you?'

'I'm Lizzie and I'm really pleased to meet you.' She smiled at me.

'Why? Why are you pleased to meet me?'

'Jean is my mother.'

I shook my head; I didn't understand. 'Who's Jean?'

'Jean is Arthur's sister, your granddad's sister. Violet was sent to live with her, well us, when she was sixteen.'

Trying to take in this information, I felt Tom's reassuring touch as he squeezed my hand.

'So that makes you Violet's cousin?'

She nodded. 'Yes, Kitty, and Alice's.'

Then she paused.

I could feel the emotion rising inside me; my breath caught in my throat.

'Why do I think there's something wrong? Why do I get the awful feeling you're trying to tell me something?'

I glanced at Ted. He was staring at the floor. His face looked defeated.

For a second no one said a thing.

'Ted, talk to me.'

Ted shook his head. 'I'm so sorry, Kitty.'

Anxiety ran through my body. My eyes widened with dread.

'Kitty, I'm so sorry. Violet has passed away unexpectedly,' Lizzie said softly, her eyes now brimmed with tears.

I heard the words but didn't believe her. I shook my head. 'No, it can't be true, it can't, please, Ted, tell me someone has got this wrong?'

Ted shook his head, his eyes gleaming with unshed tears. 'I wish I could, Kitty, but I can't,' he said, placing his hand on my knee.

My throat became tight and heaviness surged through my chest followed by a pain around my heart. I gasped for breath.

'No, no, I was going to find her. We were going to find her,' I screamed at Tom. He clutched my hand tightly.

'I'm so sorry.'

The tears fell, my eyes were blurred and nausea had taken over my body.

'How – how did she die?'

'It was very sudden. Violet loved to read; it was her passion. She would spend her time reading anything and everything. One evening, early last month, she began to complain of a headache and we joked that maybe now she was getting a little older it was probably her eyesight. She told me not to be so daft. We were sitting in the living room, the night was drawing in, and as usual Violet had settled down with her book, switching on the lamp beside her. I was watching the television at the far end of the room. I heard a crash and turned round to find that Violet had knocked over a drink of water. The glass smashed on the wooden floor. I stood up to fetch the dustpan and brush but then Violet slumped forward and placed her head in her hands. At first I thought she'd cut herself on the broken glass but then she vomited everywhere. She began to scream that she couldn't see and had severe pain in her head. I immediately called for help. When we got to the hospital she was taken straight in for a scan and then transferred to the specialist neurology unit. She lost consciousness and slipped away soon after due to the bleeding around her brain. It was confirmed that her death was caused by a brain aneurysm bursting. She'd suffered a head injury from a skiing trip and they think it's possible that was the cause. There was nothing anyone could do. I'm so sorry, Kitty – it was too late.'

Tom put his arms around me and held me tight.

'Here, drink this,' I heard Ted's voice. Looking up through my tears, he passed me a small glass filled with liquid. Without thinking about it, I swigged it back with one gulp and passed the glass back to him.

'Please tell me everything, absolutely everything. I need to know – did she marry, have a family, what happened in her life?' I asked.

'Kitty, Violet was the loveliest person I've ever known. She was beautiful, loyal and instantly became my best friend the moment she walked through the door of our home. My mother, Jean, welcomed her with open arms. In all honesty she brought happiness to my life every day; you would think we were sisters not cousins. Violet never married or had a family. She never recovered from her broken heart.'

'Do you mean Ted?'

'Yes.' Lizzie nodded in Ted's direction. His eyes were filled with tears and he placed his head in his hands.

'Violet loved Ted with all her heart; no one ever came close to the love that she felt for him. She used to say that she would never settle for second best, and if she couldn't have her true love then she would have no love at all.'

'I'm so sorry.'

Ted was clearly distraught. I'd forgotten about him in all of this but Violet's loss must have hit him hard too and yet here he was comforting me. Standing up, he walked towards the fireplace. He examined his face in the mirror before placing his hands on the mantel and hanging his head low, staring at the floor. Turning back towards us, he spoke softly. 'I honestly thought we would find her, Kitty; I honestly thought I would see Violet again.'

I could feel a terrible sadness bleeding through the room.

'Why didn't she come back, Lizzie?'

'Oh, Kitty, don't think we haven't had many late-night conversations about this. I've stayed up numerous times while Violet wept through the night in my arms, wanting to come back to England. But she couldn't – she didn't come back because of you.'

'Me, why me?'

'It was too late. Alice and Julian loved you with all their heart and she knew that. You'd grown up with the security of a loving family. If she came back after all these years she didn't know what to expect. Her worst fear was rejection; the upset it would cause to everyone – Alice, Julian and you. She put everyone's happiness before her own. She thought it was better for everyone if she was unhappy and the rest of you were happy, if that makes sense. Her love for you, Kitty, never diminished.'

I nodded.

'I lived with Violet all these years. Even though she had a troubled life as far as you were concerned, she was happy in other ways. She loved her work.'

'What did she do?'

'She was a librarian. Books were her life – she could lose herself in the pages and she did.' Lizzie smiled.

I managed a weak smile too. Maybe that was where my love of books stemmed from?

'Have you got a family, Lizzie?'

'No, I haven't. I'm a workaholic, no time for that caper, and to be honest I rather liked living with Violet. Don't get me wrong – I have had a fair few relationships, but I'm quite happy doing my own thing.' She smiled again.

'Why are you here, Lizzie?'

Ted sat back down next to me and Tom perched back on the arm of a chair.

'It was a difficult call. There should have been two of us on this trip: me and Violet. But I decided to still make the trip, for Violet.'

'What do you mean?' My lips were trembling and my whole body ached with pain.

'We were coming to find you, Kitty; we booked the plane tickets at the end of May.' At this point Lizzie broke down and the tears rolled down her face. Quickly she leant down to her handbag and grabbed a packet of tissues then dabbed her eyes. 'I'm sorry – it's all very raw for me too.'

'That's OK, take your time,' I said softly, my heart twisting for her grief too.

Lizzie nodded towards the letters on the table. 'Word came through to us when Agnes passed away. Violet was unaware that Alice and Julian had also passed until recently. Agnes had lodged a letter with a solicitor and instructed that on her death the letter must be forwarded to Violet. Even though Violet was sad to hear of Julian's tragic death and your mother's illness, it was a huge relief for her receiving this letter – she saw it as a way of return. The only thing we were never sure of was whether you knew the truth.'

I shook my head. 'I didn't until very recently.'

'The letter revealed that the Lodge, her old family home, had been left to you. We knew where to find you – that was the easy part – but the hard part was guessing your reaction. Also, Violet had to lay some ghosts to rest. The relationship between her and Agnes was always a strained one, and the minute she left for Canada they never spoke again. My mum, Jean, would keep Agnes updated with how things were on a regular basis. Violet never forgave Agnes for sending her away like the black sheep of the family, but we did know that Agnes found out Ted was your father, though we never knew how.'

I looked up at Ted but he remained silent.

'I think she knew it was Ted from Violet's diary – she must have worked it out.'

'Agnes never said a word to me.'

'She would have been protecting your family and children too.'

Ted nodded.

Lizzie fumbled about on the table with the papers that were laid out. 'Here, read this, Kitty. It's a letter from Agnes to Violet. It was passed to her from the solicitor. Violet read this just before she died.'

Taking the letter from Lizzie, my heart was thumping and my hands were shaking.

'Do you want me to read it to you?' Tom asked gently.

'Would you mind?'

'No, give it here.'

I exhaled and settled back on the chair. I closed my eyes while Tom read.

'To my dearest darling Violet,

I am struggling to decide how to begin this letter. The pain is twisting in my heart while I put pen to paper.

All this time you have always remained in my thoughts and prayers. I have never forgotten you and times have been so difficult without you and Alice in my life. Alice and Julian made the decision to cut all families ties; they loved Kitty so much that they were scared the family secret would be revealed if they stayed in contact.

Being pregnant without a husband carried a great deal of shame back then, more than I think it is possible to remember today. I had to make a decision and I hope you understand what it was like in a different era. It was even more shameful that your baby's father was a married man living in the village. I didn't have the strength or wherewithal to figure out what to do quickly. It seemed like an easy option to pass the baby to Alice – she was family and could provide for Kitty in a loving home alongside Julian.

It is my sorrow that I have never seen any of you again. Over the years I began to realise it doesn't matter what anyone else ever thinks about you as long as you're happy within. I have never been happy within since losing all of you. My life has been one of existence.

You are receiving this letter because I have passed. The Lodge has been left to Kitty in my will; she will no doubt discover the truth very soon. This is my only way to make amends for my cruel actions all those years ago and bring you two back together, the way it should be.

My heart was shattered into tiny pieces after reading your diary and I couldn't bring myself to destroy it. It was the only part of you I had left. The diary is stored in the safe at the Lodge and the combination code is 1507 – Kitty's birthday.

Please believe me when I write I have always loved you.

Your mother,

Agnes

My breathing had become more erratic; I had to concentrate hard to get my natural rhythm going again. I wiped the tears of frustration away. I felt drained and battered. It was plain to see that Agnes regretted her decision; she too was pained and had lost everything and everyone.

'Are you OK?' Tom asked gently.

'Things could have been so different.'

'Yes, but we can't change it now,' Tom replied softly.

I nodded. 'I know, and out of all of this I was the one who had a loving childhood. Mother and Father did me proud.'

'That's right,' he agreed.

'Why were you at my parents' grave this morning?' I asked Lizzie, fumbling in my pocket and taking the card out and placing it on the table. 'And who wrote this?'

'Violet wrote the card. She had everything prepared for the visit. Once Violet knew that Agnes and Alice had died she thought she would take her chance to return. She wasn't going to turn your world upside down. She planned to visit Ted first to see how the land lay. The trip coincided with your birthday; she wanted to see you, Kitty, and it was more than likely you would visit your parents' grave today. We were going to sit nearby, watch and wait. Violet wanted to see with her own eyes what a beautiful young woman her daughter had become. I brought the card with me and placed it on the grave just like Violet was going to do and bought the flowers on the way. Violet even remembered which flowers your mother loved. I'd been at the churchyard for most of the morning. I sat on the bench and thought about Violet the whole time. She was truly thankful for the way Alice and Julian treasured you. As I climbed on the bus, I heard you shout but it was too late – the bus was pulling away and I saw you slump to your knees. I didn't mean to unveil all this on such a day but something was telling me to come to you here.'

Biting down on my bottom lip, I paused for a moment trying to take everything in.

'I'm glad you did, Lizzie. The hardest part has been trying to piece everything together. I'm heart broken that I'll never ever meet Violet, but I know she'll always be in my heart.'

Lizzie stood up; the tears were rolling down her cheeks. She walked towards me with her arms open wide. 'I know I'm not Violet, but I hope I can be the next best thing,' she said and smiled.

I fell in to her arms. We hugged tight.

CHAPTER 51

Five months later …

The world appeared silent and still except for the snow falling lightly all around as we drove up towards the farmhouse. All the fields around were veiled in a layer of white candyfloss snow and the frost had polished the trees and bushes with its glittering silver sheen. There was something about this time of year I loved; there was something about Christmas.

Tom pulled up and parked the car. I watched the lights twinkling away on the two Christmas trees that adorned either side of the steps up to the front door.

I noticed the smoke was spiralling out of the chimney pot and disappearing amongst the greyness of the sky. I was glad to soon be stepping inside, into the warmth. I climbed out of the car and watched the flakes fall. Tom switched off the engine and joined me. He pulled me in close, wrapping his arm around my body while we looked up at the sky. My heart swelled with happiness. I held tight to the necklace around my neck – Agnes's necklace. Tom had kindly taken it to the local jewellers and the chain had been fixed. As the snow fell all around us I thought about the last year of my life and how it had changed so dramatically in such a short space of time. I smiled and even though I would never ever be able to tell Violet that I knew about her, I hoped she somehow knew that she would have a special place in my heart forever.

'Kitty, Tom, what are you doing standing out here? Come on in out of the cold – the log fire is roaring,' Jeannie squealed excitedly, waving at us from the steps of the front door.

Turning around, I smiled and waved. 'Coming!'

'I'll just get the presents from the boot of the car and I'll follow you in,' Tom said and smiled, wiping the snowflakes from the tip of my red nose and kissing it lightly. For a second he held my gaze. 'I love you, Kitty Lewis,' he whispered softly in my ear.

'I love you too, Tom Drew.'

I skipped forwards towards the door and Jeannie wrapped her arms around me and gave me a hug.

'Wait there, Kitty,' I heard Tom shout. Looking around, he was bounding towards me. He grabbed my face with his cold hands and planted his lips on mine and kissed me.

'What was that for?' I asked, laughing.

'Ha ha, look above your head.' He laughed, bounding back towards the boot of the car. Looking up, I giggled – a huge bunch of mistletoe was hanging down from the old oak beams above.

Jeannie was standing there smiling. 'Merry Christmas, Kitty!'

'Merry Christmas to you too, lovely. You're looking fantastic! Now where is that little chubbiness of delight? Aunty Kitty wants a cuddle!'

Stamping my snowy boots on the mat, I unbuttoned my coat and threw it over the banister. I could hear Christmas carols playing throughout the house already, adding to the festive feel.

The excited chatter from the living room was echoing up the hall as I followed Jeannie into the living room.

'Kitty and Tom have arrived,' Jeannie announced.

All heads turned towards me.

'Merry Christmas everyone!' I smiled as I walked into the room. 'Now where's Harry? I need a cuddle from my favourite nephew.' I kissed Danny on the cheek. 'You don't mind if I pinch your son for some Christmas kisses, do you?'

'Not in the slightest!' Danny grinned, handing me over the little bundle of joy. 'It'll give me a chance to refill my glass! Would you like a drink, Kitty?'

'Yes, please. I would love a mulled wine if it's not too much trouble.'

'Here you go, Kitty, I've already poured you a glass,' Lucinda said, placing it down on the table next to me.

'Thank you. So, Lucinda, were you on the naughty or nice list this year?' I grinned.

'Naughty,' Robin said, giving her shoulder a friendly punch, then topped up her glass.

'The nice list of course,' she replied playfully. 'Look,' she said, thrusting her hand forwards to reveal a very expensive-looking bracelet.

I nodded. 'Wow, that's absolutely beautiful.'

'Where's Tom?' Robin asked.

'He's enjoying playing Father Christmas. He's bringing in the presents from the car. I think we may have gone over the top a bit and spoilt this little one,' I said, wrapping my fingers around Harry's little hands, 'but he's worth it.'

'Ho, ho, ho.'

Everyone laughed as Tom walked through the door wearing a Father Christmas hat and a white beard, carrying an old hessian sack filled to the brim with presents. He placed them down next to the Christmas tree that stood the height of the ceiling, its branches covered in silver and purple tinsel that glittered brightly. The aroma of the real pine swept through the room.

'Take off that silly hat and beard quickly before you frighten the baby,' I said, laughing.

'Spoilsport. Harry doesn't mind, do you, Harry?' Tom peered over at the baby.

Harry's eyes widened and he let out a cry.

'Sorry, sorry,' Tom said, rapidly whipping off the costume.

'Would you like a drink, Tom?' Robin asked.

'A glass of red would be lovely,' he replied, standing in front of the open fire, which fizzed and spat as he thawed from the wintry chill outside.

'How come I'm always late to the party,' said Ted, popping his head around the door.

'Because you're always cooking!' Jeannie and Robin replied in unison.

'You're probably right,' he said, laughing.

Ted bent down and kissed me on the cheek while ruffling the hair of his newly born grandson. 'Merry Christmas, Kitty.'

Patting Tom on the back, he then shook his hand firmly. 'Merry Christmas to you too, Tom.'

'Thank you, and the same to you.'

'Dinner will only be a couple of minutes, so chat amongst yourselves until I'm ready.'

'Do you want any help, Ted?' I offered.

'I wouldn't dream of it. Don't worry, it's all under control.'

'Ted, I forgot to give you this; it arrived a few days ago,' I said, retrieving a card from my handbag.

'What is it?'

'It's from Lizzie – a Christmas card.'

Ted took the card from me and opened it, then smiled. 'It's a shame she couldn't extend her visit when she was here.'

'I know, I agree; it would have been wonderful if we could all have spent Christmas together, but we speak on the phone every week and hopefully, fingers crossed, Tom and I are going to go and visit in the summer. It'll be great to see where Violet lived and hear more about her.'

Ted touched my arm affectionately. 'We'll toast her at the dinner table.'

Even though tears welled in my eyes they were happy ones.

Ted disappeared back into the kitchen and I joined Tom in the living room; he was now making Harry smile with his funny face-pulling.

A few moments later Ted announced dinner was served. The table looked magnificent. It was decorated with individual place settings, Christmas crackers and a small present for each of us was wrapped and rested on top of our serviettes. I had never seen such an abundance of food.

'Ted, this looks amazing,' I said.

He smiled. 'I wanted it to be special.'

We settled at the table and Jeannie balanced Harry in her arms. I watched her as she cuddled her baby and smiled at him the whole time. She suited her new role and I'd never seen her so happy.

'Is it possible I could say a few words before we start?'

'Oh go on then, if you must,' Jeannie joked.

We all turned towards Ted, who was standing up and holding a glass of red.

'I would just like to say I never ever thought I'd see the day that we'd all be gathered under one roof celebrating Christmas together. First of all I would like to make a toast to absent friends,' he said and raised his glass. The whole table echoed his cheers and raised their glasses too. Tom squeezed my knee. 'And secondly I would like to welcome my grandchild, Harry, into the family and Danny, both of whom are spending their first Christmas with us. Jeannie and Danny, you have both made me very proud. Robin and Lucinda, you are both going from strength to strength. Lucinda, your business has doubled in size and is extremely successful – not to mention you make the most perfect cakes!' He laughed, patting his stomach. 'I hope someone has bought me a larger belt for Christmas!'

Everyone laughed.

'Robin, I haven't bought you a Christmas present this year because I'd like to give you a little bit of family history and I hope you'll accept my kind offer of taking over the farm from me?'

Robin gasped. His jaw fell open. 'Are you kidding, Dad?'

'No, not at all, son. I think the time is right, if you would accept?'

'Yes, yes of course.'

Robin's beaming face said it all as he stood up and wrapped his arms around his father in a bear hug then promptly sat back down at the table.

'Well done you,' Lucinda whispered in his ear.

'And I know it's been an emotional year for all of us, especially for Kitty and Tom.' He smiled at us both. 'And I'm delighted we've been reunited after all this time. And I believe Tom has a little surprise for you, Kitty. Over to you, Tom.' He raised his eyebrows at Tom and sat back down in his chair.

I looked at Tom, startled. 'What are you up to?' I gave a nervous laugh.

Tom gazed at me then paused.

'OK, here goes. I think we've both come such a long way in the last twelve months and, Kitty Lewis, I never believed in love at first sight until I met you. I'll never forget the day we met – the day you ran Dotty over when you first arrived at the Lodge. The moment I hauled you off the ground and looked into your eyes was also the moment I knew I wanted you in my life forever.'

'What are you saying?' I gave Tom a quizzical look.

Tom stood up from the table and I turned to face him. He bent down on one knee in front of me.

'What's he doing?' Danny whispered to Jeannie.

'Shhh!' Jeannie shot him a stern look.

'I am saying, Kitty Lewis, will you do me the honour of becoming my wife?'

The whole table fell completely silent.

I clamped my hand to my mouth. 'Are you serious?' I gasped.

'You better believe it.' Tom waited patiently for an answer.

'Yes, yes, YES!'

I slipped my arms around his neck and hugged him tight, tears of happiness brimming in my eyes.

'Now stand up and kiss me.'

He brushed his lips against mine and I melted into his arms. Everyone let out a cheer and applauded.

This was it – I knew everything in the past had happened for a reason. Tom was mine and I was his and I wouldn't have it any other way. I knew there would never be anywhere else I'd rather be than with my new fiancé and my new family.

LETTER FROM CHRISTIE

Dear all,

Firstly, if you are reading this letter, thank you so much for choosing to read *Kitty's Countryside Dream*. I have without a doubt enjoyed every second of writing this book.

Over twelve months ago when I first started writing, I never in a million years thought I would already be releasing my third book. This time I wanted to write a book that was filled with friendship, humour and genuinely loveable characters, and Kitty Lewis and Tom Drew have become my new best friends. Every character in this book was full of such warmth and belonging that I have a little confession to make ... I have totally fallen in love with them all and I hope you did too.

Secondly, I would like to say a heartfelt thank you to everyone that has been involved in the project – my publisher Bookouture, my family, friends, book bloggers and readers. I adore you all. Writing fiction can be a lonely job but your texts, tweets and emails along the way make me smile on a daily basis. Hearing what readers think is an absolute joy and makes all the hours spent tapping away on my laptop with only my mad cocker spaniel Woody for company truly worthwhile.

I sincerely hope you enjoyed *Kitty's Countryside Dream*. **If you did, I would be forever grateful if you'd write a review.** Your recommendations can always help other readers to discover my books.

To keep right up to date with the latest news on my releases just sign up using the link below:

www.bookouture.com/christie-barlow

I would love it if you could all keep in touch.

Warm wishes,

Christie x

84235639R00188

Made in the USA
San Bernardino, CA
05 August 2018